Help! I'm a Pastor

A Guide to Parish Ministry

Richard Stoll Armstrong
with
Kirk Walker Morledge

Foreword by George H. Gallup Jr.

WJK
WESTMINSTER
JOHN KNOX PRESS
LOUISVILLE • KENTUCKY

Book design by Sharon Adams
Cover design by Mark Abrams

First edition
Published by Westminster John Knox Press
Louisville, Kentucky

This book is printed on acid-free paper that meets the American National Standards Institute Z39.48 standard. ♾

PRINTED IN THE UNITED STATES OF AMERICA

05 06 07 08 09 10 11 12 13 14—10 9 8 7 6 5 4 3 2 1

Library of Congress Cataloging-in-Publication Data is on file at the Library of Congress, Washington, D.C.

ISBN 0-664-22895-X

This book is dedicated to
our long-suffering spouses,
Margie Armstrong
and
Faith Morledge,
without whose loving support
and patient understanding
we could not survive,
let alone thrive,
in ministry.

Contents

Foreword

The thousands upon thousands of churches of all shapes and sizes that dot the American landscape from coast to coast represent the heart and soul of the nation. Churches are places where people worship God and connect with fellow seekers. They are way stations for rest and renewal in a broken and troubled world.

Gallup's extensive studies of religion in America have consistently shown that Americans deeply value their churches, generally hold the clergy in high esteem (despite the adverse publicity in recent years relating to reports of child abuses by some clergypersons), and give good marks to faith communities for the job they do in meeting the physical and spiritual needs of their constituents.

Churches provide the basic infrastructure of our society, and spur much of the volunteerism for which our nation is well known.

These houses of worship are, however, only as healthy and vital as their leadership—the pastors and others who are in clerical authority—and here there is clear cause for concern. Our studies and other surveys have pointed to a serious condition of "clergy burnout." Nearly one-third of persons in pastoral ministry have, at one point or another, thought of leaving this ministry.

The clergy are asked to be all things to all people all the time. Discerning people recognize this, and they continue to name the parish ministry as one of the most demanding and stressful of all occupations.

If the local clergy falter in their leadership under the burdens of their calling, the churches they serve are at risk of losing their impact on both their own members and the world about them. So it is a matter of urgent necessity to clear away any impediments to the clergy's using their special gifts to the fullest, as they seek faithfully to fulfill their high calling.

Now comes a timely and much-needed book: *Help! I'm a Pastor: A Guide to Parish Ministry.* Here is a desktop resource for pastors that identifies the challenges, demands, and frustrations, as well as the satisfactions and rewards, of pastoral ministry, and provides solid and practical advice on how to live with these realities with theological integrity and spiritual stamina. This book will save pastors precious time and energy, and most important, it will help them to be more fully responsive to the God they serve.

I'm impressed by the scope of this volume, which is a compendium of parish ministry. It covers a wide range of topics relating to the pastor's personal life and professional ministry. Parish ministers of every denomination who read this book will be forced to think more deeply about and perhaps be moved to change how they manage their financial affairs, work with staff and committees, balance their personal lives with their pastoral responsibilities, and deal with conflict. Lawsuits and other legal issues; the use of computers (our studies indicate that a surprisingly large number of churches are not yet online); spiritual, mental, and physical fitness; relationships with one's predecessors and successors; ethical considerations; support groups and prayer partnerships; and many other vital topics are discussed. An inclusive index makes all these topics easily accessible.

Clergypersons need to bear in mind that church members, according to our surveys, are ready, willing, and more able than some pastors realize to support them in their struggle to meet the challenges of parish ministry. Our studies have revealed that a high percentage of the "very active" members on the church rolls not only believe that the laity should have greater influence in their churches but appear prepared to take on a greater share of the leadership of churches than is now the case.

The authors of this comprehensive view of parish ministry—Richard Armstrong, a distinguished professor, preacher, and author, and Kirk Morledge, a former student of Armstrong's and a thriving pastor himself—are well qualified to write this book, which is rooted in solid experience. It can be fruitfully read by clergy spouses, as well as by church officers and members, who need to know the kinds of demands and pressures their pastors and pastors' spouses are having to cope with. It is a guidebook for pastors starting out in ministry, a manual for those who are seeking to reexamine their present ministry, perhaps toward making a "midcourse correction," and a textbook that should be required reading for seminary students who are heading toward parish ministry.

This book is a gift of love arising from the deep desire of the authors to free up ministers to do the work of the Lord. For pastors the book is a wonderful reminder that they are never alone in their struggles, and as an Episcopal layman I am moved to underscore the authors' concluding word of advice to pastors, for whom I have the greatest respect: "Do the best you can and leave the rest to God. Trust in God's promises, pray for God's wisdom, and rely on God's strength."

George H. Gallup Jr.
Chairman, George H. Gallup International Institute

Preface

Our readers might be interested to know how this book came to be written. It is based on the lecture notes of a course I taught annually, as Professor of Ministry, at Princeton Theological Seminary. The course was called "The Parish Minister." It was an introduction to the life and work of a pastor. The course was in turn grounded in my own experience as a pastor for sixteen years of two quite different churches and as an interim preacher at various times in urban and suburban congregations for periods of from six to eighteen months. I have been with the congregation I am presently serving as supply preacher for more than two years.

My students often asked why I did not publish the lectures as a textbook. It was something I indeed intended to do but had to keep postponing because of other commitments. Former students, now pastors, have continued to express appreciation for the course, and have kept urging me to write the long-delayed book.

Although they convinced me that it could be a useful resource for many pastors, I was beginning to despair of being able to complete such a project at this latter stage of my life. But one day while I was fast walking, a time when my creative juices seem to flow more readily, a new thought occurred to me. Why not ask one of my former students to take on the project? I immediately thought of my good friend and former student Kirk Morledge. He was one of the most outstanding students I've ever had the privilege of teaching, and after he became a pastor, he also served as my teaching assistant for the Parish Minister course. The students responded to him readily. He was doing (and doing effectively!) what they were learning to do. As a pastor he was practicing what I was teaching!

Kirk and I have long shared the same theological convictions, the same commitment to the church, the same concerns about ministerial practice. We have the same approach to ministry. Kirk has served both urban and suburban congregations. He has served a church overseas. He has served in interdenominational settings. He has worked closely with pastors of other denominations. His ministry has crossed racial/ethnic lines. He has been a solo pastor and part of a staff. He has been a youth minister, an associate pastor, a "senior" pastor and head of a staff. He has worked with and without a secretary or a custodian. He has served churches with no money in the bank, and churches with multimillion-dollar endowments.

Kirk has worked with both male and female clergy colleagues. He has mentored seminarians. He has served as a chaplain in a psychiatric hospital and is currently a (reserve) chaplain in the Navy. For the first ten years of his ministry he was single. He is now a happily married husband and father. The congregations he has served have been small and large. His work as a pastor has been and continues to be fruitful and effective in every setting.

The church he now pastors has quadrupled in size since he came. His congregation has been bucking all the downward trends plaguing most mainline churches. His people are beginning their second building program under his leadership, while remaining first in mission giving in their denominational region. His congregation's youth program was chosen by the Lilly Foundation as among the top fifty in the nation for "exemplary youth ministry." The Spirit of the Lord is alive and at work in his flock. I know that he gives God the glory for the remarkable growth that has taken place in his church. And as his close friend and one who has observed his ministry for many years, I know that his constant prayer for the people he serves is, "Lord, help them to see Jesus!"

He was the ideal choice and I was thrilled when he readily agreed to take on this project. We met shortly after that to discuss how to proceed, and there have been many telephone conversations, letters, and e-mail messages back and forth since then. Kirk worked with my lecture notes to produce the first draft, which I then revised and edited, and sent back to him. He added his editorial suggestions, and then together we worked on the final draft, page by page, paragraph by paragraph—a time-consuming but most enjoyable and agreeable effort.

Because of our theological compatibility and similar styles of ministry, we decided to write in the first-person plural. As a thriving pastor in a thriving church, Kirk brings a fresh and relevant perspective to this project. Some things about parish ministry have changed, but many things remain the same. When I taught the course I was constantly updating the material, and Kirk and I have tried to do that too, based on our current experiences as active ministers, our current involvements with churches of various denominations, our conversations with innumerable pastors, and our observations of the way things are.

Our project was interrupted when Kirk was called into active duty by the Navy after 9/11. After serving with distinction overseas as a Navy chaplain for a year, he returned to take up again his duties as pastor of the First Presbyterian Church of Waunakee, Wisconsin. We picked up where we had left off, and pushed ahead with the project until it was finally completed.

In this book we look at matters pertaining to the call, the pastor's ministerial style, and the personal life of a pastor. We also examine the various professional roles of a pastor and the kinds of things a pastor needs to know about each role in order to thrive and not just survive in ministry. We have footnoted our sources as appropriate. Biblical quotations are from the New Revised Standard Version, unless otherwise noted.

This has been a challenging assignment, but we have enjoyed tackling it. I'm speaking for Kirk too when I say it has been fun working together, and we hope what we have done will prove helpful to our readers and beneficial to the churches they serve.

So, thrive on, friends!

Richard Stoll Armstrong

And a Postscript from Kirk:

I'd like to say something about my mentor before we move on. Dick has said some nice things about my pastoral work. Allow me to say something about his work: The Rev. Dr. Richard S. Armstrong knows ministry! He has done it. He has taught it. He has inspired and influenced thousands who pursue their callings faithfully, around the world, today. God has used Dick Armstrong in my life—more times than I can count—to point me in the right direction, to guide me in my pastoral work. And I know I speak for countless other pastors and church leaders who have benefited from his writing and teaching.

I was green as grass the first day I sat in Professor Richard S. Armstrong's class. I had signed up for it because it sounded like something I needed. I was in my last year of seminary and wondering what church I would find on which to inflict all my book learning. I began to think about the fact that I had not learned very much yet about the specifics of pastoral work. I hadn't learned much about the pastor's personal life as it related to his or her ministry, or about running a board meeting, or living in a fishbowl, or perching on the pastoral pedestal, or falling off! I hadn't thought much about how I would begin a new ministry, or about the burden of never really being "off duty." I hadn't had much time to think about my own personal stewardship, my own pastoral "style," my relationship with pastors who came before me or who would follow after me, my specific approach to counseling appointments. I had never formulated a church policy for weddings or funerals, or considered the matter of staff communication. I had never attempted the weekly preaching task. I had no idea of the demands on a pastor's time. I had never considered a proper approach to interruptions!

Dick's class was a look down the road ahead—with a map, an experienced guide, and a compass! The course was called "The Parish Minister." I learned as much from Richard S. Armstrong, the man, as I could have from any treatise or book. Hardly a week has gone by in the two decades since I knelt for ordination to pastoral work that I have not thought about something Dick Armstrong said, or taught, or showed us.

I have thanked God for that class, for the man who taught it, and, in the ensuing years, for that man's friendship. He preaches weekly. He teaches around the globe. He continues to write. A number of his books have become ministry classics.

But most of all, he continues to love the church of Jesus Christ, and to aid those whom the Lord calls to serve it. It has been a joy for me to work with him on this important project. May it serve the church and may it help those who have to find and claim their own way as pastors.

Kirk Walker Morledge

Chapter 1

Wondering What This Book Can Do for Me

Our Purpose

We hope this book will help make better pastors, and help make pastors better. We hope it will help pastors and future pastors be more effective and fulfilled in their work.

Most pastors we talk to find great satisfaction in ministry. They say there is nothing else they would rather do. Our impressions were confirmed by the National Clergy Survey conducted at Duke University Divinity School. The survey was part of "Pulpit and Pew," a four-year research project on pastoral leadership. The findings as initially reported in March 2002 indicated a high level of job satisfaction among clergy of all denominations, with six out of ten reporting that they have never had doubts about their call to ministry, and seven out of ten indicating they have never considered leaving pastoral ministry.[1]

The survey results prompt us to ask, What about the four out of ten pastors who *have* had doubts about their call to ministry? That's a high percentage! And what about the 30 percent who *have* considered quitting pastoral ministry? Those statistics confirm our other impression: too many pastors are *struggling* in ministry. Too many are wrestling with too frequent frustration. Too many are hanging up the pastor's mantle and looking for other kinds of work. Too many are departing the pastor's calling or questioning their own commitment to it.

"Consider the burned-out parish pastor," commented one highly qualified observer in an article reprinted by the Free Methodist Church in the Summer 2003 issue of *Benefit Insights*, "feeling isolated, invalidated, trapped, empty, worn down and beaten up. We see the desperate-determination/hidden-despair

1. According to the authors, the survey was "the most inclusive and representative of clergy ever undertaken, with responses from leaders in over eighty different denominations and faith groups."

of the lonesome loser. It is easy to understand why clergy morale is low, why clergy are leaving ministry. One can also see how clergy, in such a depleted state, might fall victim to improper relationships (the 'temptations of the flesh'), which are displayed so prominently in all-too-regular media coverage."[2]

It is not just American clergy who are experiencing low morale. "It is unarguable," wrote the Rev. Robbie Low, commenting in *New Directions* on the state of affairs in the Church of England, "that in many areas clergy morale is low. The often illegal and persistent abuse of the Pastoral Measure by successive diocesan bishops nationwide has asset stripped rural communities, in particular, and bequeathed an intolerable workload on country parsons."[3] And Archdeacon Rod Gillis, of Halifax, Nova Scotia, stated in a letter to the *Anglican Journal* that "the problem of clergy morale is hardly limited either to this diocese or to Anglicans."[4]

Increasingly, seminary students are saying they hope to serve somewhere other than in the local church. One disgruntled Lutheran pastor in a letter to his denominational publication concluded: "The church may be full of more hatred and venom than any other institution, despite the fact that its members proclaim love and mercy as primary ways of practicing their faith. So I ask: Why would any pastor want to encourage young people to take up a career as a pastor?"[5]

We don't share that pastor's pessimism about the church. We note, however, that congregations of every shape, size, and denomination are finding it harder and harder to find (and keep!) good pastors. In a fragmenting culture, local churches are pleading for them, and *needing* them, as never before. But fewer people seem to be hearing the call to serve, and those who do respond feel inadequately equipped.

If pastoral ministry is becoming a lost art (and we hope not!), we want to try to help recover it before it's too late. We believe in ministry in the local church! We are committed to it. We love it. We believe the parish minister is on the front lines of the work of Christ's kingdom. This book springs from the study, experiences, observations, and lives of two who have joyfully undertaken this calling: one who, after many years in the parish, was summoned to teach seminary students the theory and practice of effective ministry, to

2. From "The Life of the Lonesome Loser: Beating Clergy Burnout," by the Rev. Gregory A. Hinkle, PhD, Executive Director of the Samaritan Center, a nonprofit mental health agency in Elkhart, Ind. Dr. Hinkle's observations are based on his many years of counseling pastors. This article appeared in the Summer 2003 edition of *Benefit Insights*, published by the Free Methodist Church of North America, Indianapolis, IN.

3. The Rev. Robbie Low is vicar of St. Peter's parish in Bushey Heath, Hertfordshire, England. He is a member of the editorial board of the magazine *New Directions*.

4. Published by the Anglican Church of Canada, October 2001.

5. *The Lutheran*, March 2002.

become a "shepherd of shepherds," and to write extensively. The other, one of his very first students, who after two decades of serving Jesus Christ and his church still loves being a pastor.

We hope this book will encourage you to think more deeply about what it means to be a pastor, and about how to handle the pressures, pitfalls, and rewards of this demanding (and *fulfilling!*) vocation. There are few callings in life that will challenge and test you more thoroughly and steadily. At the same time, there are few callings in life that will satisfy you or enrich you more profoundly.

The Stresses of Ministry

Regrettably, many pastors today are more aware of the stresses than the satisfactions of ministry. In his book *Transforming Congregations for the Future*, Loren B. Mead commented: "No one needs to underline the pressure pastors are under today. As paradigms of ministry change, clergy are also buffeted by financial pressures, insecurity regarding their professional futures, and a diminished public image of their role in society. The multiplicity of changes that have simultaneously hit clergy leave them stressed and feeling burned out as they try harder to accomplish their work with reduced resources. All too often," he observes, "I find clergy almost immobilized—they are so aware of their pain and need."[6]

What has *happened* to them, one might ask! Church conflict has robbed them of some of the joy they looked for, and hoped for, in ministry. They have felt the frustration of too much to do and not enough time to do it. They have tasted the isolation and loneliness that often come with being a pastor. Their spiritual highs are countered by too many spiritual lows. They have searched in vain for true friendship, fellowship, or relationship with others in ministry. They have prayed and worked toward goals that have eluded them and their congregations. They have wondered whether or not they are serving in the right place, whether or not they have found the right congregation. Some have even wondered whether or not they have pursued the right vocation.

Those who have tried it know that the life of a pastor can leave you feeling like a ringmaster—scrambling to run a three-ring circus and keep all the tigers and clowns in their places. Others have found out that a pastor's life is often lived in a fishbowl, with folks looking on, and looking *in*, all the time.

6. P. 80. This book was published by the Alban Institute of Bethesda, Maryland, in 1994 as the third volume of Loren Mead's Once and Future Church series. The Alban Institute is a church research, resource, and publishing organization founded in 1974.

Some have learned that a pastor can be idolized, set up on a pedestal—a perch from which there's only one direction to go, and that direction is down! Others have felt the heat of the hot seat, the withering blast of criticism. Still others have sat on the mourners' bench, bothered by guilt, self-pity, or envy.

For Whom Is This Book Written?

This book is intended for them, but not *just* for them. We also write for those who may one day embark on this holy path of Christian service. This is not a book on stress or burnout,[7] although we hope it will help our readers to live with the former and avoid the latter. It is the inability to deal with stress that leads to burnout. We sincerely believe that if pastors can learn to do their work better, then their joy in ministry can also increase—and the joy of their congregations as well.

Who is offered more opportunities to employ all of his or her talents, abilities, and gifts than a pastor? Who enjoys a more immediate entrée into people's lives, hearts, and affections? Who finds such built-in support from a group of people wanting to love, to encourage, to *befriend* her or him, wanting simply to be close? Who but a pastor? Who is granted the immense satisfaction of serving as an instrument of God at the most acute times in people's lives? Who indeed but a pastor?

It is for pastors and pastors-in-training, then, that *Help! I'm a Pastor* is written. To those who are paddling desperately to keep their head above water, we are tossing some lifelines. We're not trying to teach you all the different strokes; we're trying to keep you from drowning. We also want to help you enjoy the swim. So this is a book for those who are yearning to thrive as well as for those who are struggling for survival. Our purpose is to identify and hone some of the practical tasks and skills required of pastors. So if you are a pastor or a pastor-to-be, we hope this book will help strengthen the connection between what you learned in seminary and what you do in your congregation. We also hope our thoughts will help you sharpen your own beliefs

7. Burnout can best be understood as a loss of ideals and hope. Stress can best be understood as a loss of fuel and energy. Burnout is a defense characterized by disengagement; stress is characterized by overengagement. In burnout the emotions become blunted; in stress they become overreactive. Burnout produces demoralization, a sense of helplessness and hopelessness, leading to paranoia, depersonalization, and detachment. Stress produces disintegration, a sense of urgency and hyperactivity, leading to panic, phobic, and anxiety-type disorders. The exhaustion of burnout affects motivation and drive; the exhaustion of stress affects physical energy. We are indebted to Dr. Archibald D. Hart for these distinctions between burnout and stress, quoted in part from a very helpful online article entitled "Stress and Burnout in Ministry," by Rowland Croucher, Director, John Mark Ministries (home page: http://jmm.aaa.net.au/).

about ministry and help you shape your ministerial style, so that your joy and satisfaction, and that of your congregation, may increase to the glory of God.

The Focus and Scope

Our intention is to look at the big picture of parish ministry, to get a broad view of what it means to be a pastor. Our focus is on the *pastor*, the ordained minister or priest serving a congregation, not on the lay minister. We offer some practical suggestions about different aspects and dimensions of a pastor's life and work. Obviously, we cannot cover everything, nor can we cover anything in depth. Our Contents table is not exhaustive. There are many other topics we could have considered. We feel the ones we have selected are important, and we have tried to present them briefly but thoughtfully.

Those who have taken courses or had experience in various phases of ministry will be in dialogue with these pages. We welcome the conversation! We are proceeding on the assumption that you do not consider yourself to be an expert in every aspect of ministry. Even if you have been a pastor for many years, we hope you will find it beneficial to check out your ways of doing things. Maybe you will discover some new ideas or insights as you read.

Then, too, we do have some ideas of our own to share—plenty of them, in fact! Together, we've been in ministry for a combined total of more than sixty years. We have spent much time reflecting on what we've seen, and learned, and done. We don't want simply to be imparters of facts and ideas. Rather we want those who read this book to be encouraged to think, to see things in new ways, to be creative. We believe the church needs self-reflective pastors who feel confident about what they are doing, and who are equipped for the glorious but demanding calling of ministry to and with a congregation.

Thinking Theologically about Ministry

We want you to think *theologically* about the varied tasks and roles pastors are called on to assume, and about the challenges—both professional and personal—that pastors must face every day. A theological understanding of what you are doing and why you are doing it will help you sort out some of the pressures and demands inherent in ministry. Some who read this book will be generalists, needing a little knowledge about a lot of things. Others will be specialists who need to see how their ministries fit into the big picture. Everyone will have specific interests, such as the relationship between preaching and pastoral care, or between evangelism and social action, or Christian education and worship. Most importantly, we hope this book will help you integrate your professional life with your personal life. How will you deal with the demands every pastor must face, particularly as they impact your personal life? Is it possible to be an effective pastor, a devoted spouse, and an available parent simultaneously?

Integration is always a pastor's task: integrating theory and practice, integrating the infinite facets of parish ministry, and integrating one's personal life with the full-time nature of every pastor's calling.

There are challenges confronting men and women alike as pastors and as human beings, but there continue to be special challenges presented to women in ministry. Unfortunately, stereotypical thinking persists among some parishioners even today as to roles and expectations, though increasingly those outmoded perceptions appear to be waning. Such thinking places a special challenge on all of us who share the pastor's calling, both male *and* female, to stand together, to support one another, and to lead by example.

We hold high hopes and great expectations for all who seek to live out the pastor's calling. We want to present to future ministers a high ideal of what a pastor should be and can be. We do this not to alarm you, but to inspire you; not to intimidate you about all a pastor needs to know, but to make you aware of what a tremendous challenge you are undertaking. We certainly don't want to shake your confidence in your ability to be a pastor. God cares more about our availability than about our ability. We *do*, however, want to dispel any illusions you may have about what a pastor is or should be. One of the best ways to avoid being disillusioned in the ministry is to avoid laboring under any illusions from which you will have to be "dissed"!

Nor do we want you to be frustrated about not being able to do everything. We do want you to learn to *live* with that frustration. We don't want you to be burdened by the overwhelming demands every pastor faces, demands that will claim everything you have to give and more. We do want you to be excited about discovering or *re*-discovering your unique gifts, and using them for the glory of God so that you can have the same love for the church, the same joy, the same satisfaction that we and many other pastors have had and continue to have today.

If this book can help you know who you are as a pastor, to remember whose pastor you are, to remind you "whence cometh" the inspiration, strength, power, and gifts to be a pastor, and to recall who alone is the ultimate Judge of your life and ministry, then our efforts will not have been wasted and the church of Jesus Christ will be all the better served.

At the end of each chapter you will find one or two "Pastoral Pointers." These are miscellaneous practical suggestions relating to pastoral ministry. We offer them hoping that some of the ideas will be helpful.

Pastoral Pointer

The clue to learning the names of the people in your congregation is not your ability to remember the names and faces of those you see at the door of your church. It is, instead, your inner commitment to be thinking and praying about your people throughout the week. Their names will come to mind on Sunday because their faces have been in your heart throughout the week. They will sense and appreciate this. Let your church directory be part of your intercessory prayer list.

Pastoral Pointer

Congregations like to think of themselves as "a friendly church." Worship leaders and preachers can greatly add to or detract from that impression. Friendliness begins in the pulpit. It doesn't hurt to smile once in a while! The pulpit is no place to keep a stiff upper lip.

Chapter 2

Shepherding a Flock

The Perfect Pastor?

The perfect pastor, as far as anyone knows, has yet to be born. If you spend any amount of time serving in a particular church, before long your people will know that God has sent to be their pastor one of those "earthen vessels" the apostle Paul talks about. There is nothing like being a pastor of a local church to stretch even your most considerable gifts, and, similarly, nothing quite like it to expose your frailties and weaknesses.

It is to be hoped that, after a while, congregations and pastors will learn to accept the fact that Christ called and still calls ordinary human beings to serve him. There is a wonderful grace and mystery in this, a maturing of the relationship between pastor and people. The clay feet of every pastor, matched by those of the pastor's people, serve as reminders that "the transcendent power belongs to God and not to us" (2 Cor. 4:7 RSV).

Yet some church members still hold out hope that, one day, the perfect pastor will be found. They're looking for someone who is young and good-looking with twenty-five years of experience as a pastor, who will be available to the congregation 24/7 but is a role model as a spouse and parent, who can delegate well but never does, who is in the office ten hours a day but is always out making calls, who is paid the minimum salary but is the biggest contributor to the church, who believes in evangelism but never expects anyone else to do it, who believes in stewardship but never mentions money in the pulpit, who preaches prophetically but never steps on anyone's toes, who is . . . you get the picture.

The word "pastor" is a transliteration of the Latin word *pastor*, meaning shepherd. It is derived from the Latin word *pastus*, which is the past participle of the verb *pascere*, "to feed." It was a rural term having to do with feeding or nourishing a flock. Hence the adjective "pastoral" pertains to shepherds or herdsmen. The New Testament Greek word for pastor is *poimen*, which is usually translated "shepherd." Jesus was the good *poimen*, the good shepherd. The shepherd-flock relationship became a key metaphor for parish ministers and their congregations.

In today's usage the term "pastor" identifies a position as well as a function of the one holding that position. Unlike the word "minister," it is a title as well as an office. So it is proper to address a parish minister as Pastor Johnson, but we don't say Minister Smith. Incidentally, it is grammatically improper to address a minister as "Reverend Jones." It is correct to speak *about* the Reverend John Jones or to refer to the Reverend Dr. John Jones or just Dr. Jones, but it is not really correct to say, "Good evening, Reverend Jones." Most of your congregants and not a few ministers are unaware of these distinctions, or they simply pay no attention to them. Nor are ministers who *are* aware likely to be offended by what has become a common practice.

Inasmuch as a pastor is called to serve, and employed by, a congregation, it is appropriate for us to make a few comments about the local church as a particular expression of the whole church, the worldwide communion of saints.

The Local Church

The New Testament presents various images of the church: the body of Christ, the bride of Christ, the flock of which Jesus is the Good Shepherd, the branches of which he is the true vine, the building of which he is the cornerstone. The disciples referred to Jesus as their Lord and Master and to themselves as his servants. Jesus, in turn, called them his "friends," but he was also their Redeemer, their Shepherd, their Savior, Teacher, Prophet, Priest, and King. He was the "only begotten Son of God." They were children by adoption, yet with him "joint heirs" of the kingdom of God.

We begin with the affirmation that Jesus Christ is head of the church. The church belongs to him, it exists and is sustained by the power of the Holy Spirit, who came to bear witness to him. Jesus promised that wherever two or three gathered in his name and for his sake, *there,* indeed, is the church!

The New Testament tells us the church is Christ's *body* on earth. If so, what should the local church be doing? What is the purpose, the raison d'être of the church? The Gospels remind us that "the Son of Man came not to be served but to serve, and to give his life a ransom for many" (Matt. 20:28; Mark 10:45; cf. Luke 22:27). Therefore, whatever else we believe a particular church should be and do, we must never forget that the church exists to *serve*, to minister to people in Christ's name and for his sake!

Think of the potential that exists in any local church. Think of the talent, the expertise, the accumulated experience that resides in your congregation. Your people's gifts, their pooled know-how, represent an immense resource for ministry to one another and to the wider community. The church is where the action is! Or at least where the action *should* be. Not all churches are living up to their potential. Some have no sense whatsoever of the possibilities for service and for growth. They are barely surviving, and, in their struggle for survival, they have lost their vision, their perspective, their hope—their reason for being a church!

The Size Factor

Whatever the size of the congregation, every church has its own potential. Every church faces its own set of challenges, as well. Pastors and church members are all too aware of the problems, which can cause them to lose sight of the potential.

Small churches have their own unique problems, such as the tendency to be preoccupied with their own survival. They have fewer leaders to draw on, limited resources and programs. But small churches have their own strengths as well, their own possibilities: a depth of intimacy, an immediacy of caring, a deep connectedness that can be harder to achieve with a large congregation. Small churches possess a stubborn and steadfast survivability, a high level of member involvement, and a deep sense of belonging.

Large churches also have their special challenges, and their own unique potential. Sunday mornings can seem impersonal, the worship services a sea of anonymous faces. Greater numbers can produce an illusion of "success," when little of substance is happening. A church may be growing because of the population explosion taking place around it, without engaging in any evangelism or outreach to unchurched neighbors. Meanwhile, internally factions can form and fault lines develop as the membership grows and communication becomes more difficult. Feelings of anonymity can discourage the involvement of marginal church members.

Large churches have their obvious strengths as well. Their greater personal and financial resources permit a wider array of programs, their leadership rosters have greater "bench strength," they can offer newcomers a multiplicity of plug-in points, with a variety of avenues for exploration, connection, and assimilation. They can benefit from the fact that growth begets growth.

What is the ideal size congregation for a pastor to serve? It depends on the pastor's particular gifts and emphases. There are different strokes for different folks! This is a question every pastor has to decide for himself or herself. When it comes to pastoral shoes, one size does not fit all. Some pastors serve best and are happiest in churches of 150 members or fewer. Their gifts are ideally suited to ministry in this more intimate sort of setting. These pastors, to be effective, should have strong pastoral gifts, a genuine love for people, an ability to demonstrate care and compassion. They should be good listeners and enjoy pastoral calling. They need to be "generalists," who are able to function well and be comfortable in a variety of ministry situations. They have to be Jacks or Jills of all pastoral trades, though admittedly they will be better at some than at others. They need to be less afraid and resentful of having to live in a fishbowl, for their lives are generally an open book in their communities. They need truly to have a shepherd's heart, and a desire to know and call each sheep by name.

Pastors of larger churches frequently need a slightly different set of gifts. They may find themselves excelling or specializing in specific areas of ministry: preaching, or Christian education, or pastoral care, or church administration, or youth ministry, or mission and outreach. They may prefer the opportunity, typically found only on the pastoral staffs of large congregations, to focus on their special gifts, or on areas of ministry not generally required in smaller congregations, such as personnel supervision or financial management. They may be inventive designers or planners of programs aimed at specific segments of larger congregations.

Be it to a large church or to a small church, neither calling is better. But one may be better for you. Neither calling is higher, but one may be a higher priority for you. It is important, therefore, to know yourself well, to consider the gifts God has given you and how the skills and interests God has blessed you with match the needs of the particular congregation whose call you may be considering. What kinds of people do you relate to best? What kinds of people respond best to your style? What are the expectations of the congregation you are thinking about when it comes to the person who will serve as their pastor? What kind of church will make best use of your gifts? Where are you needed most?

Pastoral Pointer

If in the polity of your denomination the procedure for calling a pastor involves a vote by the congregation, and if you are invited by their search committee to be their candidate, ask for an opportunity to speak informally with the congregation *(before* the congregational meeting) about your hopes and dreams for your ministry there, your vision of the church and its mission, your leadership style, and why you are open to a call. Share the enthusiasm that has made you receptive to the committee's invitation to be their candidate, but explain that you are not anxious to go anywhere God doesn't want you to be. Their decision will be God's word to you. You have made yourself vulnerable by speaking this way, but that kind of honesty is not only important but refreshing, for you want the congregation to know the kind of pastor you are and what you believe. If they don't want the real you, then that's not the church for you.

Chapter 3

Struggling to Survive

The Survivability of the Church

There have been and probably always will be prophets of doom who predict the death of the institutional church. Notwithstanding the growth of some congregations and the megachurch phenomenon, there are today critics ready to discard the church as we know it, arguing that it has outlived its usefulness, or that it has become so weakened and infirm as to jeopardize its very survival.

But until God reveals some other form by which to transmit God's truth from one generation to another, the church remains, for all its shortcomings, the community of faith of which Jesus Christ is still Lord in the mystery and power of the Holy Spirit. Our task is to be *faithful* and to entrust the future to God. We believe, furthermore, that *any* church that has a community to serve, a "parish," if you will, can not only survive but grow—spiritually and numerically. Circumstances beyond its control may limit its potential for numerical growth, but it can reach, maintain, and, yes, often exceed that potential.

Churches usually reflect the population trends of their communities. Whether particular churches are living up to their potential, however, depends primarily on their self-image, their self-perception, their openness to God's Spirit, and their depth of faith, and on the leadership of their officers and pastor(s). In other words, the survivability of a particular church depends to a large degree on the *ministry* of that particular church, and on both the pastor's and the people's enthusiasm for the work of Jesus Christ in their lives and community.

Whether you serve an inner-city parish, a suburban church, or a rural church, a large church or a small church, a "yoked" parish or a multistaff ministry, an African American church, a Hispanic church, a Korean church, or a church full of WASPs[1]—whatever the setting, whatever the location, whatever the size of the congregation, it is still the church of Jesus Christ. Faithfulness to Christ and his work is and always will be every church's primary calling.

A pastor's work in the local church has changed as times have changed. But the essentials have remained the same. There are still preaching, and teaching, and pastoral care. There are still education, and administration, and outreach. The world has changed and is still changing, but people's basic needs remain the same. There are new theories of church management and administration, but the Lord of the church is the same. There are new techniques in pastoral counseling, but the good news of Jesus Christ has not changed.

Will the church survive? "I am the Alpha and the Omega, the first and the last, the beginning and the end" (Rev. 22:13). Jesus Christ is "the church's one foundation," its eternally secure cornerstone. "I will build my church," Jesus said to Peter, "and the gates of Hades will not prevail against it" (Matt. 16:18). Yes, the church will survive. Congregations may change—and they should, if they want to thrive—but the church will survive!

The Survivability of the Pastor

Being a pastor looks easy . . . until you try it! It is not an easy calling. In their wake-up call to the local church entitled *Your Pastor Is an Endangered Species*, H. B. London and Neil Wiseman paint this picture of the realities of a pastor's life:

> Pastors live in a world that never stops, where the light never goes out, and where the average work week is between fifty-five and seventy-five hours. Seventy percent of their spouses work outside the home, meaning both are employed to keep themselves in ministry.
>
> Pastors dwell in a world of the unfinished tyranny, where they can't shut the door, walk out of the office, or know something is completely finished. There's always another Bible study, sermon, phone call, committee, hospital call, home visit, or gathering clamoring for attention. When someone dies or gets married or is hospitalized, the well-crafted schedule has to be abandoned and caught up later. Sometimes later is a long time coming.

1. White Anglo-Saxon Protestants. Although there are reasons why so-called ethnic churches may be needed for a time, we hope all congregations will strive to become more inclusive. Our point here is simply that Jesus Christ is Lord of the church, no matter what the makeup of the congregation, and the essentials of ministry are universally valid, though there may be cultural or ethnic differences in their application.

> Pastors live in a world of guilt about their families. Most want a family life that models marriage and parenting for their congregation. But that's tough to accomplish when they often spend more time with other people's kids than they spend with their own, and more time with other adults than with their spouse.
>
> Pastors live in a world of decreasing approval. . . . They serve in a "me-centered" world where church members and others are becoming more apathetic. . . . Some doubt whether they can make much of a difference in times like these. Consequently, pastors who want their lives to count are asking if ministry is worth the effort when compared with the results.[2]

A Three-Ring Circus

In chapter 1 we used some images to describe the challenges every conscientious pastor faces. One challenge is the sheer magnitude of the work. There are so many things going on at the same time. The image we suggested was that of a **three-ring circus.**[3] It symbolizes the busyness and the immense variety of demands on a pastor. An Episcopal priest was overheard to say his work made him feel, sometimes, as though he were "trying to herd cats." Sometimes it seems the pastor's main task is to bring order to this widespread confusion.

The sheer breadth of skills and knowledge expected and required is immense. As a pastor, you may find you are your own secretary, in which case, can you . . .

master word processing?
handle desktop publishing?
do the layout for the church's newsletter?
prepare and reproduce the Sunday bulletin?
set up and maintain a church filing system with some hope of retrieving what you have filed?

Other skills are constantly demanded as well. Can you operate a VCR or DVD? compile the denomination's annual statistical report? plan and carry out a stewardship campaign? prepare a budget and monitor it? set up financial

2. *Your Pastor Is an Endangered Species*, by H. B. London Jr. and N. B. Wiseman (Victor Books, 1996), pp. 31f.

3. Some have suggested that the church is more like a carnival than a circus, citing the fact that the various booths and rides at a carnival have little if any coordination or connection. There are a variety of unrelated activities taking place on the same grounds. But we prefer the circus analogy, because circuses, like churches, have structure, program, and organization. The main point is that there are many things going on in the church at the same time, and the pastor has the burden of keeping up with and helping to coordinate all of them.

controls and cost-accounting systems? write and submit a press release in proper form? establish and practice personnel policies that keep you within the law?

It goes without saying that you are expected to be able to conduct funerals and weddings, administer the sacraments, teach a church officer orientation class, visit the sick with a good bedside manner, befriend the elderly, encourage the young, comfort the grief-stricken, give hope to the hopeless, plan a preaching schedule, organize an evangelistic calling program, advise a young couple struggling with infertility, help a couple on the verge of divorce, counsel an alcoholic, set up a church library, develop a deferred giving program for your church, deliver the commencement address at the local high school, offer the invocation at a Rotary Club meeting, chair the church board and/or help guide its business, conduct a church officers retreat, mediate church conflicts, spend time with your family, exercise regularly, and get adequate sleep. It sure feels like a three-ring circus!

Your parishioners will often assume you are an expert in these and many other areas. Some, if not most, of their expectations will be impossible to fulfill. They would like you to be available in your study at all times, but also to be out calling in homes. They would like you to be a public figure, visible, involved, and active in important work beyond the church, but they complain if your involvements take you away from your duties with the congregation. They are anxious for you to bring new members into the church, but they prefer you not to be spending too much time with new folks, time that you could be spending with your present church members!

On it goes. Not every congregation is as understanding of these tensions in a pastor's life and work as some of the ones we have been privileged to serve. Being a pastor in parish ministry is not a nine-to-five job. It's a calling, not a job. You don't stop being their pastor when you leave your study. You are their pastor twenty-four hours a day. As we said earlier, you are much less likely to become disillusioned about ministry if you don't enter it with any illusions.

No one should "choose" to be a pastor expecting a life of tranquillity and ease. Some lay folks like to joke about the easy life we pastors have. "You work an hour or so on Sunday and drink tea and do a little reading to get ready for next Sunday. What a life!" We have never known a full-time pastor who had that job description. No congregation would tolerate it. The pressures of life today will not allow it. The fractured lives of families deserve something better.

Four More Images

If you have yet to become a pastor, there are some other realities of the pastor's calling of which you should be well aware so that you may be prepared for their impact on you (and on your family, if you live with one). We have expanded on the image of a three-ring circus. Let us do the same for the other four images we used in chapter 1 to symbolize these realities:

There is the image of the **fishbowl**, which reminds us that the pastor is a high-visibility person. While this image is often useful in terms of ministry, it points to a hard reality. Living in a fishbowl can be hard on you, hard on your spouse if you're married, hard on your children if you have any. As a nation we are seeing the perils of the fishbowl with great regularity today, as the lives of celebrities, politicians, and others become more and more the object of public scrutiny.

But if you are a pastor, fishbowl living comes with the territory. It is part of every pastor's calling. You may resent your lack of privacy, but a pastor cannot always claim that right. Very few if any pastors have unlisted addresses or unpublished phone numbers! Where you live will be public information, as will the kind of furniture you have, the kind of car you drive, and the kind of clothes you and your spouse wear. Your health and the health of your family (if you have one), your children's behavior, the movies you see, the places you go on vacation, what you do on your day off—these are all perceived to be matters of public information and legitimate topics of conversation.

This invasion of your private life is harder on the pastor's family, sometimes, than it is on the pastor. A subtle tug-of-war can develop over who "owns" you: your family or the church! Your children may view the church as a competitor for your time, and your spouse may view the congregation as a rival for your affection.

How grateful we can be for congregations that have allowed us, in our callings as pastors, to have family time, time away, time for our loved ones, time for ourselves! Even Jesus needed this kind of time. "In the morning, while it was still very dark, he got up and went out to a deserted place, and there he prayed" (Mark 1:35). We see him seeking the relaxation and refuge of time apart from the crowd, enjoying a meal with close and comfortable friends like Mary, Martha, and Lazarus.

But not every congregation is sensitive to the reality of the fishbowl. It is up to you to determine reasonable boundaries, to know what amount of privacy you need, to consider the feelings of your spouse and/or children, and to guard the boundaries you set. Your visibility as a pastor can be a wonderful asset to your ministry. It can be a solace to the flock, a source of encouragement, guidance, and strength. But if we are so available to our people that we are never fully available to our loved ones, to God, or to ourselves, in the long run we will serve no one very well. We become empty shells. The key is finding a workable balance.

Another image is that of the **pedestal**. It symbolizes the peril of misdirected adoration. You may find, to your embarrassment, that some people will seem more intent on idolizing you than on worshiping God! Particularly in a day when our culture seems to search more and more for heroes—having been disappointed by politicians, professional athletes, celebrities, and, in many cases, by their own family members—some will be tempted to put their pastor on a high pedestal. They will forget, for a moment at least, that God, in God's own perfect wisdom, and for God's own unfathomable reasons, decides to draw pastors from the ranks of human beings. Those whom God calls are imperfect, clay-footed sinners who need grace and forgiveness along with everyone else! Parishioners can easily forget the First Commandment, which cautions them to have no other gods but God.

True, a pastor *is* called to encourage others, to be an example, a humble example. But the pastor is never the *standard*. Only *Christ* is the standard. By lifting you up too high, well-meaning worshipers can set you up for a fall, not only in their eyes but in yours as well. They can tempt you to become proud, vainglorious, overconfident. It's lonely up there on the pedestal. You become isolated, and once you are up there, you soon find yourself hanging on for dear life!

Some years ago a study sponsored by the Association of Theological Schools in the United States and Canada (ATS), which at the time was composed of some two hundred Protestant, Catholic, and Orthodox seminaries and one Jewish seminary, pinpointed the number one quality American and Canadian congregations were looking for in their pastors and priests: "a willingness to serve without regard for acclaim." That perch on the pedestal is indeed a dangerous seat to occupy!

Two other images of every pastor's life come to mind. One is that of the **hot seat**, which symbolizes the reality that pastors are constantly being evaluated, compared, critiqued, and criticized. When things go wrong the buck stops with you. The hot seat is not a comfortable place to sit, but a pastor is often on it.

Drawing on a custom from old time revival meetings, where a bench for mourners and repentant sinners was placed at the front of the tent or hall, we use the **mourners' bench** as a final helpful image. It symbolizes the fact that the other realities we have mentioned can cause some pastors to moan and groan. The hot seat evokes their self-pity. The pedestal syndrome subjects them to the temptation of pride. The three-ring circus arouses their guilt about what is not getting done and their resentment, because they feel they're not getting the support they need. The reality of the fishbowl tempts them to be angry about their lack of privacy. All of these feelings can drive them to the mourners' bench. Nobody knows how hard I work. Nobody cares. Nobody understands. Poor me!

Rewards and Satisfactions

That's the bad news. The good news is that no other professional role offers more rewards and satisfactions than that of pastor. Yes, it is a three-ring circus, but where else can you find such an opportunity to use every talent God has given you for the good of other people and the glory of God? Yes, you live in a fishbowl, but what other profession gives you such an entrée into people's homes and hearts? You have a built-in community of people waiting to welcome you and be your friends. The parsonage, or manse, or rectory, or whatever the pastor's home is called in your denomination, can be a tremendously positive environment for raising a family, entertaining parishioners and friends, and sharing the joys and sorrows of life with one's spouse and children. Congregational life can provide children and youth with many positive role models. Spiritual themes, so often forgotten today in an increasingly secular world, simply become part of the tapestry and pattern of family life in a pastor's home.

Yes, there is the pedestal danger, but you don't have to remain on it. Put positively, what other work provides you with such a built-in support group, surrounds you with people who love, respect, and trust you instantly, simply because you are their pastor? Yes, you may sit on the hot seat now and then, but what other profession provides such opportunities for reconciliation and redemption? Where else can one experience the same spiritual satisfaction one receives from leading worship, administering the sacraments, preaching and teaching the love of Christ, and seeing the Holy Spirit at work in people's lives? A pastor's psychic income is tremendous!

Yes, you may be tempted to sit on the mourners' bench once in a while, but that very temptation forces us pastors to depend on God. We can resonate with the apostle Paul, knowing that when we are weak, then we are strong, for our strength is in God, whose grace is always sufficient.

So, all is not lost! We believe wholeheartedly in the survivability—indeed, in the *thrivability*—of the local pastor! As long as there are sheep there will be a need for shepherds. As long as there are human beings, there will be spiritual needs to be met! And as long as there are spiritual needs to be met, there will be a need for caring pastors to help meet them! It has been so since the dawning of Christ's kingdom. Until his kingdom work is accomplished, there will be a need for pastors to serve the church of Jesus Christ. As the apostle Paul noted twenty centuries ago, "the gifts he gave were that some would be apostles, some prophets, some evangelists, some *pastors* and teachers, to equip the saints for the work of ministry, for building up the body of Christ" (Eph. 4:11–12).

We are thankful to be among those who have been called to be pastors. The blessings have been innumerable, the compensations countless. Though the demands have been great, we can truthfully claim the satisfactions have been greater. We have both been in ministry long enough to have encountered plenty of high hurdles and lonely valleys. There have been occasions for personal and family sacrifice. But God has been faithful. God's grace has been *more* than sufficient, God's promises totally reliable. We have loved parish ministry, and still love it today! To use the vernacular, being a pastor is "where it's at"! Though one of us was eventually called to teach future pastors, he would be the first to agree that to serve as the pastor of a particular church is to be *on the front lines, in the trenches*, of Christ's kingdom work. To be ordained to pastoral ministry without ever serving a church would be like being in the Navy without ever going to sea!

So you *can* survive as a pastor, and what is more, you can actually *thrive*! You can come to love and enjoy the work that God has called you to. You can learn to look forward to each new day, not knowing what it will hold, but knowing that God holds you, that Christ has called you, equipped you with certain gifts, and promised to work in, with, and through you.

Pastoral Pointer

If in the calling process in your denomination you are required to preach a "candidating sermon," here are three DON'Ts and three DOs to remember:

DON'T . . . . *DO*
Perform . . . . Preach!
Pretend . . . . Be yourself!
Pontificate . . . . Relate!

And above all, you need to have

A SENSE OF THE OCCASION!

That's an important rule for every preacher, and every public speaker!

Chapter 4

Rethinking My Approach to Ministry

Understanding Your Role

*Y*ou will have greater staying power as a pastor, find greater meaning in your work, and find your life more satisfying and more purposeful if you have a solid theology of ministry. If you are not clear why you are doing what you are doing, if you are not charting your course with some kind of ministry map, some theological understanding of your role, your purpose, who you are, what it is that God wants you to do and why, your life as a pastor will lack the confidence, conviction, and strength it could otherwise have. If you lack a biblical/theological basis for your ministry, we urge you to do some reading in this foundational area.[1]

Do you embark on your work as a pastor with a sense of "call"? On what theological presuppositions or assumptions is your work as a pastor based? How do you understand your pastoral authority? How does it differ, if it does, from that of the laity? What, in your mind, are the unique contributions you are called to bring, as the *pastor,* to the life and work of your congregation? How do you understand your various pastoral roles—as preacher, teacher, administrator, overseer, planner, helper, guide, listener, learner, leader, follower? What biblical insights inform your understanding of each of these roles? Assuming you have been, are, or will be ordained, what do you believe about your ordination?

These are the kinds of questions every pastor needs to wrestle with. Your own ecclesiastical tradition will influence your response. How do you understand,

1. See, for example, *Pastor: The Theology and Practice of Ordained Ministry*, by William H. Willimon (Nashville: Abingdon Press, 2002). W. T. Purkiser's classic text, *The New Testament Image of the Ministry* (Boston: Beacon Hill, 1969), provides a helpful and still relevant overview of various biblical concepts and images of ministry. See also Willimon's book *Calling and Character: Virtues of the Ordained Life* (Abingdon Press, 2000).

for example, "the priesthood of all believers"? And how does that understanding inform your role as an ordained pastor?

Have you been shaped by a mentor, guide, or teacher who has influenced what you believe about being a pastor? How similar are you to your mentor? In what ways are you called to be different? If you have never had a mentor, can you think of a more experienced pastor whose approach or whose "style" and substance you admire?

Give thought to these questions as you read on, so that you can formulate your answers clearly. This will add strength and depth to your ministry and enable you to do what you do with integrity. Is your methodology consistent with your theology? That is a matter for continual self-examination and reflection.

Desirable Traits

If, as the ATS study referred to in chapter 3 indicated, the most significant trait that parishioners across denominational lines were looking for in their pastors was a willingness to serve without regard for personal acclaim, then humility certainly becomes a pastor. When it comes to "getting the credit," it is a wise and humble pastor who can whisper the prayer, "God, give me the willingness to be anonymous," and mean it!

According to that same study, people next wanted a pastor who has personal integrity, one who follows through on commitments, keeps promises, and does what he or she pledges to do. The ability to set a Christian example was the next most desired trait. Then came the desire for a pastor with good pastoral skills, and the ability to lead in building community within the life of the congregation. Other high-ranking qualities included those of a perceptive counselor, described as "one who reaches out to persons under stress with a perception, sensitivity, and warmth that is freeing and supportive." Also sought were qualities of a theologian and thinker, wherein the pastor's "basic intelligence is demonstrated in his or her communication." Parishioners wanted pastors "who are able to handle stressful situations by remaining calm under pressure, while continuing to affirm persons," and "who are able to acknowledge limitations and mistakes, and recognize the need for continued growth and learning."

On the opposite side, survey respondents did not want pastors who are self-serving, who avoid intimacy with people, or who involve themselves in illicit sexual relationships or other actions that "irritate, shock, or offend." They did not want pastors who are "emotionally immature, insincere, or insensitive."[2]

2. The results of the survey were reported in a document entitled *Readiness for Ministry*. The quotations are from Samuel Calian's discussion of the report in his book *Today's Pastor in Tomorrow's World* (Westminster Press, 1982), pp. 4–5.

As you consider your own approach to ministry, take a moment to reflect on these qualities. Discuss them with someone you trust who will be honest with you. As we have said, no pastor is perfect. It is quite likely the apostle Paul himself would have come up short on some of the qualities mentioned. But, as one ancient philosopher put it, "The unexamined life is not worth living."[3] A healthy self-awareness of your approach, your pastoral style, will help you *and* your congregation, and it will keep you mindful of areas in which you need to improve.

What Kind of Pastor Will You Be?

This, of course, is a critical question—critical to your pastorate, to the effectiveness of your work, to the work and witness of your congregation, and to the level of satisfaction you find in ministry. The answer will come first and foremost from you, as you consider your reasons for becoming a pastor, the gifts that God has given you, the things that you do best, the needs of your church, and the ways God's Spirit leads and guides you.

If you do not take the time to answer this question for yourself, or at least to think about it, then it will be answered for you by the demands and pressures of your church, the agendas of particular parishioners, the crises of the moment, the latest ministry fad or prepackaged program, the blur of circumstances, or even by the agendas of well-meaning family members or friends. Far better that you take the time to think about how you will deal with the pressures, the temptations, the successes, and the failures that will inevitably come your way in the course of your life as a pastor. There are some things to consider.

Interruptions

Jesus was always being interrupted. One day, for example, he was on his way to heal the desperately sick daughter of Jairus, a leader of the synagogue, when he was stopped by a woman with a hemorrhage (Mark 5:22–34; Luke 8:41–48). How did he respond to such interruptions? He commonly stopped what he was doing, turned his attention to the immediate need, and responded appropriately with a thoughtful word or a healing touch.

At other times, however, he did go off to be by himself. He was able to draw apart from the crowd and take time to be alone, hoping to avoid interruptions. But even his quiet times were subject to interruption! He went by

3. Socrates (470–399 BC).

boat to a secluded place to be alone, but the crowds followed him on foot from the towns. When he saw them, what did he do? Send them away, saying, "Can't you see I need to be alone"? No, Matthew tells us "he had compassion for them and cured their sick" (Matt. 14:14).

This tension exists in every pastor's ministry. Who of all people needs more time to be alone—time to be with God, to commune with God, to think about God, to drink deep from the wellsprings of Scripture and prayer—than a pastor? Yet who of all people needs more to be with others, connecting with people as they live their lives, providing that ministry of presence and pastoral care that is so vital to all God's people? No one more than a pastor!

How is it possible to be so available to others without sacrificing one's availability to God? Jesus managed it. He balanced his availabilities! We see him slip off by himself before daylight. We find him drawing apart from his disciples to be alone with God. We catch him asleep in the stern of a boat in a storm. Jesus found his own small sanctuaries of uninterrupted time. Somehow we who minister in his name must learn to find (or make!) ours, too.

It is never easy. Learn to expect interruptions in ministry. Ministry is full of interruptions. And don't be surprised when you discover that the interruptions *are* your ministry!

Still, to be effective, a pastor must have time for study, for personal devotions, for scriptural exegesis and sermon work, for letter writing, for telephone calls, answering e-mail and voice mail, sorting through messages, and for the myriads of tasks that accompany church administration. A pastor who shortchanges sermon writing in order to be with a church member in need has done a good thing and a not-so-good thing. One of the sheep of the flock has been helped, but all the others may be shortchanged by an inadequately prepared sermon or service that Sunday! A well-meaning church leader, attempting to help his overburdened pastor, offered this advice: "Pastor, you need to budget your time." The frustrated pastor replied, "The problem is not *budgeting* my time. It is *controlling* my time!" The schedules of conscientious pastors are in large part driven by the needs of others.

As a pastor, you will be called on regularly by members of your congregation when needs arise, and often by members of the community, who will turn to you for help in an emergency. People's needs don't honor your schedule. No pastor has invented a way to get people to confine their emergencies, or even their routine concerns, to his or her office hours. The secret lies in finding a happy balance you can live with. If you don't find that balance, you (and your spouse and children, if you have them) will struggle with ministry. The driven, "workaholic" pastor who complains about never having time to take a day off is not necessarily advancing the cause of the kingdom by his or her frenetic pace. Sometimes these driven pastors are serving their own need to be needed, or their own inability or unwillingness to establish appropriate boundaries. We pastors must learn how to be available to our congregation when we should be, to our family when we should be, to ourselves when we should be, and to God when we should be—the God who alone can help us find the balance that works for the kingdom, our family, and us.

Increasingly, today's congregations need to see this balance modeled. They have the same problems we do. In many cases their own lives are out of control. They are running breathlessly. They need to believe that balance is possible. They need to see it lived out in their spiritual leaders. And most importantly, they need to find it for themselves.

Criticism

Negative criticism can come crashing into your ministry when you least expect it, and from the people you least expected. Constructive criticism is helpful and nonthreatening; it keeps you humble. But negative criticism can suck the wind right out of your sails. It puts you on the defensive, tempts you to justify yourself. Whether positive or negative, criticism will keep you from ever doubting that the work you do is for the Lord alone, and that you need his help!

Criticism imposes on us ministers the burden of professional omniscience. We think we have to know it all. We do not, we cannot, we need not! A pastor who lives with a sense of his or her own infallibility teeters on dangerous ground. One of the most freeing admissions you can make in your work as a pastor is a simple, candid, "I don't know." Note that this is an *admission* and not a *confession*. There is no sin in not knowing everything. In fact, sin lurks in the *other* direction, that of hubris, of feigned omniscience, of wanting, as the serpent promised Eve, to "be like God."

Next to "I love you" and "I'm sorry," the simple statement "I don't know" may contain the three most important words in a pastor's vocabulary. Thank God that throughout your ministry honest critics will give you occasion to make holy use of all three of those statements.

Criticism also imposes on us the burden of moral perfection. Pastor Know-it-all often contends with the burden of trying to be Pastor Sinless as well, hiding his or her humanity, trying to project an example of moral perfection for the world to see. This was the Pharisees' bondage. Don't let it become yours. Remind yourself from time to time, if you have no one else to remind you, that you are *not* perfect. You cannot be. You need not be. You are human. You have clay feet. From dust you have come, to dust you shall return. You live and move and have your being, and your ministry, by God's grace.

What your people most need to see modeled by you is not how to live sinlessly, but how to live joyfully, freely, abundantly, having been redeemed, delivered, and accepted by God's amazing grace. They need to see what it looks like to be on the journey the apostle Paul calls "sanctification," growing from grace into grace by the power of God's indwelling, empowering Spirit. They don't expect to witness your "arrival" in the land of perfection this side of the River Jordan, because no human being this side of heaven will reach that land of perfection. "Not that I have already obtained this or have already reached the goal," confessed Paul, "but I press on to make it my own, because Christ Jesus has made me his own" (Phil. 3:12). The same forgiveness and grace you preach to your people they need to see finding a welcome place in your life too.

> Of all the miracles I've known
>   the greatest one must be
> that God in Jesus Christ can love
>   the likes of you and me![4]

Couple the burdens of professional omniscience and moral perfection with the burden of emotional invulnerability, the burden of always trying to be the tower of strength, the emotionally self-sufficient rock of Gibraltar. We are not, we cannot be, we need not be. It takes a while to be willing to reveal our emotions. Revealing them is not reveling in them. There's a big difference between genuine emotion and emotionalism. We need to be honest about our feelings, not brutally frank, but tactfully honest. It requires the willingness to be vulnerable.

To be sure, some kinds of criticism are easier to take than others. If someone criticizes the dress or suit you have on, you may let it roll right off. If they criticize your sermon, it may hit closer to home, especially if they do it minutes after you finish preaching it, like a parting shot as they go out the door of the church. That is a vulnerable moment for most pastors, who have just exposed their souls, their faith, their hearts. Their guard is down, their soft spots are exposed. Most parishioners do not realize that the best time to engage the preacher about something she or he said in a sermon is on Monday or Tuesday, perhaps by a phone call, not at the church door on Sunday. Criticism of this nature, though usually painful, is not as hurtful as criticism aimed at your family or loved ones, if that type should ever come your way. Similarly, no criticism will ever hurt your loved ones as much as criticism aimed at you.

4. This is the title poem of *Now, THAT'S a Miracle!* (CSS Publishing Co., 1996), by Richard Stoll Armstrong, p. 11.

Our advice on this matter is to decide whose opinions matter most to you. To whose criticism will you give the greatest weight? Whose opinions will you trust the most, and whose comments do you need to take most seriously? Fielding criticism is like shopping at a flea market: not everything is of equal value. Listen to people whose intentions you trust, who you know care deeply for you and for Christ's work. Pay heed to those whose intelligence and integrity you respect, whose Christian spirit you sense and appreciate. Constructive criticism can be among the greatest blessings you receive in ministry. What athlete could ever improve if the coach never offered any suggestions for improvement? What writer could ever win a Pulitzer prize if his or her editor were permitted no correcting marks? What performance could ever bring an audience to its feet if those on stage had never had any direction?

So distinguish your critics carefully, and decide whose opinions you are able to trust. Because, in truth, nearly every activity in the church, every change, every new direction, every initiative, every vision, will invite criticism. As the comedian Bill Cosby once put it, "The only boat that doesn't make any waves is the one that isn't going anywhere."

The temptation, as we have said, is to react defensively to criticism. The beast in us wants to lash back at our critics. But in a very real way they are our allies. They see to it that the suggestion box of the church never has a padlock on it. So we need to learn to digest criticism and grow from it, as bitter as it often can be. Throw away the bones, the indigestible parts, but chew on and digest the meat!

And thank your critics. They have cared enough to talk to you, to make their views known, to suggest better ways. They could simply have given up on you. They could have thought their comments not worth the trouble. They could have thought you to be unapproachable. (You might want to ask a trusted church member about that, someone who will tell you the truth.) So be thankful if they have chosen to come to you. Far better they talk *to* you than *about* you. Their willingness to sit down and confer with you testifies to their belief that you are approachable and willing to listen. If your critics *are* talking about you, but not to you, consider reaching out to them, letting them know you want to hear their concerns and that you are willing to discuss things with them.

Remember, too, that the ultimate judge of your ministry is the One who called you into it. Because of the nature of pastoral work, where few things ever please everyone, you will need continually to submit your labors to the God who has set you apart for the work of the kingdom, the God whose Son is the chief Shepherd of the flock, the cornerstone of the church. As God gives us light to see the Light, we must learn to judge our work as Christ would judge it, not as a self-flatterer, but as a self-critic, hoping that when all else is said and done, we will hear him say, "Well done, good and faithful servant."

And never forget, God sees into our hearts. God knows our intentions. God alone understands what we're trying to do and be. God knows our abilities, our limitations, the obstacles with which we are contending. God does not judge us the way some of our church members do. They may judge us by how well they like or don't like our sermons. But Christ uses a different measure. He expects our sermons to represent our best efforts, our sincere convictions, our compassionate concern for people, and our genuine love for him, his words, his world, his church. We can't guarantee that people will like our sermons, but we can and should promise them that our sermons will be carefully and prayerfully prepared, biblically based, theologically sound, and existentially relevant!

Christ expects us to use all the gifts God has given us for the upbuilding of his church. He expects us always to be open to the leading of the Holy Spirit, to keep an open mind and heart, that we might be faithful channels of his grace. Some of our sharpest critics in the pews may not realize that God is expecting the same of them too!

Doubts and Disappointments

One other thing we suggest you think about is how you will handle the setbacks that inevitably occur in ministry. How will you deal with your own faith struggles? your failures and disappointments? The integrity of your ministry stands or falls at this very point. It has to do with your devotional life, your own spiritual pilgrimage, and the honesty of your witness. We shall have more to say about this later on.

For now we want merely to underscore the need to determine your *style* of ministry. How you deal with interruptions, how you react to criticism, and how you handle your own doubts and disappointments will reflect your pastoral style. It's crucial that you get your act together before you plunge into the parish. Style is more important than method, and integrity is much more important than technique.

The Essentials of Ministry

Given the above realities, what are the essentials for effective pastoral ministry? Three come immediately to mind: first, *a strong personal faith in God*; second, *a sense of call*; and third, *an honest assessment of one's strengths and weaknesses*. An obvious fourth essential is *thorough training and preparation*. The last implies a well-rounded theological education, including a strong biblical foundation, the requisite ministerial skills, and a disciplined devotional life.

A Strong Personal Faith

You can't preach with integrity if you yourself don't believe in the God who has revealed himself in Jesus Christ and who calls us to place our trust in him. This does not mean doubt is banished. It does mean that you know at some level *that* you believe, *what* you believe, and *why* you believe it. It is virtually impossible to maintain this faith without a steady and consistent devotional life. It is your devotional life that empowers and energizes your witness.

As we've already stated, it is not necessary for the pastor to appear to be an emotional rock of ages. You aren't trying to teach people to sing, "A mighty fortress is our Pastor, a bulwark never failing." We can't deny our humanity. The great biblical heroes and heroines of the faith were fallible human beings. Throughout his letters the apostle Paul speaks candidly of his sufferings, his infirmities, his weaknesses, his own struggles with sin and temptation. He refers to himself as the chief of sinners, the least of the apostles, unfit to be called an apostle. We hear him agonizing, "I can will what is right, but I cannot do it. For I do not do the good I want, but the evil I do not want is what I do" (Rom. 7: 18b–19). Yet it is in his very *weakness*, that *God's* strength is revealed and made perfect (2 Cor. 12:9–10). The invincible pastor who appears to feel no pain, who seems to be immune to the ordinary struggles inherent in living the Christian faith, may even intimidate his or her parishioners or cause them to question their own faith.

We need to be honest in our ministry and not afraid to let people know how we feel—even when we're struggling. Our honesty helps make us, and the faith we profess, more real. That doesn't mean we have to spray our doubts over those sitting in the pews or pour out our personal troubles on those who come to us for help. It does mean that we need to let people see that pastors do have feelings. The shortest verse in the Bible may be one of the most poignant: "Jesus wept," John tells us, when Jesus saw his friends weeping at the tomb of Lazarus (John 11:35 RSV).

Because people are different, they will respond to you and your ministry in different ways. Just as no teacher is equally liked by all students, no coach equally respected by all players, no general equally revered by every soldier, no author equally enjoyed by every reader, so no pastor is equally loved by all of his or her parishioners. Pastors have to liberate themselves from the impossible task of getting everybody to like them. Peter and Paul didn't accomplish it. Neither did Jesus. If you are conscientious, most people will probably appreciate your ministry, but some may not. Some people, for a variety of reasons, may resent you or even thoroughly dislike you. That's hard to take.

And guess what: you won't like all of them either! As their pastor you are called to *love* them all, but you may not necessarily *like* them all. You certainly will like some better than others. You minister to everyone. You pray for everyone. You seek everyone's welfare. You're available to everyone. You deny no one your pastoral services. But there may be some individuals you find hard to like. And some may find it hard to like *you*.

> Just preach what they like and how lovely it goes.
> The honeymoon lasts till you step on their toes![5]

Every congregation has its share of "prickly pears," folks who are a little bit harder to like. One teacher of pastors has called them "E.G.R.s"—Extra Grace Required! But they need love just like everyone else. And, as their pastor, you need to love them—if not with your own love, then with the love flowing forth from the springs of Christ's love, as it flows through you. We must never forget that Jesus died for these folks too!

What is most important, ultimately, is not that all your people love *you*, but that they love *God* and are engaged in the work to which Christ calls them. If you minister with integrity and sincerity, most will respect you, even if they happen to disagree with you.

There is *one* person, however, who you need to be sure always, or almost always, likes you. For if this person begins to despise you, your ministry will soon be over. That person is the one who stares back at you every morning when you look in the mirror—you!

A Sense of Call

Another essential of pastoral ministry is a strong sense of call, a belief that God has drawn you to this work and commissioned you for it. Few pastors today claim to have heard God audibly speak, that is, in a way that someone else could have overheard in the same room. Not many pastors report visitations from angels who have addressed them face to face. But nearly every pastor with staying power, with a sustainable commitment to the work, with perseverance, conviction, and the ability to weather the ups and downs, no

5. *Enough, Already! And Other Church Rhymes*, by Richard Stoll Armstrong (Fairway Press, 1993), p. 24.

matter how he or she may have reached the conclusion, will report, "I am doing this because God wants me to be doing this."

Even if you are in an appointive system (e.g., Methodist) it is still important for you to believe that you are doing what you are doing because God wants you to, and that you are willing to remain an instrument in God's hands to be used as God sees fit. Don't let the human elements in any situation cloud your strong conviction that God has called you to minister wherever you are appointed!

Be honest and knowledgeable about your own strengths and weaknesses, always open to the possibility that God may have a new assignment waiting for you, whether it comes via the call of a congregation or the appointment of a bishop. This requires constant self-evaluation, a continual assessing of your gifts, your skills, and the needs of your congregation. Where and how can you best serve Christ? Where can he make best use of your gifts? Have you finished all the work you believe God has called you to do where you are right now? Or have you barely scratched the surface?

Some feel God's call to serve a particular church for a short time; others may sense the same call for a lifetime! Wherever we may be on the Master's course, we need to keep an open stance! We have to be careful not to hamstring the Holy Spirit. We can be grateful for our gifts and for whatever God has accomplished through us, without becoming proud. We pray for God to fill us with assurance, courage, and determination to serve to the best of our ability, until the Holy Spirit lets us know God has other plans for us.

Pastoral ministry is a vocation. The word itself means "calling." Without a sense of call it is extremely difficult if not impossible to sustain effective, fruitful ministry.

An Honest Assessment of Your Strengths and Weaknesses

A third and obvious essential of ministry is an honest assessment of your strengths and weaknesses. One's natural response to a call of God may be a feeling of unworthiness. One does not aspire to be a minister; one is *called* to be a minister. In most communions that call must be confirmed by the judgment of the church. In considering our call to ministry, we must listen to the voice of the church, including those who teach us and those who examine us. Is it a genuine call, or is it our own starry-eyed desire to be somebody others will look up to and admire? Do we see ourselves one day filling some prestigious pulpit in a church of five thousand members?

As pastors, the flattery of our congregants can blind us to our own inadequacies. Well-meaning but undiscerning church members can tempt us to think we are better preachers than we are. We may not be the scintillating teacher, the stimulating worship leader, the sharp administrator, capable counselor we think we are. This is when the constructive criticism of those we trust and respect can be most helpful.

Thorough Training and Preparation

While some aspects of ministry may look easy to a casual observer, effective pastoral work is complex, multilayered, and often dizzily demanding. Even the best training leaves one only minimally prepared to meet all the challenges of pastoral work. Ongoing training and continuing education must be lifelong if one is to remain proficient. Seminaries, divinity schools, and denominations continue to wrestle with what is needed to prepare someone to be a pastor today.

Most would insist that a pastor's preparation include solid theological training. Pastors need to know what they believe, and, too, how their understanding of the faith relates to the understandings of other branches of the Christian family. In our increasingly pluralistic world, we believe it is important for pastors also to have some understanding of the beliefs of other faiths.

Pastors need a strong biblical foundation, as well. They need to have a solid knowledge of the Bible. They don't have to memorize its contents, but they should know where to find what they're looking for. They also need to know and to be able to articulate what they believe about the authority and inspiration of the Scriptures. They need to be able to teach others why and how the Bible should be used in the life of the believer, and of the church, and they should have a clear understanding of how they will interpret and use the Bible in their own preaching and teaching ministry.

Of all people, pastors should know the importance of a disciplined devotional life. Habits of personal study, devotional reading, meditation, and prayer should be developed in seminary. A devotional life is not something that begins after one becomes a pastor. It is in the devotional center of a pastor's life that the power for ministry is generated and replenished. It is frighteningly easy for pastors to become "professionals" who do not practice what they preach. We in the ministry can be so busy talking *about* God that we never talk *to* God; so busy telling people what the Bible says that we fail to hear what it's saying to *us*; so absorbed in rummaging through the Scriptures for sermon material that we never really *study* them for ourselves! It is the pastor's devotional life that counteracts these temptations.

So the question for those who want to be ministers is, What kind of minister do you want to be?

Pastoral Pointer

Have a church officers retreat soon after your arrival at your new church, and covenant with one another regarding your common ministry, your dreams for the church, and how you will relate to and work with each other. The purpose is team building and faith sharing, not planning. If you are an associate pastor, ask for a staff retreat for the same purpose. Share with one another what it will take for each of you to be fulfilled in your ministry together.

Pastoral Pointer

If a particular hymn would make a perfect conclusion or closing prayer to your sermon, consider having the organist play the tune *very softly* as you speak the words. You will find that you can speak two stanzas while one is being played. When some pastors or lay people do this they make the mistake of trying to say the words exactly as the notes are being played. The pace is awkward and the effect is lost. If it's done properly, the impact is powerful. Practice with the organist ahead of time.

Chapter 5

Beginning a New Ministry

A Word of Caution

*P*ermit us to offer a word of caution to every pastor beginning a new ministry: Don't begin your ministry by disparaging something that might be important to people in your congregation. You may be sorely tempted, early on, to speak critically of a style of worship, a particular program, a church office procedure, or some other feature of your church's life that, unbeknownst to you, has great meaning or value to people in your congregation. You may be justified in your criticism, but *resist the temptation.* **Take time first to listen**! Learn the history of what is being done, and why it is being done that way. You may lose some time but you will gain the appreciation and earn the trust of your new congregation. Honor their traditions until you've had time to evaluate and decide with their official board what new directions, if any, the congregation should take.

Similarly, think twice before introducing something that may offend or disturb the sensitivities of your new congregation. There are always exceptions to this caveat, but generally it's good to wait until you've had time to get to know the lay of the land, and until you *have earned the right to be heard.* Things are seldom as they seem at first glance. You will need to set a prudent pace for progress, or your best-laid plans may never get off the ground. Some would argue that during the "honeymoon period" is a good time to make changes, but we respectfully disagree. Building up the church takes time and patience. It is always wise to listen before you speak and to look before you leap. Your ordination gives you the right to speak, but you have to win the right to be heard. Trust is something that can only be given, not demanded.

The Call to a Parish

We have mentioned the importance of knowing yourself. This is especially true when considering a call. Your resumé or dossier should reflect the real you, not a false or inflated you. It is unfair and even unethical to present a false picture of yourself to a prospective congregation. What if they call you and you turn out to be someone quite different from the person they expected? Sad but true, that happens all too often. You owe it to God and to the congregation to introduce them to the authentic you. If they don't want the person you really are, then that's not the church for you.

So, try to acquaint them with your theology. Give them a sense of what you believe. Share your personal faith. Explain and illustrate your ministry style: Are you formal, informal, driven, relaxed, gracious, demanding, spontaneous, planned? What excites you about pastoral ministry? What is your vision for the church? What special gifts do you believe you have, at least as you now perceive them? What are your weaknesses? What are your strengths? What do you do best? Where do you need to grow?

What do you want them to know about your personal needs and those of your family? Does one of your children need special medical care? Are you concerned about an aging family member who may soon be living with you? Congregations almost always do better knowing these things up front. The grace, acceptance, understanding, and support of God's people can be remarkable. As in any marriage, however, it helps to let your potential partner know your situation and your needs before you tie the knot.

You also want the search committee to know what it takes for you to feel fulfilled in your ministry. And what are the church's needs and expectations? Do you see a match or mismatch forming? The more you know about yourself, as a person and as a pastor, and the more clearly you can conceptualize and articulate your self-understanding, the less likely you are to deceive yourself about a church, or to mislead a church about you!

Of course, ultimately, matching congregations and pastors is God's business. It is up to us to seek to discern and be open to God's wisdom and sovereign will. God sees far more clearly than we do! The process of discernment requires us to be aware of our gifts, to seek a sense of how our abilities and training and interests align with a particular opportunity or need. We're often inclined to run ahead of the Holy Spirit in this process and peer over the next hill to see what's on the horizon. This is a time for us to *follow* the leading of the Spirit, to be diligent in the practice of prayer, and to remember that one of the fruits of the Spirit is patience.

Then, too, we must know the individuals whose responsibility it is to call us to a new ministry, whether our faith tradition presents us with a pastor-nominating committee, a pulpit committee, a pastor-parish relations committee, a bishop, a district superintendent, or some other individual or group. The search committee will give you your first real sense of the life and tone of the congregation they represent. In your conversations with them, be mindful of who is interviewing whom. It should be a two-way street. They will be seeking to learn more about you, of course, but you will want to take advantage of this time to learn more about them and about their church. How do they describe the corporate personality and temperament of their congregation? What do they say about the congregation's vision, hopes, and dreams, about their faith in God, about the spiritual temperature of the congregation, about the challenges they have met and must meet, and about their openness to new ideas and perhaps a new style of leadership?

The purpose of both sides in their conversations about a new call should be to see if this feels like a match. Does God want to bring you and this congregation together? If you don't sense a clear yes, then the answer may be no. We believe strongly in praying for and being open to God's leading, God's presence, God's peace. Often in these conversations you will discover that you need to take charge of the interview at times; that is, it may be up to you to steer the conversation, gently and tactfully, so that your time together will be most useful for them and for you. If you make it a *faith-sharing* conversation, it will indeed be a meaningful experience for you and for them, regardless of the outcome.

If there are other staff members, you will want to find out as much as you can about them. This is most important. If the church you are considering has a good staff made up of people who love what they do, who are committed to the work of the church, and who enjoy one another, if morale is high and if a spirit of teamwork abounds, then you are looking at what may be a great situation! If, on the other hand, you discover that there has been high staff turnover and low retention, if you sense that morale is low, and if there are simmering conflicts or personality clashes that have not been resolved, then you can be quite sure that whoever comes to serve this church will be facing a difficult situation. Arguably the greatest problem facing multiple-staff churches everywhere today is troubled staff relationships. This may come as a surprise to some, until they remember that two of the disciples infuriated their colleagues by confronting Jesus with the question of who would be at his right hand and who at his left in his kingdom (Mark 10:35–45; cf. Matt. 20:20–28 and Luke 22:24–27).

In asking about the church staff, you need also to strive for role clarification. What would be your primary responsibilities? What would be handled by others? Are there written job descriptions? If so, are they set in concrete, or are they flexible? What are the lines of accountability? By whom and by what criteria and process will you and others be evaluated?

In multistaff churches, some of the things you will want to look for that make for good staff relationships include a theological compatibility among church staff members (especially the pastoral staff), affinity of lifestyle, congruity of work habits, a high level of trust, and a common concern for maintaining good relationships. It is a positive sign when you find a church staff that prays together and plays together. Praise for work well done should be frequent, and expressed both publicly and privately. Criticism should usually be offered privately. A good rule for heads of staff is: public praise, private reprimand. Psychic income factors, such as adequate recognition of one's work, are extremely important for maintaining high morale.

There should also be an expectation that church staff members have their days off, and that they take the vacation time due them. See if you can discern how the congregation (and the staff!) regard the staff members' responsibilities as spouses and parents. Congregational attitudes may have been shaped for good or for ill by the practices of a previous pastor. Excessive work habits should not be the standard. Beware of the congregation that expects its staff members to be workaholics! Those who have been brought up with the so-called Protestant work ethic have no trouble remembering there are commandments against stealing, against bearing false witness, and against adultery. They seem to forget there is a commandment about keeping a Sabbath.

In your discussions with the search committee you will also want to find out about the community where the church is located. This information will not magically tell you whether or not to minister there, but it *will* help you to be better informed and more knowledgeable in your thinking and praying about a call there.

Learn what you can about the political climate and the demographics of the community. Is the population increasing or decreasing? Is the community changing? What kinds of people live in the vicinity of the church? College students? Elderly? Suburban families with two working parents? Farmers? Ranchers? Yuppies? What are the ethnic, and religious, and linguistic, and social, and cultural demographics of the community? A young Lutheran pastor we know discovered pastoral ministry felt completely different when he moved from a large Lutheran congregation in Wisconsin to a small Lutheran church in a predominantly Hispanic neighborhood of South Los Angeles.

These are just some of the factors relevant to your consideration of any call. They set the stage for your ministry. The more you can discover about a particular church and its community, the more clearly you will be able to tell whether or not your gifts match that church's needs. You will sense an answer forming in response to your question, "Is God calling me to this church?"

It's like Courtship and Marriage

The matching of pastors and congregations has been likened to the process of courtship and marriage. In some branches of the Christian family the pastor-parish marriage is essentially arranged by somebody else, a bishop perhaps, who has, we would hope, *both* parties' interests at heart. In other branches of the Christian family, with their differing polities, pastors and churches somehow manage to find one another, through some formal institutional process or through divine serendipity! Some denominations use various forms of computer screening and matching. Whatever the method, we must believe God is at work and guiding the process for the good both of the pastor and of the particular congregation.

The courtship is the period involving letters, phone calls, meeting each other, trying out each other's names. A church committee may ask you about your family. You may ask about *theirs*—the congregation! The engagement comes when you have reached the point of sufficient comfort—even joy—with each other that you decide to "make it legal" and enter into a committed, faithful relationship. Announcements are sent out, a ceremony is planned. Now you are eager to meet each other's families! If you have been courting any others, you should let them know you are now spoken for. (The church should do the same!)

The installation ceremony serves as your wedding day. You are now joined, pastor and church, in ecclesiastical wedlock. You are hitched. You are mated. Both you and the congregation want to believe it's a match made in heaven. You say your vows and make your commitments in a service of worship. Church bells ring. Music plays. Cameras flash. You alert your friends to your change of address. Your father may smile, your mother may cry. There may be a cake to cut. Some of your friends or family wonder what you see in her anyway (this particular church). Others may wonder what the church (or the committee or the bishop) sees in you! Most of the church members will rejoice that they have found someone who will truly love them, someone who thinks they are wonderful, and who believes in them.

Meanwhile, close friends of the church, denominational officials, and others are hoping that you will be loving and kind to your new congregation, and faithful to them, and that they will blossom in their new relationship with you. Your relatives and friends and all those who love you are hoping the church will be good for you, and that you will be happy too. One New Testament image of the church is "the bride of Christ." Sometimes it seems she's the *pastor*'s spouse too!

Next comes the honeymoon phase, which varies in length. Some honeymoons are in trouble before they even get off the ground. But others keep going, in some cases for years. The honeymoon period is marked by an almost giddy joy, a feeling of euphoria that this was indeed a marriage made in heaven.

Then comes reality, as with most marriages. That's not necessarily bad. Indeed, it can and should be a time of maturing love, growing trust, and deepening friendship, when pastor and flock become aware of each other's humanness and imperfections, and learn to accept and embrace each other with love and grace. Your relationship with a congregation is deeper and more honest in this phase than in the courtship, more sustainable and abiding than the honeymoon, more intimate and binding than either. It is also more dependent on grace and acceptance than on perfection and performance. In a sense, in the reality period your marriage is now free to be more truly Christian than it has ever been before. It is the way the relationship between a pastor and a congregation should be. You are becoming one in Christ.

In the reality phase you learn to deal with conflict, with disappointed hopes and unfulfilled expectations. Churches learn their new pastor may *not* be all they had hoped for. Pastors learn this of their churches, too. It is living with this reality that causes you sometimes to picture Jesus, near the end of his life, looking sorrowfully on those with whom he had lived, traveled, eaten, slept, taught, and worked for three years. "Have I been with you all this time, Philip, and you still do not know me?" (John 14:9).

Pastor and people learn each other's limitations, each other's gifts and joys. You are made aware over and over again that God is a God of surprises. God is not bound by our expectations, and God is able to do more than we could ever ask or think, if we remain open to him. The reality phase is a time of deep understanding, of trust, of forgiveness, of mutual encouragement and amazing grace. It is a time of second chances. You learn that it's possible to work things out. You realize that you can get through trying times together. You learn to encourage each other's faith and to rely on each other's faith. You learn to grow together.

The reality phase leads, it is to be hoped, to a period we might call the "compatibility phase." Its hallmarks are mutual acceptance and appreciation. Pastor and congregation learn to appreciate each other not for what they wish the other *could* be, but for who the other is. You and your flock value what

God has done and is doing in and through you, together. A sense of balance, a feeling of gratitude, characterize this compatibility. You have learned to accept, embrace, and appreciate each other, just as God in Jesus Christ has accepted us all. The trust level is high. You can each almost predict what the other is going to do. This high level of trust and mutual awareness enables you to accomplish, during these years, some of your most important work together.[1]

You have attained true maturity in your relationship. You have been through much together. You have seen firsthand the steadfast love and faithfulness of God in your lives. The maturity phase is a time of quiet rejoicing, a time of thanksgiving for what God has enabled you to accomplish together, a time of looking ahead to the next generation and to those who will come after you. It is also a time of recommitment, of recalling the journey, of dreaming about tomorrow and about what God may have in store for you and for the church. It may be the prelude to the time for parting, when you conclude this chapter of your ministry and prepare the scene for whoever will come after you.

Not every pastor-parish relationship goes through all these phases. As we have said, you must always be listening for God's marching orders, and at the same time watching for the confirming evidence of God's call to stay where you are. We can never know for sure how long we will serve in any given situation. But however long God may give you in a particular church or ministry, don't forget: it's the simple things in a marriage that help keep the honeymoon going! Just for fun, try remembering your anniversary date each year and let your congregation know how much you love and appreciate them.

Pastoral Pointer

Early on in your new pastorate, establish contact and rapport with the in-folks and the out-folks of your predecessor, preferably by personal visits in their homes. Win over the special friends and win back the alienated, by being a good listener and without ever being critical of your predecessor.

1. We note at this point that virtually all commentators on church life and pastoral work emphasize the importance of long pastorates for optimal congregational growth.

Pastoral Pointer

Keep and remember to use a guest book. Have people sign it every time they visit. It is a most useful reminder, and a permanent record, of those who visit you and when.

Chapter 6

Trying to Balance My Personal Life and Ministry

Your Name Is Legion

*I*t is sometimes hard to know where your professional (pastoral) life ends and your personal life begins. That's because the two are so often intertwined that it's impossible to separate them.

It's your day off. You and your spouse take your small children on a long-awaited outing to the zoo. You run into a church member at the concession stand. She wants to talk. Who and what are you at this moment? Are you primarily a parent, a spouse, or a pastor? What and to whom are your primary obligations?

Or how about this: It's Friday night, the first night in a week that you are free from church meetings, hospital visits, or home calls on church members. You and your spouse decide to take in a movie. You've spent too little time together lately, and you need to have a "date." You enter the darkened theater, popcorn in hand, and are finding some seats when a friendly tap on your elbow turns your attention to a couple seated directly behind you. They are from church. They want you to join them. Later they whisper they're going out after the movie and would like you and your spouse to accompany them. Who are you at this moment? Are you primarily a spouse or a pastor? What about that time alone with your spouse, to which you both have looked forward? What do you do?

Or envision a Saturday luncheon program for the retirees of your church that has been in your date book for weeks. The planning committee has asked you to lead an opening Bible study, and to pose for a photo with five saints who will be celebrating fifty years of church membership. One of these dear elderly people will be brought to the luncheon from the local nursing home in a wheelchair-equipped van. The local paper will be covering the event. The luncheon is scheduled to begin at 11:30 a.m. At 11:20 a.m. the church office phone rings.

Your school-age daughter is calling from home. She says water is spraying out of the hose connecting the washing machine to the wall. No one else is at home at the moment. Her voice is edging toward panic. She has tried turning off the washing machine. She has thrown towels on the floor to soak up the flood. But your family-room carpet is already wet, and the leading edge of the water is spreading. Who are you at this moment? Are you primarily a parent, a spouse, a homeowner, a damage-control specialist, a pastor—or all of the above?

Your pastoral identity overlaps everything—even your civic life! Suppose a school bond referendum is coming up for a vote in your community. A yes vote will expand the high school, which is crowded beyond capacity. As a parent of two school-age kids, you strongly favor expansion. And you strongly believe it to be in the best long-term interest of your community. But many in your community oppose it. A yes vote would raise everyone's taxes. Opinion is divided in your congregation, and you know it is. You feel a civic and parental obligation to work for the referendum's passage. A member of the "Vote Yes" committee calls you at home one night and asks if you would put a "Vote Yes" sign in your front yard. She informs you a "Vote Yes" rally will be held that Saturday in front of the Town Hall. She invites you to be there, and hopes you will come to show everyone your support. She says she knows your presence "would say a lot to everybody." She invites you to speak at the rally. Who are you at this moment? Are you a parent, a voter, a citizen, a taxpayer, a homeowner, an advocate, or are you a pastor? Or are you all simultaneously?

The answer in each situation above is that your name is Legion! There will be countless situations in which you will find you are many things at the same time. This is a fact of every pastor's life. It is one of the challenges of ministry! Here are some thoughts to help you align your personal life with your pastoral identity.

Family Matters: Your Spouse

Let's begin with your spouse, if you are married. It *can* be a great joy to be married to a pastor. It can also be terribly difficult and trying. Remember, your spouse will feel the effects of the occupational challenges you face—of living in the fishbowl, in the limelight, under the spotlight, atop the pedestal, on the mourners' bench, and, yes, especially on the hot seat. You will help your ministry and your marriage if you remember to fulfill your obligations as a spouse. You have a duty to protect him or her from unreasonably demanding, overly inquisitive, hypercritical parishioners. Interpret and defend the role he or she chooses to play in your congregation. Don't force or push your spouse into ill-fitting involvements. Remember, you are dealing with people's *images* of your and your spouse's roles, images that are sometimes unspoken, sometimes uncertain, and sometimes unrealistic, given the nature of people's lives and of our world today. Times are changing. Expectations are changing. But congregations still have expectations. They have expectations of you as pastor and expectations of your spouse, even if they are not fully aware of it. You can help inform and guide their expectations by letting them know what *you* expect of your spouse, and what your spouse desires, needs, and deserves in his or her own church involvement.

A Pastor's Expectations of His or Her Spouse

Most pastors want and need their spouses to offer a sympathetic ear. Ministry is a lonely calling. It helps to have someone to talk to, someone who is willing to listen, someone who understands and can keep confidences. Most pastors want and need their spouses to provide them with honest, constructive criticism. As the book of Proverbs reminds us, everyone's way is right in one's own eyes (Prov. 21:2), but an observant, thoughtful spouse can point out the things we're doing (or *not* doing) that may not be proper or helpful. Thoughtful criticism, to be most productive, should be offered privately and lovingly, and should be accompanied by affirmation of what was good, successful, or effective.

Most pastors want and need their spouses to play a supportive role in the life of the church. That means at least being present, actively involved, and enthusiastic. They don't want their spouses to be bossy, officious, or usurping. Most pastors hope their spouses will understand the pressures they are facing, the 24/7 nature of the job, the fishbowl/pedestal/hot seat/mourners' bench/three-ring circus pressures of pastoral ministry, the demands of dealing with people's physical, spiritual, and emotional needs, the burden of leadership and decision making. Pastors want their spouses to be patient when their pastoral schedule gets overfull, when their stress level seems to be rising, when the demands of ministry test their humanness and they become tense or short-tempered. The same pressures, of course, can afflict the pastor's spouse too. We'll say more about that later.

The remarkable truth is that God uses us earthen vessels, flawed human beings that we are, to carry his treasure, to do his work, to lead his people, to shepherd his congregations. What Jesus said to his first disciples has been true of every follower since: "The spirit indeed is willing, but the flesh is weak" (Matt. 26:41; Mark 14:38).

At times like these—and there *will* be times like these—pastors need their spouses to be patient and encouraging. It is so important for a pastor's spouse to keep faith in God and not to see the church as a rival. The church can be a demanding mistress, indeed. While she gives life and joy and hope, she demands a great deal of those whom God calls to be pastors. What is true of Christ is true of his church: with the life he offers comes the burden—and the glory—of his cross.

Sometimes a pastor needs nothing more from a spouse than tactful silence. Some things cannot be shared at home, and they should not be discussed. An inquiring, controlling curiosity on the part of a pastor's spouse does not help a pastor and is inappropriate. What people tell a pastor in counseling, for example, is strictly confidential and should never become a topic of conversation at the pastor's dinner table. Church members frequently assume their pastors' spouses know more than they actually do. They assume that pastors tell their spouses about church members' cares and concerns. Quite the opposite is usually the case. Pastors' spouses, therefore, need to learn how to respond sensitively and tactfully to church members who assume they are in the know.

Pastors and spouses must understand and respect each other's needs for both space and intimacy. Pastors spend so much of their time with people, many of whom are beset with pressing needs, that a measure of solitude, time alone with God, is essential for survival and effectiveness in ministry. Pastors need their quiet time to meditate and pray. For pastors faced with the daunting task of crafting a sermon every week, time for reading and reflection is an occupational necessity. Mark tells us that "in the morning, while it was still very dark, he got up and went out to a deserted place, and there he prayed" (Mark 1:35). If our Lord needed his quiet times, how much more do we! Pastors expect their spouses to understand and respect their need for solitude *as well as* for togetherness and intimacy. This is an ongoing give-and-take in most clergy marriages. *Balance* is the key.

Finally, pastors who are parents want their spouses to join them in the responsibilities and commitments of parenthood. (Spouses, as we will note below, need their pastor husbands or wives to be committed to the task and privilege of parenting too!) Those who have attempted to do both know that parenting and pastoring are both full-time jobs! They are both full-time challenges demanding total concern. Each calls for around-the-clock energy and attention. Since we are focusing here on the pastor's needs, we must emphasize that pastors have a right to expect their spouse to help shoulder the demands, if they have children, of parenting.

A Spouse's Expectations

What does a *spouse* have a right to expect of the pastor to whom he or she is married? Our availability, to begin with—our *presence*, not our relentless, oblivious absence. In writing this, both of us want to state publicly that our own wives, Faith Morledge and Margie Armstrong, have every right to expect us to be husbands and fathers in more than title only, despite the fact that we have been called to the Lord's work and are never finished with it. Nobody marries with the intention of being alone all the time, and that includes the spouses of pastors!

If you are a busy pastor—and what conscientious pastor isn't busy?—there are numerous occasions when your spouse has to take second place to some pressing demand in your pastoral work. A church member is rushed to the hospital. You go to be with that person. Someone is suicidal. You go. Parents of a teenager in your congregation call. Their daughter has run away from home. You go to be with them. A church member fighting an addiction calls and wants desperately to talk with you. You can't say no. A couple on the verge of divorce call. Someone dies on your spouse's birthday. You go to be with the bereaved family. A church board meeting falls on your anniversary date. You have a decision to make! Many dutiful pastors will show up at that meeting.

To compensate for these continual interruptions and to fulfill your own responsibilities as a spouse, and for the continuing strength of your relationship, you need to think seriously and creatively about what you can do to give your spouse an extra bit of you from time to time. A couple of ideas we have found useful in our ministries have included setting aside a regular "date night," when your spouse can count on being with you. Put it on your calendar. Circle the date in red. Let your spouse know that you will hold that date sacrosanct, and only under the rarest and most pressing circumstance will you break it. If you must break it, you will *immediately* schedule a makeup date.

Special "getaways" with your spouse can help immensely. If you haven't tried it, you'll be surprised how refreshed your relationship can be after a Friday and Saturday getaway. If he or she is employed, arranging such getaways can be more difficult. But the two of you may need a little time away from the children. It is exciting for both of you, if on occasion, you can be spontaneous! Call your stay-at-home spouse in the middle of the day, and do something you enjoy doing together. Escape to the park for a picnic or walk. Go to a movie. Have a lunch date.

Pastors' spouses have a right to expect their mate's support and interest in *their* lives, *their* activities, *their* careers or professions. They need sympathy and understanding for the burdens *they* carry, for the challenges God has called *them* to face in this world. They may need your patience and forbearance in matters of faith. Just because they are married to a pastor does not mean they will have the Bible memorized or have special eloquence at prayer. It doesn't mean they will be expert counselors, or proficient problem solvers, or competent chairs of committees, or stellar additions to the choir. It means, rather, *they will be who God made them to be.* They will have their own gifts, their own interests, their own callings, and their own places of service in the life of the church. They need the pastors to whom they are married, therefore, *not* to force the church, or any part of it, down their throats. They're entitled to share in the decision-making process where the family's involvement in the life of the church is concerned.

Pastors' spouses need and deserve tact and diplomacy from the pulpit, when it comes to family matters. Their permission should be secured before they or the family are used as a sermon illustration!

They should expect to be protected, to the extent they want to be, from the impositions of parishioners who may decide to ring the pastor's doorbell at any hour of day or night. They should expect family meals not to be interrupted by every ringing of the phone, and to enjoy at least some degree of family sanctity. It is not unreasonable for your spouse to ask that all but emergency calls be returned by you after family mealtimes are over. They should expect to be safeguarded, to whatever extent they wish to be, from the overly curious and sometimes prying types that exist in every congregation. In every church there are those who would love to know all the details of the pastor's private life, and pastors' spouses are constantly being scrutinized by some overly curious and less than tactful parishioners.

Pastors' spouses should also be safeguarded, to the extent that they wish to be, from those we will call the "recruiters." They are found in every congregation. They are the ones who feel the pastor's spouse should be asked to serve on every board, every committee, activity, task force, or project group in the life of the church. Pastors' spouses should also be shielded from the "monopolizers"—those who have no compunction about taking up all of your spouse's time. Monopolizers can't take no for an answer.

Spouses of pastors have their own need for intimacy, togetherness, and time to be alone. They have a right to expect their pastor spouse to be sensitive to those needs. They will sense whether or not you are, and they can easily tell if you are seeking to maintain a workable balance. They have the right to expect that the little things that help any marriage to thrive will not disappear from your marriage—even though you are a pastor. We are talking about evenings out, birthdays and anniversaries remembered; gestures of caring and affection; notes of endearment and appreciation.

Finally, pastors' spouses need to know and be reassured that they will not *always* play second fiddle to the church. They will discover soon enough that there will be frequent times when the demands of the church will come first. They will see you head down to the hospital in the middle of the night. They will hear your car in the driveway as you pull in from a late meeting after they've gone to bed. They will learn your weekends are not your own. They will get used to your leaving the house to head over to the church. It will be a common sight.

But, *when you make a commitment* to them or to the whole family, do your level best to keep it! By any measure of fairness, they have a right to expect you to—unless you encounter something extremely urgent or extraordinary. They should know that when their names are on a page in your appointment book, that commands as much respect and attention from you as the name of any church board member would. Indeed, they should know that their name commands even more! They should know that when you are home you are *home*, and not tied up with church business on the phone all night. They should know that when you go on vacation as husband and wife, or as a family, you are *theirs*. They should know that you belong to them in a special way during these sacred times, that they have you wholly to themselves for this respite of days. They should not have to wait in the car at each rest stop as you check in with your church office by phone. They should not have to sit on the beach watching you plan the fall preaching schedule on your laptop computer.[1] Nor should they have to feel as if they are competing constantly with your cell phone or pager for your attention.

In other words, your family should sense that *they* are your priority during these special times, that your commitment to them is of supreme importance to you. If you have children, they will remember these times all their lives. They will remember, too, if you violate these principles. How will you preach the importance of marriage and family if your behavior says otherwise?

Some pastors operate under an illusion of their own indispensability. They believe their churches can't function without them. They believe they are shirking their duty if they don't carry a cell phone, wear a beeper, and stay clipped to a pager. In the eternal span of Christ's kingdom, however, great saints, faithful servants, wise and wonderful pastors have come and gone, but the work of the kingdom goes on. An exaggerated sense of one's own importance can be idolatry in subtle disguise. It can mean that the creature, the servant, is trying to stand where only the Creator should be. A moment of discovery occurs when a congregation—the *laos*, the people of God—find they can function without their pastor, at least for a time. They are still the church, still the body of Christ. And they can still do the work of the church. Sometimes a pastor's *absence,*

1. Some pastors use their vacation time to plan their preaching schedule for the coming church year. That's OK, as long as you have negotiated with the family to do this in a way that does not encroach on your time with them. It is possible to build time into your vacation program for you to do something that will save you hours, even days, of work later on, and which will give you more time to be available to your family throughout the rest of the year.

for the sake of being present to *others*—to family, to God—does more than anything else to encourage the saints to do the work of ministry.[2]

Determining one's degree of "indispensability" is important, to be sure, but it should be done with humility. You will have to decide that for yourself. If you feel your "pastor pager" needs to be with you as you vacation on the beach, or perched on the nightstand next to you as you rock your new baby to sleep, here are some things to consider: First, our society today is awash in examples of people undercommitted to their family, their spouse, their children, their parents, and overcommitted to work. We search in vain for those who have found a balance that seems to work. You can serve your church members well by showing them what that balance looks like in *your* life. Your example can offer them hope that it's possible to be faithful both to one's work and to one's family.

Second, we know that Jesus found time to get away by himself, not because all of the work had been done, but because he wanted to spend time with God. He set aside time to be alone and time to be with his friends. And Jesus had a whole world to save!

Toward Strengthening the Pastor's Family

As pastors' family ties are strengthened, pastors themselves are strengthened too. Our comparison of several recent studies by various family research

2. A note from KWM: When I was mobilized for active duty as a Navy chaplain soon after the 9/11 terrorist attacks, I learned I would be sent overseas just before Christmas to minister to those in uniform. My orders read "one year, extendable to two." That meant my congregation of ten years would be without their pastor for many months. Their response to the news of their pastor's call-up was both inspiring and gratifying to me. It was an example of the people of God being the church!

As it turned out, I served overseas for nine months. During that time, the congregation rose to the challenge. One of their strengths for many years had been knowing that each one of them had a ministry. So now they shifted into higher gear. Every member pitched in wherever help was needed. They pulled together. They practiced the priesthood of all believers. There were fits and starts and some tough terrain, but the staff stepped up, and neighboring pastors helped out with pastoral services. The lay leaders worked well together, carrying on their responsibilities.

During my time away the church celebrated Christmas and Easter, observed Holy Week, confirmed a large class of young people, continued to take in new members, purchased property for future expansion, ran a highly successful capital campaign, conducted a wonderful summer Bible school, and in every way demonstrated what it means to BE the church of Jesus Christ.

The preaching load was carried faithfully and ably by an associate pastor, along with supply clergy from the area who were contracted by the church board to help share that important responsibility. There were also some gifted church leaders (elders) who discovered, developed, and exercised wonderful gifts of leadership in worship. The flock was well fed!

What a happy homecoming it was for me and how excited and justifiably proud our church leaders and members were about all their accomplishments! We had been keeping in touch by e-mail, but what a thrill it was for me to come home and see for myself! How grateful we all were for the abundant evidence of God's providential care and gracious love. They admitted it had been a challenging time, but a time of spiritual growth for the entire congregation. What more could a pastor want for his or her flock?

organizations and consultants confirms what most thoughtful parents would agree are the essential qualities that build strong families. Certain qualities appear on everyone's list. If you want to help other families and keep your own home fires burning brightly, you will want to be mindful of the following:

Communication

Good communication is essential to strong families. Family members try to be good listeners. They take a genuine interest in one another. They learn to communicate in positive ways. They ask questions about one another's lives, interests, and activities. They sense that other family members respect them enough to care about them.

Commitment

Members of strong families sense that their life together is a priority. There is an internal commitment that binds the family together and resists the efforts of outside distractions to undermine or dismantle it. Family members take reassurance from their common commitment to one another and to the family as a whole. They are patient with one another, and forgiving. They persevere in their relational efforts. They rejoice with each other, and grieve with each other.

Cooperation

Commitment to each other implies cooperation among the members of the family, including respect for each other's schedules, needs, and obligations. Rules for the use of the telephone, for example, must be fairly and clearly defined. Whose needs take priority and when? Children, especially teenagers, need to know when and for how long they may use the phone. It is annoying to parishioners, or to others who may have an urgent need to speak with you, to be unable to get through because your tenth-grade son is chatting interminably on the phone with a friend or is instant messaging his buddy list on the computer. Young people need to have access to a computer these days and should have their own, if you or they can afford it. But be sure to monitor their use of it (see p. 99)! If you can afford to have a second telephone line for your professional use, that is a tremendous help. A spirit of cooperation is essential to the peace and harmony of the family.

Ability to Deal with Crises and Stress

Because of their commitment to each other, members of strong families are able to cope with major and minor crises. They recognize when someone is under stress, and they don't allow that stress to tear them apart. They try to find some positive element in every situation, no matter how small. Crises draw the family together. There certainly will be times of conflict and fighting. Disagreements can even be pronounced. But conflict is open and family members try to deal with issues rather than indulging in personal attacks. During times of conflict, family members try to identify the problems and issues at hand and find alternatives that will work for everyone.

Appreciation

Members of strong families develop ways of affirming one another, of building one another up, of expressing appreciation. This is in contrast to problem families, where a pattern of continual put-downs, criticisms, complaints, and the like seems to prevail.

> Among the blessings God bestows there's one we recommend.
> Appreciation is a gift of God, we do contend.
> Just think about it, and you'll see exactly why we say,
> appreciation is a gift God gives to give away.
> How few there are who bother to express their gratitude.
> Their failure to give thanks reflects a thoughtless attitude.
> Why, hardly anyone these days will take the time to write.
> Folks act as if each favor they receive is theirs by right.
> The people who express their thanks give other folks a lift,
> and that is why we view appreciation as a gift,
> that one both has and also gives, as faithful stewards do.
> So when God's gifts you're listing, add "appreciation," too.[3]

Activity Sharing

Members of strong families place a high value on doing things together, work-related as well as recreational activities. They have fun together. This does not just happen. Family members are intentional about it. They organize their lives, their plans and schedules, so that they can spend time together, including mealtimes.

Spiritual Well-Being

While some of our sources were not church-related organizations, even the secular studies we looked at included "spiritual well-being," or "shared spiritual values," or "high religious orientation," or some similar phrase as one of the key qualities of strong families. Family members belong to an organized

3. "Appreciation Ratio," from *Now, THAT'S a Miracle!* (CSS Publishing Co., 1996), p. 48. At the poet's suggestion, we have changed the personal pronouns in this poem from "I" to "we."

church or faith community, or are committed to a spiritual lifestyle. They live with a sense that God is very much a part of their lives. They pray together, if only at mealtimes. They know that faith in God is essential to a happy, fulfilled life.

As a pastor who is searching for ways to build up and strengthen your congregation, how about intentionally working to strengthen family life throughout your congregation—starting with yours! We believe healthy families help make healthy churches, and healthy *pastors'* families help keep pastors effective!

Children

The pressures on pastors' children can be enormous. Without intending to, well-meaning church members and others in the community will hold them to a different standard. "I never would have thought that of *you*, Janie—and you, a minister's daughter!" Because they live and grow up in a pastor's home, your children will be assumed by some people to be more inclined to like church, be more fond of the Bible, be more sensitive to spiritual things. With a moment's reflection, these same people would realize it is not always the dentist's children who most enjoy brushing their teeth, or the music teacher's children who most like to sing.

In some ways a pastor's children grow up with ample reasons to resent, even distrust, the church. After all, is it not the church that always takes daddy or mommy away? You can soften this attitude and ease the strain by the things you do and say. Your children will observe your attitude toward the church. Is it grudging, resenting, critical? Or is it thankful, enthusiastic, affirming? Take care not to speak critically of the church or church members in front of your children. Try to interpret your ministry positively to your children. Instead of saying, "I have to go to a meeting at church tonight," say, "Daddy (or Mommy) is going to help some people learn about Jesus tonight," or "meet with some nice people who want to join the church," or "to meet with members who want to figure out how to help hungry people."

Help your children to enjoy the church. When they are little, let them come over to see you at church. Let them climb up behind your desk and sit on your lap. Let them talk on the "pastor's phone." Let them listen to the organist practice. Show them the baptismal font, and tell them about baptism. Let them sense your excitement for church festivals, special events, or special seasons. On your way home from a family vacation, let the children know why you are looking forward to and excited about getting back to work at the church.

Try not to let them feel cheated out of your time as a parent because of the church. While it is true you may be called at any hour of the day or night to respond to an emergency involving some church member, it is also true that ministry offers you some flexibility in how you parcel out your day. You may find, if you have small children at home, that you are able to see them for lunch on a regular basis. If you have a full morning of appointments and a full evening of meetings, you may find time in the afternoon to get away from the church for your daughter's soccer game or your son's football practice. You may find time for a family bike ride. You may have to *make* the time. And when you do, *make the most of the time!* The years fly by, and before you know it your nest is empty. The children's bedrooms are quiet. You will treasure the memory of every moment you had with them!

New research has revealed that children who partake of regular meals with their families are at *significantly lower risk* for drug abuse, alcohol abuse, antisocial behavior, delinquency, truancy, depression, teen pregnancy, and promiscuous sexual behavior. Family mealtime is an important time. Make it consistent. Make it regular. Take advantage of bedtime, too. This is a wonderful time to read with or to your children, and to share a bedtime prayer.

At special school events your children will look to see if you are present. Show them how important it is to you to be there for them. They will remember your presence for the rest of their lives. They will also remember your absence.

If you leave a church you have been serving, after a while the congregation will find another pastor. If you should leave your children, where would *they* be? They can't replace you.

We do not intend this section to be a study on child rearing. We are not experts. We are pastors who have been there, who are there, and who wish to underscore from our experience (including our mistakes) the uniqueness of family relationships for those in ministry. Special pressures bring special challenges, but there are ways to deal with them successfully.

We pastors have to be mindful of what we are teaching our kids (or our grandchildren!), and of what we are communicating about our beliefs and values. They are usually listening to what we say. They are always watching what we do. What do we want to teach them about stewardship, for example? The lesson each of us has sought to convey to our own children is that God comes *first*: we give the church the firstfruits of what we receive. We wanted our children to develop an appreciation for the music of the church, to the point where they could sing many of the hymns and spiritual songs with us and know what the words mean. We wanted them to know that Christmas and Easter are great holy days of the faith, not just secular holidays. We wanted them to know the reasons for the seasons!

We also wanted them to know that prayer is an indispensable part of our lives. We shared family prayers before departing on trips, in restaurants, at every meal, at bedtime, and other times. We wanted them to relate to the idea of thanking God for blessings received and to be grateful to God for the good gifts of life. We wanted them to seek God's help in trying or difficult times. We wanted them to see *us* do that in the face of death or accident or disappointment or tragedy. We wanted them to sense in us a love for the Bible, and our belief that it is the guide and sourcebook for life.

Family traditions are very important. Develop your own. Your children will love them. They become reminders in a child's life that the family is stable, that life is secure. They can be as simple as sharing grace at the table, as elaborate as repeated family vacations to what become sacred family places of shared memories throughout the years. They can be as routine as having the same seats at the family table when you sit down to eat, or as playing the same family games in the car. They can be as unique as a family outing to find this year's Christmas tree, or helping out as a family at the homeless shelter during the Christmas holidays.

For Pastors Who Are Single

Jesus was single. So was the apostle Paul. The New Testament speaks approvingly of the advantages of singleness in ministry. But there are special considerations that need to be taken into account if you are an unmarried pastor. If you are young and just starting out in ministry, some of your older parishioners may act like parents. This could happen whether you are married or single, but it is especially true if you are single. We are told that people tend to attribute a higher level of maturity to young married pastors than to young single pastors. That kind of bias is unfortunate, but it exists. If you're young and single, don't be surprised if it happens to you. You may resent being treated like somebody's little girl or boy, but bite your tongue. Just remember that your call and your ordination are the basis of your authority, not your age or marital status. If you act professionally, you will be treated accordingly. As you perform your pastoral and ministerial duties, you will gain the respect of all. One thing is certain: if your young age is a problem, it will be solved in time!

There are other non–age-related considerations for single pastors. It is also true that being a single pastor can be lonely. Getting married does not vaccinate a pastor against loneliness, of course. The loneliness of an unhappy marriage can be more isolating, and more bereft of hope sometimes, than the loneliness singles encounter. The antidote for loneliness is not simply marriage per se. It is connectedness, genuine intimacy, and communion with God and with others. As a single pastor you may need to work harder than some of your married colleagues to find that listening ear, that caring friend, that place of acceptance and understanding. But you may trust God to provide what you need. Demographic trends show an increasing number of Americans will be living alone in the coming decades. To experience that as a pastor, to know what it *feels* like, can be both an enhancement and an entrée to ministry.

Many congregations are so family-focused and family-oriented that they barely notice the single people occupying their pews from Sunday to Sunday. In a typical congregation there are probably some who have never married, some who are widowed, some who are divorced, some who are seeking a meaningful relationship. According to the latest U.S. Census Bureau statistics, fewer than 25 percent of American families are traditional nuclear families, consisting of husband, wife, and young children. Increasing numbers of women never marry. Recent studies reveal that increasing numbers of women in their twenties will never marry. Yet many congregations continue to act and to speak out of the nuclear family context. Single persons will increasingly seek faith communities that understand their situations and speak to their needs. Single pastors can look at these folks and say, "I understand."

Some fear single pastors will be more prone to illicit involvement with married church members or others seeking inappropriate intimacies. Clinical studies have not justified this fear. Actually, *married* pastors engage in proportionately more affairs. Others suggest single pastors cannot comment on family life or parenting with any authority. Why not? They've all had parents, they've all seen parents (good and poor), they've all been raised in families, they all have powers of observation, inference, and conclusion. The mere fact that a pastor is married is no guarantee that pastor will practice or even know the things that make for a strong marriage. The mere fact that a pastor has children is no guarantee that pastor will practice or even know the things that make for good child rearing. There are unmarried pastors who could teach some of their married colleagues a thing or two about marriage. There are similarly childless pastors who could teach some of their parenting colleagues a thing or two about raising children.

So do not, single pastors, feel inadequate just because you're not married, or disqualify yourself from children's programs or ministries just because you don't have children. Don't let people's unthinking comments bother you. Accept the fact that because you are single you will have greater credibility with some members of your flock, and less with some others. Don't be resentful. Just try to be who you are. Allow God to use you. God will!

Be prepared, too, for the matchmakers who will try to "fix your problem." Every church has matchmakers. Be grateful for their spirit, for they have your best interests at heart. But beware of the gossips who monitor your personal life.

They watch to see who it is you speak to at coffee hours, put two and two together, and come up with five! Be discreet in your calling and counseling. Avoid situations that could invite criticism or gossip. And be aware lest there be some extra transference happening, particularly if the person you are counseling or visiting has a notion that someone like you would make a good catch. Be aware of and comfortable with your own sexuality. You may discover that single persons in ministry can be a threat to some people, for others of your gender may resent the attention they fear you are getting from members of the opposite sex. You just have to learn to deal with these dynamics without being intimidated. It can make ministry more complicated sometimes, as any single pastor could testify.

It is regrettable that in some churches both single and married women must still deal with stereotypical attitudes toward female pastors. If you are a female person called to such a church, the battle is half won. For those in the congregation who objected to calling a woman, you have an opportunity to help change people's attitudes, which in time will be shaped by the kind of minister you are. So handle it well. Don't be defensive or belligerent. Just be yourself, and realize that it's their problem, not yours.[4]

All ministers, male and female alike, have to be doubly discreet in today's environment. You may view the fact that you are not accorded, without suspicion, the same freedoms that other singles are as one more expression of our litigious, sexist culture. But that's the way it is at the moment. So you and your married colleague had better not stay too late too often at the church. Be discreet!

We hope our readers who are single will talk to as many different single persons in ministry as possible, to see how others are dealing with these realities. Pay attention to those who have it all together, those who know themselves well and are comfortable with their personhood. They are the ones who by not having to prove anything are able to prove something very important! So, once again, be yourself, but try to be your best self.

For both female and male pastors, there are also decided advantages to being single; for example, most single persons with no spousal or parental obligations have greater freedom of movement and more flexibility timewise. If you live alone, you are not answerable to anyone in your domicile with respect to your comings and goings. Your congregation is free to become your "spouse" in a very special way. You will undoubtedly be invited to dinner in the homes of church members. You may be invited for an evening out or a day at the lake or shore. Thoughtful church members will check on you at holiday

4. A note from RSA: My daughter, the Rev. Elsie Armstrong Rhodes, who is a solo pastor, can attest that people's attitudes about female ministers can change for the better!

times to be sure you're not having to celebrate by yourself. You may be invited into people's homes on Sunday afternoons or evenings. All of which is to say that you will be viewed as belonging to your flock in a very special way. They look out for you. Don't resent that. Enjoy it, and make the most of it. It can enrich and deepen your ministry.

One more word of caution: Being single can tempt you to become a workaholic. If you are accountable to no one at home, it may be easier for you to stay out or up later than you should. It also may cause some church members to feel they can call you at any time of the day or night. If people impose on married pastors, they are even more likely to impose on single pastors. And single pastors may impose on themselves; that is, they may neglect their own health and well-being out of concern for the flock they have been called to serve.

Relatives

Single or married, male or female, you may have parents or other relatives visiting you from time to time, or even living with you. They can be an asset or a liability to your ministry, a cause of embarrassment or of joy and gratitude. That is true of any person in public life, as some presidents of the United States have discovered to their great chagrin. Your relatives have to be sensitive to the fact that what they say and how they act in public may have unintended consequences that could be detrimental to your ministry. You want to be supportive of your relatives, of course, and help them to feel they are part of your church family. At the same time, as the one most affected by their indiscreet conduct or remarks, you need to help your relatives to understand the need for discretion.

Whoever may be living with you also needs time alone. Live-in relatives, like spouses, are entitled to their independence. They, too, need to maintain a proper balance between intimacy and privacy.[5]

Pastoral Pointer

Sometime during your first year in a new church, teach a course in church polity. Help your church officers and the congregation at large to appreciate

5. For more discussion of the pastor's relationship with and the role of live-in relatives, see *The Pastor as Evangelist*, by Richard Stoll Armstrong (Westminster Press, 1984), chap. 6, pp. 88–94.

their heritage and to understand the ways their denomination differs from or is similar to other denominations in its beliefs and practices. Whether people were born into their present denomination or adopted it, they will appreciate such a course. It will facilitate your ministry and greatly enhance the church's evangelistic efforts.

Pastoral Pointer

Are you behind in your pastoral calling? Is your list of persons you need to visit growing longer every day? Do you feel as if you'll never catch up? Join the crowd, because that's a common source of worry and stress for most conscientious pastors. Here's a suggestion: Use the telephone! It's not the same as a personal visit, but it's a lot better than no contact at all. The telephone is a wonderful medium for prayer, and you can make many phone calls in the time it takes for one in-person visit, if you include travel time.[6]

6. For some more thoughts on how to use the telephone, see Appendix B.

Chapter 7

Worrying about My Finances

Pastors at Risk

An undisciplined or distressed financial life undermines a pastor's effectiveness in ministry. It tears at the fabric of family relationships. It erodes personal integrity. And, of course, it affects personal stewardship, which is a cornerstone of ministry. A pastor in financial trouble is a pastor at risk—the risk of poor decision making, the risk of losing one's concentration or misplacing one's focus because of being preoccupied with one's own financial worries, and in extreme situations the risk of committing an act of misconduct.

For married pastors, when it comes to dealing with your family finances we recommend openness, honesty, and thorough communication. Financial misunderstandings are a real problem for many couples. How you allocate the responsibility of keeping the books at your house is obviously up to you, but we urge you to work out a plan with your spouse, so you know who pays what bills, who writes what checks, who makes what deposits, who is responsible for what. Plan your work and work your plan. And, if you run into snags, make the necessary adjustments. Your plan should allow for contingencies.

It isn't always easy for a pastor's family to balance the budget. There may be times when you will reach the end of your paycheck before you reach the end of the month. The years when many pastors were paid barely a subsistence wage were a most unfortunate and regrettable period in the employment history of the church. Many were living in church-owned houses as well, and would come to the end of their working years with no equity to put toward the purchase of some place to live out their retirement years. It was not uncommon to find pastors and their families severely strapped financially, despite Jesus' instruction that "the laborer deserves to be paid" (Luke 10:7). While the Christian church has been at the forefront of improvements in American society in notable areas—civil rights, education, health care, penal reform, among others—the church has often been lax in matters relating to the care and equitable treatment of its own staff.

Other Staff Members

As a matter of fairness and justice, you want to do all you can to ensure that your congregation is not paying your youth director a part-time salary while expecting full-time work. If there is a full-time secretary, you want to ensure that the church has a pension plan or is providing for some kind of retirement fund for him or her. Do all you can to ensure that church employees have health insurance, that inadequate compensation is not impeding their work, and that they are earning a salary commensurate with their education, training, experience, skills, and abilities. Make sure that they have adequate vacation time, that their days off are protected, and that they receive ample recognition and expressions of appreciation, publicly and privately, for the work they do. Take care that your congregation has not hired one person, expecting that employee's spouse to be a full-time, nonpaid church worker too. And you want to be sure that no church staff member can be fired without some type of due process.

Sadly, corporate America, the government, and other branches of our society have often been more considerate in their treatment of workers than has the church. *Every* church worker deserves to be treated fairly and equitably, if not generously and graciously! The church can set an example for the employers and bosses who occupy its pews Sunday by Sunday. The welfare and well-being of its staff members should be a priority for every church. It is mission-enhancing! In the long run, it saves money. Cared-for workers are more productive and effective than neglected, mistreated, overextended employees.

Unfortunately, the church has been neglectful and heedless in many of these areas. To ask why is to ask a difficult question. Perhaps church people have assumed that if someone is working for Jesus, he or she needs no other compensation. We make that assumption about church volunteers, but there is a world of difference between a volunteer who has another source of income and a full-time church employee who has no other income.

There are countless motivations for going into church work, but no one chooses a church vocation expecting to get rich. That fact does not relieve the people of God from their responsibility to compensate their staff members fairly and equitably. We are happy to observe that churches have made progress in these areas in recent years. But there is still a long way to go for many.

As we have implied, money is not the only motivator or even the primary motivator of those who work for churches. A feeling of being appreciated for one's efforts is extremely important to most. Reasonable flexibility of time and schedule is also important. Sensing that one's labors are advancing the work of Christ and providing a witness is probably the most important factor of all. Do those who work for your congregation feel appreciated? Do they have sufficient time off and flexibility of schedules? Do they believe their work is advancing the cause of Christ? Do they understand how it is? Do they have opportunities to learn and grow? As pastor, if you supervise a church staff or even one church worker, it is your responsibility, in collaboration with your church board or personnel committee, to see to the proper treatment of the other members of the staff.

Your Family Finances

Whether anyone is seeing to *your* and your family's welfare is another question! It is to be hoped that some committee or leader in your church is fulfilling that responsibility. It is *your* responsibility to be a good steward of whatever compensation you receive. In that regard, be careful with your use of credit cards. If you run up an unpaid balance, the interest charges can be as high as 20 percent! Finance charges have to be taken into account as well. They can be deceptively high. Paying only your card's minimum amount monthly greatly increases the cost of that television set you buy on credit.

If you buy a home, you will probably need a mortgage, and an auto loan to purchase your car as well. Apart from those two large purchases and perhaps some furniture items, try to pay cash whenever you can. If you use your credit card, pay off the balance each month to avoid the exorbitant interest charges. You will save an enormous amount. If you can't pay for something, question whether you actually *need* it right away, or just *want* it. This is a distinction increasingly lost on the typical consumer.

Ben Franklin urged people to save. Someone else said, "Always pay yourself out of your paycheck first." We would amend that to say, "Always pay *God* first." We have always tried to set aside at least a tithe of our income for the church and Christian causes, and to have a certain amount deposited into our savings account. You may believe this is impossible in your situation, but we would challenge you to try it, at least for a year. Those who accept the challenge will learn some rather remarkable lessons: that it's impossible to outgive God; that the measure you give to others is the measure God uses to give back to you; that you really don't need all the things you thought you needed, that you are capable of a simpler lifestyle, that you actually grow to enjoy it, and that you *can* make some of the changes you once feared you could not. To borrow a line from a familiar commercial, "Try it! You'll like it!"

It is important, too, for pastors (and their spouses, if they are married) to have a last will and testament. It is wise to seek good advice in planning for the disposition of what the law calls your estate. What will happen to it when something happens to you? Well over half of all Americans die *intestate* (i.e., without a will). If you don't decide what to do with your estate, the government will decide for you!

You also need adequate insurance to meet the needs of those who depend on you, in the event of your death. That calls for an insurance agent who really wants to understand your needs, not just sell you a policy. Many people buy insurance over the Internet now, and close a deal with the click of a mouse. We encourage you to invest enough time in this important transaction to be sure you understand your and your family's needs, and to be clear about the specific features of the policy or policies you're getting.

The fact is, we live at a time when many people have never been taught how to balance a checkbook. A little ignorance can go a long way toward impairing one's financial situation. There is nothing spiritual about neglecting this area of life, or about remaining ill-informed. A pastor's financial knowledge, planning, and management relate directly to her or his stewardship, which, of course, relates directly to her or his preaching and teaching, and directly to her or his walk with God. If you have questions about a pension plan, or an IRA, or a tax-sheltered annuity; if you don't know the advantages and disadvantages of using a credit card vs. a debit card; if you wonder whether you have the right kind of checking account and if you need a better system for balancing it; if you are unsure about how to fill out a Schedule C form on your federal income tax return; if you don't know the difference between an adjustable and a fixed-rate mortgage; if you wonder how best to invest what little you have in order to start saving for the future; if you are uncertain about whether it would be better to buy or rent a home; indeed, if any of these matters are foreign concepts to you, we strongly recommend that you seek the financial advice of a reputable, trustworthy person.

You should also know the tax implications of a pastor's housing allowance, whether or not you live in a church-owned home. You must give the official board of your church *in advance* an estimate of how much it is going to cost you to provide a home in the coming year. This estimated amount must be recorded in the official minutes of the congregation as the pastor's housing allowance. The amount cannot exceed the fair rental value of your residence plus utilities. Your actual expenses at the end of the year are tax deductible up to that amount. If your actual expenses are less than your original estimate, the difference, of course, is taxable. This is a real benefit to ordained ministers. Ask your church treasurer, your district superintendent, or presbytery, or diocese, or conference headquarters, or the local IRS office, or any tax consultant, to explain the advantages of the pastor's housing allowance and how to handle it on your income-tax returns.

Your Own Home?

An important question for every pastor is whether to live in a church-owned home or a home of your own. There are advantages and disadvantages to each. If you live in a manse, a rectory, a parsonage, or whatever your denomination calls the home it provides for the pastor, the church pays all upkeep. You have no owner headaches, at least theoretically. You have no worries about having to sell the place when you leave, no cares about finding a buyer. Nor do you have the problems of finding and buying a house you can afford when you first arrive. Some pastors like to live next door to the church, which is where the church's house is usually located if not across the street. They like the convenience of being able to scoot home for lunch, of being close to the family, and of being able to get to the church in bad driving weather. Some pastors like the total identity feeling of working and living close to the church. This arrangement is easier for some pastors just starting out, who might have a hard time mustering up the down payment for a home, or securing a mortgage.

The disadvantages to living in church-owned housing are essentially the advantages in reverse. While it's true you have less owner upkeep, and theoretically fewer owner headaches, it is sometimes hard to get the church to do the upkeep required to keep the place looking nice! Sometimes, in fact, it's hard to get the church to do *anything*! Not every congregation has someone skilled at and committed to property management. While it is true that you have no *owner* frustrations, it is also true that you do not have the satisfactions that come with owning your own home: the satisfaction of fixing it up the way you like it, the satisfaction of putting your own thought and effort into improving a place that you and your family think of as *your* home. The financial advantages of not owning a home are offset by the fact that you are not building any equity toward any home you might want to buy someday.

Then, too, the advantages of living next door to the church are countered by the fact that you and your family have no choice about where you're going to live. The church has already decided that. Also, some pastors' families prefer more privacy than the parsonage affords, and some pastors prefer more space between the church and their home. They don't like living "above the store," so to speak. Some find out, when they live next door to the church, that they become the unofficial custodian, called on every time some church member, repair person, or passing visitor needs access to the building. They become the unofficial monitor of the church's light switches, the one who has to check out the building after every nighttime meeting or other activity. And some pastors' families, who struggle to cope with the fishbowl effect of simply *being* the pastor's family, chafe under the added stress of having their lives, their comings and goings, and all their family events and activities taking place under the constant scrutiny of the entire congregation!

The question of where you live is not a question to be decided simply on the basis of practicalities, however. You want to think about this in terms of what's good for your church, what's good for your spouse, if you have one, what's good for your children, if any, what's feasible for you financially, what will best enable you to fulfill your ministry. You want, above all, to think about this matter theologically. How does what you *believe*—about God, about family, and about ministry—guide and influence the decisions you make?

Entertaining

It is important that you have an understanding with your church board about entertaining. You may or may not be surprised at how expensive it is to entertain the church officers and their spouses for dinner, or to host church members frequently in your home. If your family is on a tight budget, as most pastors' families are, you may spend a week's grocery money in one night. If no allowance has been provided for the professional entertaining you do, or if your expenses exceed the allowance, that amount is a deductible item on your income-tax return.

Think about how you want your home to be used. We two and our wives have always believed that our homes were God's gifts to us, to be used not only for family life but for hospitality in ministry. Our homes have routinely been places where church members can gather or meet, where church boards can come for meals or Saturday retreats, where confirmation classes meet, where churchwide open houses take place, where church members break bread at our tables. We give thanks for the joy of the ministry of hospitality!

Make sure, however, that you never *impose* this practice on your spouse, if you are married. Such entertaining is too time-consuming and takes far too much effort to press anyone to take it on unwillingly. Your spouse has to be part of the decision to open your home, and has to *want* to do it. If not, your spouse will end up resenting you, your congregation, and your ministry. And *if* your spouse wants to open your home in these ways, be sure you thank her or him for it!

Privacy Matters

We have found that most church members are gracious and considerate, and will not violate their pastor's privacy. Believe it or not, it's an adjustment for some of them to think of a pastor as having or *needing* privacy. But most of them readily understand, appreciate, and respect this basic human need.

There are some who don't, however. You may have to say, when the phone rings during mealtime, "Uh, actually, we're at dinner right now. May I get back to you as soon as we're finished?" Be sure you do call them back. Never lie about it. For example, never have your spouse or children say, "He's not home," when you are. Have them say instead, "She can't come to the phone right now. May I have her call you back?"

You will also need uninterrupted time to study, to prepare your sermons, to get ready for the Bible classes you teach, and for other speaking engagements and creative writing, not to mention your devotional time. The telephone can be an annoying deterrent to steady, focused concentration. Whether you do this work in a home office or at church, devise some method of protecting your study and writing time—again, without asking someone to lie for you. If the church secretary is answering the phone while you work, don't ask the secretary to tell folks you're not there. One of our secretaries used the expression "He's in the 'sermon cave' right now. I can put you right through if it's urgent." Callers always got the message. If it *is* urgent, you want to take the call, of course.

Pastors have to learn to live with the tension between their need for privacy and their pastoral obligations, between protecting their family and encouraging their involvement; between their desire to entertain and their stewardship commitments and family budget; between their need for time to be alone with God and the Bible and their desire to be available to the members of their flock. The only way to deal with these constant tensions is to stay close to God, and pray, pray, pray!

Pastoral Pointer

Equip some of your lay members to work with you in visiting shut-ins and those in hospitals, assisted living, and skilled nursing facilities. To that end, do you know a hospital chaplain whom you could ask to help train your lay hospital callers? Such training could be invaluable to laypersons who may not know all they need to know about calling on those who are hospitalized or bedridden. Those who are sick or incapacitated will be visited more frequently if you are not the only one doing such calling.

Chapter 8

Trying to Be Spiritually Disciplined

Your Devotional Life

*N*othing is more essential to your survival in ministry than your devotional life. The most important thing we can say about it is, START NOW! Don't wait for some envisioned ideal time—"after I get settled in my new church," "after I finish this project," "once the children are back in school." Some fail to begin because they think they don't have time to do what they'd really like to do. You will never have as much time as you'd like. Life and ministry are always busy.

The time to begin is NOW. If you haven't already opened your heart, soul, and mind to the presence of God, the time to do that is not later, but NOW. Your devotional life may not be what you want it to be, but something is better than nothing! We have been through times in the ministry when we could not have endured the struggle without a sustaining faith in the God to whom we prayed regularly! Every pastor encounters problems and takes on burdens which he or she must learn to turn over to God. Our ability to persevere depends on our remembering that it is not our church but Christ's church, and that apart from him we can do nothing. We face every challenge as best we can, but the outcome is up to God.

We sincerely believe that prayer is more than a psychological exercise, more than an attitude adjuster, more than an effort to make oneself "feel good." Quite the contrary—it is our pipeline to God, a source of spiritual power, in which the human heart rises into the very presence of God. It's a summoning of the powers of heaven in the name and for the cause of Jesus Christ and his kingdom. "More things are wrought by prayer," wrote Alfred, Lord Tennyson, "than this world dreams of."[1] God answers prayers. We

1. From *Le Morte d'Arthur.*

believe that, because we have seen how God has answered *our* prayers, and we can attest with the apostle Paul that "in everything God works for good with those who love [God], who are called according to his purpose" (Rom. 8:28 RSV).

Reading the Bible devotionally should be one of the disciplines of your spiritual life, and that reading should be more than your merely mining it for sermon material! We recommend using a Bible in which you can write your reflections and notes. Date the passages as you read them. Note the meaning for you at that point in your journey with God. You will be delighted to observe, as the years go by, how God has been working in you!

Regarding your intercessory prayers, consider using your church directory as a prayer list, so that you are praying for every member of the church by name. Invite your congregation to do the same. Imagine the spiritual power generated when all the members of the church are praying regularly for one another! For parishioners who need help learning how to pray, a good suggestion is to pray aloud, alone. This helps to keep one's mind from wandering while one is learning how to talk with God. Neither of us authors has the spiritual gift of praying or speaking in tongues—unless one of them is English!—but we both have had the experience, over and over again, of God's putting thoughts in our minds and words in our mouths, so that we have the amazing feeling that we are speaking God's thoughts back to God. It doesn't happen all the time, but we can tell the difference when it does. Some find it also helpful to sing or pray aloud the great hymns of the faith, or other spiritual songs. The words take our devotional lives to a deeper level. The melodies help us to remember. It is helpful to remember Paul's promise that even when we don't know what to pray, "[the] Spirit intercedes for us with sighs too deep for words" (Rom. 8:26).

When should you have your devotional time? Whenever it works best for you. But we urge you to practice the discipline of having a regular quiet time set aside every day. Some like to start their working day with a Bible reading and prayer. Both of us have been in the habit of doing this when we first sit down at our desk in the morning. If you do this, you have to start early enough to avoid or at least lessen the likelihood of interruptions. If it's later, you can ask the church secretary, if there is one, to see that you are not disturbed, except for an emergency. There is something about practicing your devotional life right at your desk that brings God into your daily routine. It's a way of dedicating your working day to God, for your time is in God's hands.

The Bible enjoins us to pray without ceasing. You will sink your spiritual foundations into deeper and firmer ground by taking advantage of other opportunities to pray. For example, while you are driving your car is a good time to pray, especially when you are alone. You can pray aloud for long periods without disturbing anybody. Try thanking God for everything you have to be grateful for, or confessing everything you have to be sorry about, or naming everything and everyone you would like to lift up to God in intercessory prayer. You'll be amazed how quickly a trip of several hours can go when you are praying. It actually keeps you more alert and makes you a better, safer, and more courteous driver.

You can pray when you run, jog, or walk. You can pray during the time you ordinarily spend *waiting* for something or someone—at the doctor's office, at the airport, standing in line at the grocery store or the bank—or riding on a train, or plane, or bus, or subway.

If you are married, we encourage you to have devotional times with your spouse. Spouses make wonderful prayer partners if they are comfortable in that role. If not, you may want to seek out another pastor or colleague to share prayer time with. You certainly don't want to force it on your family, spouse, or friends. One of the most powerful spiritual examples you can offer your children is your own authenticity and integrity as a person of faith. We believe, as we have said, that saying grace, when you sit down to eat as a family, is extremely important. Many couples and families read a brief passage of Scripture at the dinner table. Mealtimes can be hectic, so it really takes a cooperative effort to gather as a family at the dinner table, let alone to have family devotions at dinner. While we confess that the mealtime devotions often have been limited to a rather brief grace, we believe both are worth the effort.

We have each found that much of our prayer life is related to our ministry. The challenge of preaching is a relentless and daunting one. To bring a word from the Word to the people of God, to seek and to help others to see the face of Jesus every Sunday, is an awesome responsibility. So we feel the need to surround our preaching with prayer. We pray before, during, and after the writing and preparation of each sermon. We pray as we're stepping into the pulpit and as we sit down after preaching. We ask for words, for guidance, for strength. We pray that we can be vessels of God's truth, God's love, God's amazing grace. We pray that we ourselves will hear God's word, knowing how much we pastors, too, stand in need of God's message.

Staff devotions are an immensely important part of building a collegial relationship with our colleagues in ministry. The staff that prays together gets along better. Church board meetings and committee meetings should always begin and close with prayer. Sometimes we break into a discussion in order to pray about a particular issue or need.

Needless to say, we also pray before, after, and, *during* a pastoral call in a hospital or home. You have to use your best judgment and be especially sensitive in deciding whether and how to involve the person or persons you are visiting.

Again, you don't want to impose your praying on anyone. You *offer* to pray, or ask the other person's permission to pray. It should come not as a surprise to the person you are visiting, but as the natural outcome of the conversation.

Your Personal Stewardship

If your money and possessions have not been sufficiently committed to God, *you* will not be sufficiently committed to God, and both you and your people will know it. As Jesus said in his Sermon on the Mount, "Where your treasure is, there your heart will be also. . . . You cannot serve God and wealth" (Matt. 6:21, 24c).

Stewardship is a central component of one's spiritual life. A genuine, joyous, wholehearted commitment to God in one's personal stewardship liberates, frees, empowers, and fills one with a gratitude for all of life.

Our sense of stewardship grows out of our faith in a personal God, a God who holds us with loving hands, who is able to provide for our needs, who is faithful, who will never forsake us, and who is the fount of every blessing we have ever received.

"The earth is the LORD's and all that is in it," proclaims the psalmist (Ps. 24:1). We are stewards of God's creation. Everything belongs to God. We own nothing. We manage everything. In terms of our personal stewardship, this means that all we are, everything we have and hold, comes to us from the hand of our Maker, *everything*—our time, our talents, our treasure. Since everything belongs to God, what we call "ours" is ours not as *owners* but as stewards of what has been entrusted to us. We are caretakers of the good gifts of God, and out of love for God we are called to use those gifts for the work of God for ourselves and for others.

Sin tempts us continually to want to stock our own shelves, to hoard our time, talent, and treasure. We tell ourselves we just want to have enough, but that longed-for "enough" never seems to arrive. "What does it take to make a rich person happy?" The answer to that familiar riddle is, "More of the same!"

On the joyous journey of Christian stewardship one makes the astonishing discovery that God *really is* able to provide! Pastoral ministry will claim most of your time and all of your talents for God. Ask yourself: "Have I been deliberate and intentional about my financial giving?" This is a matter for serious personal reflection, prayer, and decision. If you are married, your financial decisions should not be made in isolation. Your spouse is an equal partner in the decision-making process. Faithful stewardship is a joint enterprise for every Christian couple.

As stewards we understand that the firstfruits of our labors, not the leftovers, belong to God. We don't give Christ's church what we have rattling around at the end of the month, after everything else has been paid. Christ's church should get the first portion of what we receive—right off the top. Someone will immediately ask, "Is that before or after taxes?" That's a great question, because it shows the questioner is taking the priority principle seriously. So affirm the person who asks, and acknowledge that after taxes is a great place to start, for someone who has never tried tithing. The question one needs to ask oneself is, "Does my giving show I believe that everything I have belongs to God? Where is the church on my priority list? "Honor the LORD with your substance and with the first fruits of all your produce," said the writer of the book of Proverbs (3:9).

Assuming the church is at the top, where it ought to be, you still need to ask yourself, "How much is enough for me to give?" Many Christians begin with a tithe. We don't want to be legalistic about this. God does not force us to give. God enables us, by grace, to give. If you are comfortable with a tithe, then you may need to give more. Giving to God should go beyond comfort to the point of sacrifice. God's gift to us through Jesus Christ carried the price of crucifixion. We trivialize our response if our gifts in return are negligible or cost us little. We can learn from King David, who told Araunah the Jebusite, "I will not offer burnt offerings to the LORD my God that cost me nothing" (2 Sam. 24:24).

Another principle of financial stewardship is that Christian giving should be proportionate. "From everyone to whom much has been given, much will be required," said Jesus (Luke 12:48). In Paul's letter to the Corinthians, we read of the Macedonian Christians who gave "voluntarily, even beyond their means" (2 Cor. 8:3).

We who preach stewardship should not hesitate to talk to our people about our own stewardship. This is part of our teaching role. We teach by example. We believe that what Christians do with their money is one of the most reliable indicators of where they are in their walk with God. As a pastor you want to train your people to be stewards. You probably have preached many stewardship sermons. What do you say to your congregation? We can't preach about stewardship with integrity if we don't practice what we preach! Many churchgoers aim low in their giving to God and to the work of Christ's kingdom because they've never been challenged or inspired by their pastor's example.[2]

2. For a fuller discussion of the pastor's task of discipling people as stewards, see *The Pastor-Evangelist in the Parish*, by Richard Stoll Armstrong (Westminster/John Knox Press, 1990), pp. 143–150.

To reiterate what has already been said, our financial giving is one of the most, if not *the* most, tangible, visible measures of our spiritual growth. Our canceled checks and credit card statements tell the story of our spiritual vitality. Our monthly financial balance sheets are blueprints of our commitment and character. Unfortunately, too many churches and too many Christians confuse stewardship with fund-raising. Fund-raisers appeal to people to give to their particular projects. Their appeals are need-based. The fund-raisers who make the best case get the most money. Stewardship is about giving back to God part of what God has given us as a way of showing that everything we have belongs to God. It is faith-based. People give out of grateful obligation for what God has given them. Fund-raisers compete with other fund-raisers for their share of the gift dollar. Stewards ask, "How best can I use what God has given me, and how much should I give in gratitude for what I have been given?"

Christian stewards are concerned about need, of course. Need helps determine where our gift money is directed. For that reason it is important to inform people about human needs, and about how their gifts are helping to meet those needs. Need determines where the church directs its mission giving. That's part of the church's corporate stewardship. But *how much* a person gives to the church is based not on what others need but on what that person has. If we were to base our giving on need, we'd have to give everything we have, because the needs of people throughout the world are unlimited!

Guidelines for Christian Giving

In the light of what has been said, a pastor needs to make some decisions about his or her personal giving, both as a follower of Jesus Christ and as the spiritual leader, who wants to set a good example. You can't expect others to do what you yourself haven't done. So the next time you fill out your church pledge card, ask yourself, "What portion of my income am I going to give to God through the church?" How will you make that decision? What theological convictions will inform what you do? What about other Christian causes? What about secular causes such as the United Way, the American Cancer Society, the Red Cross, the Disabled American Veterans, the Girl Scouts, your local hospital, the institutions where you and your spouse were educated?

To help you in this soul-searching process, we offer the following summary of the basic principles of Christian financial stewardship:

- *Christian giving rests and relies on a sense of grateful obligation.* That's the steward's motive for giving. "What shall I return to the LORD for all his bounty to me?" (Ps. 116:12).

- *Christian giving is priority giving.* "Honor the Lord with your substance and with the first fruits of all your produce" (Prov. 3:9). Christian stewards put God at the top of their priority list. Their giving to the church comes first. God gets their firstfruits, not the leftovers.
- *Christian giving is proportionate giving.* "All tithes of herd and flock, every tenth one that passes under the shepherd's staff, shall be holy to the Lord" (Lev. 27:32). This Old Testament text is not cited as a legalistic requirement, but to illustrate the principle of proportionate giving. Christian stewards understand that it's not the amount but the proportion that counts with God. Those who have more should give more, according to their means.
- *Christian giving is sacrificial giving.* After watching many rich people put large sums of money into the temple treasury, and seeing a poor widow put in two copper coins, Jesus said to his disciples, "Truly I tell you, this poor widow has put in more than all those who are contributing to the treasury. For all of them have contributed out of their abundance; but she out of her poverty has put in everything she had, all she had to live on" (Mark 12:43–44). She was giving sacrificially. The rich people were not. Christian stewards don't just tip God. Their giving to God represents a sacrifice on their part. They have given up something else in order to give generously and sacrificially to God.
- *Christian giving is systematic giving.* "On the first day of every week, each of you is to put aside and save whatever extra you earn, so that collections need not be taken when I come" (1 Cor. 16:2). Paul's instructions to the Corinthians illustrate the point that good stewardship must be systematic. Pledging is a way of helping church members to be systematic in their giving, rather than sporadic. Some churches feel that pledging is not necessary. They talk about "faith" giving. If everyone in the church is giving sacrificially (at least a tithe), maybe pledging is not necessary. But in our view pledging facilitates good corporate stewardship, of which sound budgeting is an important part. Furthermore, pledging is itself an act of faith, when one challenges oneself to practice *all* the principles of Christian stewardship. Pledgers believe in "faith giving" as much as, if not more than, those who don't pledge! Anonymous givers are not necessarily giving proportionately and sacrificially, nor is God necessarily at the top of their priority list.

Christian stewards are not reluctant to talk about their giving. They want to be encouraged and inspired to be better stewards, because it has to do with their relationship to God and their commitment to the church. It is true, as some are fond of saying, that "my giving is just between me and God!" But that does not mean it's nobody else's business. Our giving to the church is a personal, but not a private, matter. There's big difference between being personal and being private.

Your Evangelistic Witness

The same is true about faith. There's a big difference between being personal and being private about faith. The apostle exhorts his protégé Timothy to "do the work of an evangelist" (2 Tim. 4:5). How do you conceive yourself as a pastor-evangelist?[3] What about your personal evangelism?[4] Pastors can easily confine their ministry to their own congregation, which in some respects is a "closed" community. They are not deliberately involved with or relating to people outside the church in any meaningful or spiritual way. Many of those people couldn't care less about the church, and give very little thought to spiritual things. But there are also people "out there" who are searching for something to believe in, some sense of purpose, a reason for their existence on earth. Something deep inside yearns to be delivered from the felt meaninglessness of modern life.

Week by week, Sunday by Sunday, pastors mount their pulpits to address an essentially captive audience. Most of the people in the pews are members of the church, or visitors who have already made some kind of profession of faith. Consequently, these pastors never feel they have to defend or prove the faith. They simply assume it! They never expose their own vulnerabilities. They never confess and examine the huge assumptions that underlie their preaching. They don't have to. They assume their congregants are already believers who share their presuppositions.

Similarly, they counsel people who come to them for help, people who have intentionally picked up the phone and sought the help of a pastor. They visit the homes of their parishioners, and occasionally the homes of those who have visited their church. But when do they ever bear witness to someone who doesn't share their presuppositions? How many unchurched people have they engaged in a faith-sharing dialogue? How many unchurched people do they have sustained contact with in the course of an average week?

As pastors we must learn to think evangelistically about everything we do in ministry, always ready, as the apostle Peter enjoins, to "make your defense to anyone who demands from you an accounting for the hope that is in you"

3. This topic has been extensively examined in the following three-volume series by Richard Stoll Armstrong: *The Pastor as Evangelist* (Westminster Press, 1984), *The Pastor-Evangelist in Worship* (Westminster Press, 1986), and *The Pastor-Evangelist in the Parish.*

4. Strictly speaking, evangelism is the act of sharing the good news. Most people, however, want to use a definition that includes something about method and purpose. We have adopted the following definition of evangelism for our purposes:

> *Evangelism is proclaiming in word and deed the good news of the kingdom of God, and calling people to repentance, to personal faith in Jesus Christ as Lord and Savior, to active membership in the church, and to obedient service in the world.* (From *Faithful Witnesses*, by Richard Stoll Armstrong [Geneva Press, 1987], p. 79.)

(1 Pet. 3:15). Are we prepared at all times to make a case for Christ when we are called on or have an opportunity to do so, in appropriate ways? This too is a spiritual discipline! We have to be intentional about it. We have to be willing to be instruments of God, always reflecting the love of Christ in word and deed in our relationships with others, and ready to share that good news as God gives us opportunity, sensitively, caringly, and never intrusively. In quoting Peter's exhortation to be ready always to give a reason for the hope that is in us, people often overlook what the apostle said right after that: "Yet do it with gentleness and reverence" (1 Pet. 3:16a). We don't cram our faith down other people's throats! But we must be ready and willing to speak with unchurched persons about the things of faith, to engage others at as deep a level of faith as is evidenced by their interest, yearning, or need. We pray that God will use us to plant the seeds of faith in others, as God used others to plant seeds in us!

And we must remember that the germination and sprouting and eventual flowering of those seeds is up to God, and not up to us.

Your Personal Bible Study

Regular devotional reading of and serious study of the Bible are another spiritual discipline that should be part of your life as a pastor. There is a close relationship but also a difference between the biblical research you do continuously in connection with your preaching and teaching ministry, and your studying the Bible devotionally, which you do for your own spiritual growth. Many sermon ideas are inspired by one's devotional reading of the Bible!

Some may prefer to see these two spiritual disciplines as one and the same, but we distinguish the two. We see a difference, for example, between reading about the psalms—their background, origin, authorship, when they were written, how they have been used—and reading the Twenty-third Psalm devotionally on a day when you will be going into the hospital for surgery. We see a difference between studying the Pauline principle of justification by faith in Romans and Galatians and reading a chapter from one of those epistles devotionally. The point is: Don't limit your Bible reading and study *either* to purely devotional reading, *or* just to the reading and study you do for sermon preparation.

Devotions with Your Church Staff

If there are other professional persons on the church staff, even if the staff is just you, the part-time church secretary, and the church organist, we urge you to consider having a daily, or at least a weekly, devotional time together. It needs to be built into everyone's schedule. Use a study guide (there are devotional publications that provide these) or plan your own format. You could simply choose a book of the Bible, assign passages, and take turns leading the devotional study. Whoever is leading could start off with a few comments, invite the others to share their thoughts, then lead in a time of shared prayer. Pray for each other and your families, pray for members of the church, pray for the ministry you share, pray for forthcoming events or activities, pray for people who are considering joining the church, pray for the church's mission in the community and the world, pray for the nation and the world, pray for anyone or anything else on your minds and hearts. Give thanks to God for the joy and privilege of being part of the work of his kingdom!

These regular devotional times build strong relationships and help foster a team spirit among staff members. They also provide wonderful opportunities for sharing the good things and the unhappy things that are happening in our lives, and for affirming and recognizing fellow staff members for special projects they have done or work they have undertaken.

Pastoral Pointer

If the church does not have a memorial fund to which people can make contributions in lieu of flowers in memory of deceased friends and loved ones, establish one. Keep a list of items to which people can direct their memorial gifts, items that the church needs. Publish the list regularly to keep the needs before the congregation. Many people like to designate memorial gifts or special gifts for specific items or needs. For example, "The new choir robes were given in memory of Carmelita Sanchez by her family."

Pastoral Pointer

Having to file income-tax returns can be stressful for busy pastors. Professional tax consultants can be expensive. If you are not already doing so, we recommend you use one of the excellent software programs available (TurboTax, for example). They make filing your tax returns so much easier, and they're far less expensive than a tax consultant. Some are free! Tax forms and regulations are at your fingertips. Answers to all your questions are readily available. Carryover information is stored on your computer. You can even file your returns electronically. Let your computer apply all the formulas and do all the arithmetic. You will be glad you did![5]

5. We discovered that even the tax consultants use these programs!

Chapter 9

Pondering My Relationships

Denominational Executives

According to Dr. Gregory Hinkle, whose article we referred to in chapter 1, many clergy feel isolated and alone: "For many, the aloneness reflects the pastor's sense that colleagues and denominational leaders have no sense of what he or she is doing. A recent pilot research effort interviewing many 'effective and successful' pastors came back with the consistent response that they desperately wanted feedback from peers and supervisors, and got none—no affirmation for successes, no support during difficult times, not even constructive criticism about their methods and performance. This left them feeling alone and unnoticed."[1]

A poor relationship with your bishop or district superintendent, or some other denominational executive to whom you are in any way subordinate, can be a source of great stress. Roman Catholic and Episcopal priests, Methodist and Lutheran ministers, and other pastors whose denominational polity calls for such offices, live with the reality that their lives are not entirely their own. Someone else is making decisions that may in certain circumstances determine where they go and how long they stay there. The political realities can be frustrating if not totally discouraging. We know pastors whose morale was so devastated by "the system" that they left their denomination, or, in a few cases, quit the ministry entirely.

"There is also considerable anxiety about how one will fare in the United Methodist appointive system," writes the Rev. Susan Harrington DeVogel. "There is often a tendency, accompanied by a great deal of anger, to blame one's ills on the 'system.'"[2]

1. "The Life of the Lonesome Loser: Beating Clergy Burnout," by the Rev. Gregory A. Hinkle, PhD.

2. Ms. DeVogel, an ordained United Methodist minister, conducted a research project for the United Methodist Board of Ordained Ministry in Minnesota. Her findings were reported in the December 17, 1986, issue of *The Christian Century*. Her article was prepared for Religion Online by Ted and Winnie Brock.

We have no magic formula for dealing with a bishop or "D.S." who is unreasonable, unfair, incompetent, uncaring, or insensitive. There is no appeal process for Methodist pastors, for example, who think they have been treated unfairly in the appointment system. Those decisions are made by the bishop on recommendation from the district superintendents. The bishop is the final authority. If you are a Methodist pastor, you do have certain rights, however. The bishop cannot *refuse* to appoint you. If your D.S. and the bishop think you are ineffective, you have the right to appear before the Board of Ordained Ministry. That would be stressful indeed!

Perish the thought, but if you are accused of committing a chargeable offense, such as preaching heresy, even that cannot be decided by the bishop, but would be referred to a Committee of Investigation, where you would have the rights of a full trial procedure.

Some bishops will allow pastors to approach them directly, but they are reluctant to countermand the decisions of their superintendents. Some denominations have a built-in process for addressing a pastor's grievances, but that process itself can be terribly stressful. "If your brother sins against you," said Jesus, "go and tell him his fault, between you and him alone" (Matt. 18:15 RSV). That's hard to do, when the person you are confronting has such influence over your life. It always helps to have an advocate. Failing all attempts to be reconciled, you have a vocational decision to make. Can you live with the situation and make it work, or is the stress so great that you need to go elsewhere?

One thing is sure: your spiritual fortitude is being tested. Stay close to God. Pray for God's guidance, and for patience and forbearance. God can work miracles. God can change human hearts in surprising ways—including yours! Seek the support and counsel of trusted clergy friends. Be discreet about taking people into your confidence about such a matter, especially members of your flock. In the meantime, accept the fact that you are where you were *sent* to be, even if you think you are not *meant* to be, and resolve to make the best of it. You will be amazed how such a change of attitude can reduce the stress level, and you can get back to thriving and not just surviving in your ministry.

Friends

Being discreet about sharing such confidences does not mean that you can't have close friends in the church. As a pastor, much of your social life revolves around the congregation and their activities. Some of your church members will become more than church members to you. They will become your closest friends. Some members will develop special friendships with your spouse, if you are married. There is nothing intrinsically wrong with being close friends with certain church members, as long as you are judicious in those relationships.

For example, don't play favorites. It stirs up jealousies among other church members. You cannot afford, as a pastor, to be "in anyone's pocket." The shepherd of the flock must love all the sheep, and must be committed to everyone's welfare, to the good of the whole church, and to the mission of Christ. To be unduly beholden to any one person or clique can make ministry very difficult. Your church doesn't need this and you can't afford it, even though as a human being you want, need, and are entitled to have friends.

That is why many pastors (and spouses, too) like to establish one or two close friendships outside the congregation they serve. They want to be able to relax and be themselves, without risking any damage or harm to the church they love and have been called to serve.

People like to be friends with their pastors. That's fine. It's good for a pastor to have lots of friends, but few, if any, confidants. Be wary of overconfiding in church members, even those whom you consider to be personal friends. And never betray the confidences of other church members who have discussed their lives or problems with you. It is unethical. It is wrong. It can and usually does backfire. It can be, in fact, illegal! (See chapter 13.) It can also destroy your credibility as a counselor. Never, but *never*, discuss someone's confidential information with another person without the consent of the one who confided in you. Be very judicious in referring to any church member in a sermon, except in complimentary or positive ways. Even that can be risky, if others are not mentioned who think they should have been! It is not only prudent but considerate to seek the permission of the person before using him or her as a sermon illustration.

You are always free to share your own confidences with church members, of course, but again, you do so at your own risk. You put the other person under the tremendous burden of temptation to share with someone else what he or she knows about the pastor! Remember: you are every church member's pastor, so try to share yourself impartially. As we have already mentioned, becoming too friendly with a few people can adversely affect your relationship with others, especially if the few "chosen ones" don't know how to handle their favored status—and they often don't! You will learn who those persons are to whom you may tell things "in confidence"—things that you *want* spread around the church! We say that partly in jest, but the truth is, it works!

The more important thing to remember is that if you are open and friendly, people will respond that way to you. If you give yourself to them, they'll return that love fourfold most of the time—but, we must add, not always! Among the things we all count on from our friends, when we are burdened with particular struggles, sorrows, or frustrations, are a listening heart and a caring spirit. It may be asking a lot to expect a church member to play this role for you. While you may be thinking of Joe or Mary as a dear personal friend, Joe or Mary may be thinking of you in the same way, but they never stop thinking of you and *seeing* you as their *pastor*! Whether they are able to hear—and handle!—that you are frustrated with the church treasurer or property committee chair, that three other churches have contacted you to fill their pulpit vacancies, that you are having a tough time getting the church youth director to show up on time for staff meetings, you can't know for sure. So be wary about confiding in church members. It's OK to develop close personal friendships with members of your church. Just don't forget you're their pastor. They never do!

The good news is that God always seems to place in your church those wonderful folks who reach out to you and care for you with a love sometimes surpassing even that of your relatives. You could never repay all the favors they do for you, all the countless things they do and say to express their caring. They are the simple saints of God who keep us pastors going! Their kindnesses, their countless expressions of love, the Monday morning notes and cards that say, "We are grateful for you, we are praying for you," those are what make up for all the disappointments, frustrations, and heartaches—and the Lord knows there are plenty of them! The rewards of being a pastor are many, and one of the greatest rewards of all is the exceptional friends we have in the church—foul-weather friends, not fair-weather friends.

When the sky is blue with clear sailing ahead,
  when your worries are few and your troubles have fled,
you can bet that you'll find you're surrounded with friends,
  as if on your favor their future depends.
When your pockets are full and the world's at your feet,
  you will get invitations to join the elite.
For it's not too hard then for some folks to be nice.
  They will wine you and dine you and seek your advice.
But the question to ask yourself once in a while,
  when you're getting a slap on the back with a smile,
is what will become of your fair-weather friends,
  when the going gets rough and your influence ends?

Can you count on them then, when you need their support?
When your luck has run out and your efforts fall short?
That's the test! And the best are the *foul-weather* friends,
who are still by your side when the fair weather ends![3]

Or to put it in the form of a prayer:

Give me a friend, O God,
not one who makes me think I'm right whenever I am wrong,
confirms me in my prejudice and pushes me along
the always easy pathway of my self-deceiving sin,
where good intentions quickly die and conscience soon wears thin.

I need a friend, O God,
not one who flatters me with praise I don't deserve,
and when I need to hear the truth, declines for lack of nerve
and tells me just what others think is music to my ears,
condoning or excusing all my failures, faults, and fears.

I want a friend, O God,
whose love for me demands I take the higher, harder way
and calls me to confess my guilt, whatever price I pay.
Far better that I choose to live with honor in defeat
than bask in fame and glory gained by falsehood and deceit.

I have a friend, O God,
who wants my best, expects my best, accepts no less from me,
who sets me an example I can follow earnestly,
expecting me to stand for truth and justice, come what may,
and judging me by what I do and not just what I say.

You are that friend, O God,
a friend whose love is life itself, whose truth has set me free,
who sees not only what I am, but what I long to be,
who knows my every weakness, yet forgives the wrongs I've done.
Such friendship is for all to share, through Jesus Christ, your Son.[4]

3. "Foul Weather Friends," from *If I Do Say So Myself*, by Richard Stoll Armstrong (CSS Publishing Co., 1997), p. 14.

4. "A Friendship Prayer," from *Now, THAT'S a Miracle!* by Richard Stoll Armstrong (CSS Publishing Co., 1996), p. 14–15.

Professional Relationships with Church Members

Another question many pastors don't take much time to think about—until they encounter a problem—is whether or not to enter into business or professional relationships with church members.

You may be in a new pastorate only a matter of weeks when a church member approaches you and says, "Pastor, you probably know I'm a dentist. Just want you to know I'll be glad to take care of your teeth and all the teeth in your family!"

What you do know at that point is that you have a nice offer. What you don't know is whether or not this particular member is offering his or her services at full price, or at a discount, or free. You're often not sure what the offer implies. Is this a church member looking for business, or simply wanting to help you and your family? You also do not know anything about the person's reputation or specialty. You don't know whether or not your spouse or your kids will like him or her—and we're speaking now strictly *professionally*. You are grateful this person is a member of your congregation. You are grateful he or she is concerned for your welfare. But you may find out later he or she is one of the higher-priced dentists in town, that he or she was giving no thought to offering you any kind of a discount (not that you deserve one, anyway), and that his or her practice is, in fact, not covered by your dental insurance policy, if you have one!

If you immediately accept this church member's offer, and encounter later problems with your teeth, or with the treatment provided for you or your family, what recourse will you have at that point? What choices could you make, particularly if you *are* receiving free service?

If your mechanic is a church member, and your car never runs properly, and that clanking noise under the hood keeps getting louder—even after repeated visits to this most gracious of church members—what do you do at that point? Do you visit a different mechanic and hope your church member never finds out? Do you go back to your church member for the fourth time, particularly if you know you're not paying? What if you're scheduled for a family car trip that weekend? Do you indicate you'd like the problem corrected right away? Wouldn't you feel guilty about continuing to bother someone who's been helping you free of charge?

If your insurance agent is a church member, and your insurer denies a claim for damages you think should have been covered by your policy, do you place your agent in the awkward position of having to go to bat for his pastor while simultaneously defending his employer, the insurance company?

If your physician is a church member and you have been trying for several days to reach her by phone to ask her a question about some medication she has asked you to take but have found her always busy or unavailable, will you be tempted to call her office and say, "But this is her *pastor* calling"? Will you be tempted to seek special attention, even though her nurse says, "I can help you with that"?

Many pastors and well-meaning church members do not always realize that the pastor–church member relationship can undergo a significant change when you shift it to a business, fee-for-service, or professional relationship. It's not because both parties aren't nice, or kind, or sincere, or well-intentioned. It's not because both parties aren't skilled at or completely professional about what they do. It's because there is a difference between a pastoral-spiritual relationship and a client-customer relationship.

This is not a hard-and-fast rule. There are countless examples of pastors who are enjoying good business or client-customer relationships with church members in churches all across the country. It is nevertheless a good idea to be mindful of some of the pitfalls in such relationships, and not merely for your sake. Keeping your relationship with church members strictly pastoral helps protect them too. Suppose a member of your church, who is a professional roofer, puts new shingles on your home at a big discount and a financial sacrifice to him, only to arrive for church Sunday morning after a Saturday night downpour to find out from one of your kids that the new roof had leaked badly?

Oops!

Handling the Problem Types: The Imposer

You will relieve yourself of some stress if you learn how to respond to certain kinds of people, and, God love them, they are in every congregation. One problem type that every pastor must deal with we will designate, for want of a better term, as "the imposer." Quite simply, this is the person who would like to monopolize all of your time. This is a tough problem. You want to be pastoral. Part of your calling is to be accessible and available to every church member. You don't want to be rude. But there comes a point at which these individuals can make it very difficult, if not impossible, for you to fulfill the many other responsibilities of your ministry in an effective or faithful way. Their incessant demands on your time and attention become an imposition, when they begin to interfere significantly with the time and attention you can give to others and to your other ministerial duties, such as hospital and other visitation, program planning, church leader recruitment, teacher training, staff or volunteer supervision, confirmation classes, worship planning, community relations, not to mention your personal study, devotional time, sermon preparation—to name only a few of the countless tasks you have to tend to.

You owe it to God and to your congregation not to succumb to the needs of the imposer. If the need is genuine, OK. No problem. Pour yourself out to this person. Be there. Be available. Try with all your heart and all the resources of your faith and pastoral skill to respond to the need. But if it's chronic, continuous, unrelenting, and draining of your time and attention, to the detriment of the health of the whole flock and of the church's mission, then you have a right—indeed, an obligation—to find a pastorally sensitive way to redirect the imposer's attempt to monopolize your time and services. Every pastor must develop her or his own style for doing this.

With some, you can simply let them run themselves out. They just need to be heard. If you take time to listen to them, they don't feel the need to keep coming back. You can facilitate the process by helping them to articulate their key points. They will feel much better. Ministry has happened.

With others this approach does not work at all. The more you give them, the more they want. If you talk with them for an hour when they call you at home in the morning, they will conclude they can call you for an hour in the evening as well. If you and your spouse invite them into your home when they stop by unexpectedly to see you on Saturday night, they will conclude you'll be happy to welcome them when they drop in any other night. You may reach the point where again, for the good of the church and out of simple fairness to the rest of your flock, you need to say, "I'm sorry, Bill. I just can't talk with you now." Or, "Do you really mean 'two minutes,' Sally, because we were just on our way out the door." In some cases, you will need to say, very honestly, "Jean, I think I've done everything I can to help you. I don't know what else I can offer you. I will always be praying for you, but if you feel you need some additional help, I'd like to give you the name of someone you can call."

Each person has his or her own ways of dealing with this problem that all pastors have to face. There is probably not a single church without at least one imposer. Imposers are likely to test you early on in your ministry to see how big a piece of you they can get. But getting that big piece is not really their ultimate goal. Holding on to it is.

We are pointing out this often unspoken problem so that you will not be caught by surprise, or feel that your situation is unique, or that you simply must grin and bear it. Imposers are not just the people who come to your study four times a week. They are also the people who monopolize your greeting time at the door of the church on Sunday morning, until other people finally give up and walk out the door before you have a chance to speak to them. They are the people who call you at home three or four nights a week, or sometimes just once or twice a week, but for an hour at a time.

Some pastors count as imposers those church members who expect you to interrupt your vacation with your family and fly back to conduct a wedding or funeral. If you want to do that, or feel the need to do that, it's OK, provided you are consistent with your policy and do not play favorites! Make sure your willingness to interrupt your vacation is sincere, that you don't do it begrudgingly or out of a sense of guilt about being available to the flock. There may be some people for whom you will and should want to return from your vacation in an emergency. But if you do it for one, you may be expected to do it for others, and if you don't, those whom you refuse may become very unhappy campers—and rightfully so!

Remember, too, that when you do accept such invitations, then *you* are imposing on your spouse and children, to whom you also have an obligation to be available. They put up with the countless hours during the year when you are not available to them because of your pastoral duties. Often you're not home when the children go to bed. They get up some days and you've already left the house for an early breakfast meeting. They look for you on a Saturday, and you are conducting a wedding somewhere. They wait to hang up the stockings on Christmas Eve, and you're at church wrapping up the late service.

Your vacation time is very important. It's *family* time. It's *renewal* time. You owe it not just to your family, not just to yourself, but also, in a profoundly spiritual way, to the congregation, to get away, to be refreshed and reenergized. In a word, you owe it to all, even the imposer, to vacate and to recreate, when you go on vacation!

The same considerations should be kept in mind with regard to your day off. You need to be more flexible here, however, as deaths, accidents, and other emergencies do not honor your days off! For that reason, one of your authors preferred not to take a regular day off. Instead, he felt free to take time off as needed, to attend his children's sporting events, for example. He preferred it this way, but others want to have a particular day each week. In either case, you need some time off, and you should not feel guilty about taking it. The Lord needed a *Sabbath,* and so do we!

The Amorous Type

A second problem many pastors encounter in their ministries is the person we'll refer to as the "amorous type." You are imagining the sort of person we mean! The amorous type presents a very real problem. The danger can be subtle. It can sneak up on you. You may not see it coming and suddenly—surprise! It is there in your face. By then others have seen it too.

Some pastors are oblivious to the fact that there is a fine and sometimes even permeable line between spirituality and sexuality, between affection and physical attraction, between *phileo* and *eros*. Some pastors, merely because they are married, mistakenly conclude that they are permanently off the radar scope of amorous church members. Regrettably, they are not.

It is important for all of us pastors to acknowledge and recognize our own sexuality. It is also important to be aware of the risks and dangers implicit in the various expressions of our caring for those whom God has called us to serve. You may intend your friendly hug to be nothing more than a spontaneous show of affection, of caring, but if you stand there hugging long enough, and intensely enough, what you intend in one way can easily turn into something else in the mind of another. It is normal, natural, and perfectly OK to be capable of being aroused sexually. If God had not made us that way, there wouldn't be any babies! If sex were not pleasant, who would indulge? As pastors we have to be doubly discreet about the signals we may be sending, lest people get the wrong message.

Prudent pastors try to be aware of how others are perceiving their best, but perhaps easily misunderstood, intentions. Innocent gestures can be interpreted as something else by affection-starved people, and if those same people have been indulging in the common practice of fantasizing sexually, your friendly embrace may be interpreted quite differently than you intended by the individual being hugged. What can begin as a desire for spiritual oneness, a reaching toward spiritual union, even a sharing of intimate concerns and needs, can sometimes become a tempting sexual or physical attraction.

If this were not the case, we would not have the sad experience of seeing the lives of so many pastors ruined by misconduct and scandal. It happens far too often, and to some of God's most effective servants. If vigilance and awareness can save even one pastor's ministry, and even one congregation from enduring the heartache and grief of a fallen leader, then let vigilance and awareness be practiced and preached.

Unfortunately, as you know, and as too many churches have discovered, pastors are too often the initiators of improper relationships. They have erred by encouraging rather than discouraging inappropriate advances. So pray hard that God will not let you enter into temptation, and that if you do, God will deliver you from evil!

Ministers, like doctors, counselors, and others in the helping professions, have to recognize and come to grips with the fact that they will always be subject to the overtures of amorous or emotionally needy parishioners. Some people fantasize about and fall in love with their pastors the way some patients fall in love with their doctors, their psychiatrists, or their nurses. There are too many doctors, ministers, and other professionals who have proved themselves incapable of coping with this phenomenon. They have succumbed to the temptation of allowing themselves to ignore or be deceived by a deepening relationship with a patient or church member.

As we have said, the fact that you may be married does not eliminate the problem. Married pastors face it regularly. In fact, in some cases your being married makes the problem worse. It intensifies the attraction an amorous church member will feel for you. In some ways it makes you appear to them less risky. They think they can titillate their sexual appetite more safely with a married person. One thing is sure: if you have a strong marriage, people aren't nearly so likely to suspect you of any "hanky-panky." If, on the other hand, your marriage is strained and if things aren't going well at home between you and your spouse, you may become a more attractive target to amorous types in your congregation, who may sense that this is the case. Your activities, furthermore, will attract closer scrutiny from church members who notice that you are paying more attention to a certain individual.

Another point: you need to be willing to talk about this subject with your spouse. Don't pretend the problem doesn't exist. Sometimes your spouse will pick up signals coming your way from an amorous church member before you do! As soon as an amorous type appears on your or your spouse's radar screen, sit down and talk about it together right then and there. Your spouse needs to understand that this problem frequently occurs in pastoral ministry.

Your spouse must be assured that you are firmly discouraging the amorous person, and that you are redirecting his or her affections to his or her husband or wife, if there is one, or to the possibility of a proper, future relationship with Mr. or Ms. "Right," if the person is not married, and ultimately, to Jesus Christ. You are the key. You must never encourage anyone to any degree whatsoever, whether for ego reasons, or personal satisfaction, or to titillate your own sexual appetite. Even though you never intend to indulge, fanning the flame is never right. You must snuff it out as soon as it flickers. If you detect it, or are suspicious, back off fast. You have your ministry to safeguard, sustain, and protect, and the calling of God upon your life. Be kind, be friendly, but be firm. If you sense something is beginning to happen between you and anyone else, shut it off fast! You'll be glad you did. So will your congregation. And, in a mysterious though possibly painful way, so will the amorous person!

Pastoral Pointer

When large groups of people are being served meals at church, you can speed up the process immensely by having more than one food table, with sets of dishes and two serving spoons for each dish, so that the lines can proceed along both sides of each table. Use rectangular-shaped dishes and divide into portions (in advance) those dishes that can be divided. It makes it easier for people to serve themselves. Think twice before providing ingredients for people to "toss" their own salads, for that can be very time consuming.

Pastoral Pointer

Many pastors have not taken advantage of the fact that some automobile insurance companies give discounts to nondrinkers. If you are a nondrinker, you may be able to save yourself a considerable amount of money on automobile insurance. Find out if there are companies that offer such discounts in your state, and check out any other discounts for which you may qualify.

Chapter 10

Needing to Stay Fit

Your Physical and Emotional Health

A pastor's health obviously bears on her or his work and witness. The effectiveness of a pastor who is physically, mentally, or emotionally exhausted or overwhelmed is limited. Taking care of your flock is part of your work as a pastor. Taking care of your family is a clear obligation. But wise pastors will also find the time to take care of themselves. Preserving and maintaining your physical and emotional health should actually be seen as part of your personal *stewardship*: the proper care and use of the good gifts of life that God has given you for his kingdom use.[1]

One need only to look twice at the word "recreation" to see that it means "re-*creation*." You must recreate for your own sanity, for your own physical, mental, emotional, and, yes, even *spiritual* well-being. All work and no play can make the dutiful parson a dull and less effective person. In addition, proper and appropriate care of yourself sets an example for the overworked, unhealthily fed, overstressed, under-relaxed, sleep-deprived, mentally exhausted, and nearly depleted parishioner who is there every week in your pews trying to figure out why he or he has no energy and wondering what to do about it!

But what about you? As a pastor, *your* work is never done. There are always pastoral calls to be made, people to be counseled, worship services to be planned, sermons to be written, meetings to be attended, articles to be written, correspondence to be answered, telephone calls to be answered, classes to be taught, planning to be done, and on and on it goes. How and when do

1. We asked a certified parish nurse, Michelle Arya, RN, what advice she, as a health care professional who has had the opportunity to observe firsthand the kinds of pressures pastors are under, would like to offer anyone considering a call to parish ministry. We thought you would be interested in her written response, extended excerpts of which we have included as Appendix A.

you find time to recreate and renew? What can you do and where can you do it? The final answer to these questions, of course, is up to you.

But here are some thoughts that may help. Your recreation should be custom-made, individualized, and tailored to suit your needs and schedule. Work out your own recreational salvation with fear and trembling. Devise a plan or routine that appeals to you, that includes activities you enjoy and look forward to. If you can't stand running, you will probably not sustain a running regimen of three or four mornings a week. If you don't like swimming, you should plan something other than regular visits to the YMCA pool. If you like to walk, put daily walks in your schedule. If you do like to swim, make time for swimming. If you like to bike, decide when you will bike. Schedule your recreation.

Your recreation often needs to be as intentional as the pastoral work you do. If you write "plan fall preaching schedule" on your calendar, you should also write "exercise!" or "morning swim," too. Consider it an obligation—one you owe to God, to yourself, and to your congregation. Then if someone asks you if you are free at that particular time, you can truthfully say, "I have a commitment." Because that's precisely what is required in this part of your life and ministry, if you are going to be faithful. You need to be committed to it, or it will never happen!

If you don't schedule it, you will find, as most pastors find, that the interruptions never end. That you will never find a good time to break away for the sake of your own health and maintenance. It's up to you to take care of YOU!

We should point out that some pastors find it useful to think in terms of a three-period day: morning, afternoon, and night. One way to thrive and not just survive in the ministry is to try *not* to work all three periods every day. Of course, you are always a pastor. In a sense, you are never off duty.

There are, to be sure, many days when you *have* to work morning, noon, and night. You will have a breakfast meeting, then morning counseling appointments, then a staff meeting at church. You'll have a sandwich at your desk while you return morning phone calls. You'll work on an article for your church newsletter after "lunch." As soon as you have finished the article, you'll leave for the hospital to visit a church member just admitted. After that you are scheduled to conduct a worship service in a local nursing home. You'll arrive back at your office to find the church secretary waiting impatiently for Sunday's worship bulletin information. You will work on that for a while and nearly finish when the couple you are marrying on Saturday show up for their last premarital counseling appointment. It is nearly six o'clock by the time they leave the church. Looks as if you'll have barely enough time to grab a few bites of supper when you get home before the 7:00 p.m. meeting of your church board begins. It adjourns at 9:45 p.m., assuming you are able to keep to the agenda. You arrive home a few minutes before 10:30 p.m. You find five messages on your answering machine, all from church members. One member entreats, "Please call me. I'll be up. I don't care how late it is." You'll feel your stomach growling.

If you try to keep that pace for very long, you may survive but you probably won't thrive in ministry. You won't thrive because you aren't catching your breath! You won't thrive because you aren't "re-creating." You won't thrive because you are trying to run the race at flank speed from the starting blocks to the finish line. Even the long-distance runner seeks ways to vary the pace and the scenery, in order to *reach* that finish line!

Some pastors, therefore, do employ the concept of the three-period day. When they can, they try to catch a breath during at least one period of every three-period day. If you foresee a long morning and a long evening at the church, try to get some exercise in the afternoon. If your afternoon and evening will both be packed, take a walk sometime that morning. Find a renewing activity that you enjoy, one that is wholesome and beneficial, rather than enervating, debilitating, injurious, or depleting. You will be blessed. So will your congregation. And so will your ministry.

Not *always* will your recreational and renewal activities be planned. Indeed, some *need* to be spontaneous! Some of your most renewing moments will be those that just happen, those completely impromptu, unplanned occasions and moments that give life zest and joy and surprise. It can be a delightful thing to come home early for lunch on some summer day and invite your stay-at-home spouse or your family to the zoo for a picnic—especially if you've done all the work to get the picnic ready! It can be delightfully spontaneous to stop the car on a long trip, just to get out and enjoy a scenic vista, or to explore an old country general store.

So you try to balance spontaneity with intentionality. Life shouldn't be all one or the other. Both make life meaningful and interesting. Find your own ways of having fun or blowing off steam or relaxing. It seems a dying art in our frenzied world is the art of simple play. Playing games, being with friends, enjoying music, playing the piano, flying kites, sitting on a porch swing, tossing a Frisbee, going fishing. These renew the spirit in ways unknown to those who sprawl in front of a TV screen.

Vacations

We made a few suggestions about guarding your vacation time under the subject heading "Family Matters." Let's think a bit more specifically about what you can do with your vacation time.

First, you have to decide to *take* a vacation! Sadly, some pastors neglect this aspect of personal renewal and family renewal, and all it can do to enrich their lives, their spirits, their ministries. They boast about never taking a vacation. In our view these pastors are setting a poor example for their families, their coworkers, and their church members. We believe they are not doing the church any favors by being workaholics. They may be jeopardizing their marriages as well as their ministries. They may be jeopardizing their own health.

We hope you are a pastor who believes in taking vacations, because you know you need them, your family needs them, and your church needs you to take them. Your right and obligation to take a vacation are grounded in the biblical/theological concept of Sabbath.

If there are other church staff members, see to it that they too avail themselves of their vacation time. A workaholic staff member is less of an asset to the church, and to you as a colleague, than one who is rested, energized, and renewed! Set your church members an example, for all these good reasons and more, that will encourage them to use their vacation time to renew their own lives too. Once you decide to take a vacation, you then have to think about *where*. The best advice we can offer in this regard is *elsewhere*! Try to get away. In our experience, if your church members know that you are home, even if you're on vacation, some who want to be sure no one bothers you will pick up the phone and call you themselves about something they think you need to know, or about some crisis they are sure you would want to attend to. They say, "I know you're on vacation, but I have something important to tell you." Or: "Could I come and talk with you? I've got a problem and I need your help." If you love your people and take their concerns to heart, as most pastors definitely do, it will be hard for you to say no. Both of us pastors have found it next to impossible. If someone dies and you're in town, it's hard to refuse when the family request you to conduct the funeral service.

Both of us have tried spending a vacation at home, thinking we'd have the opportunity to work on personal projects we never have time for the rest of the year. It didn't work out that way. We found ourselves doing funerals, weddings, taking counseling requests, making hospital visits, and even responding to lights left on at the church. Some vacation!

For your sake, your family's sake, your ministry's sake, and your church's sake, and for the sake of wanting not just to survive but to *thrive* in ministry, try to get away when you take your vacation. You will be glad you did. If you can't afford it, and some pastors can't, particularly if they have families, maybe there are relatives and/or friends who would love to have you visit them. But don't overstay your visit. Remember the saying, "Guests are like fish: you don't want to keep them longer than three days!"

Be a good guest and people will always be happy to welcome you. Not everybody knows, however, what it means to be a good guest. It means things like expressing your gratitude; writing thank-you notes to your host and hostess afterward; keeping your room neat; keeping out of the way as much as possible and trying not to disrupt the family routine, so as not to be a burden; taking your host and hostess out to dinner; and so on. When you depart after spending the night, leave the bed partly made up. To make it up all the way implies that your host or hostess doesn't change the linens after the bed has been slept in! But you do want to leave the room looking neat.

It's customary to bring a gift for your hostess—something for the home perhaps, or a box of candy, or bouquet of flowers. It doesn't have to be too expensive. If you do these kinds of things, you need have no qualms about accepting invitations to stay with friends when you're traveling. But always be willing to return the favor. Invite those who host you to stay at your house the next time they come your way.

Another thing you can do to help pay your expenses is to offer to preach at a friend's church or at a church without a pastor in some part of the country you'd like to see. Often this will help with your lodging, or with some of your other expenses being paid. Frequent-flyer miles, accumulated from previous trips and from special credit cards, can save you lots of money too. Sometimes church members with cabins or vacation homes will offer you and your family the use of their getaway place.

Once you have figured out where you will go, what you do is also up to you, of course. If you are married, try to make sure it's a vacation for your spouse (and your children, if you have any) as well as for you. A vacation for the purpose of your visiting three or four dynamic churches you've heard about and always wanted to see may *not* be the sort of vacation that will excite the rest of your family! Joint family planning for a vacation can be almost as much fun as the vacation itself. Anticipation can be half the enjoyment. Let the kids pore over the maps with you. They'll love helping to plan the route and what to see and do along the way.

Some families love to go on camping trips, which offer many benefits. Few activities can match the extended quality time, the togetherness, the accepted need for the equitable sharing of chores and responsibilities that camping affords, not to mention the marvelous opportunities to learn about and appreciate nature, to talk, and pray, and laugh, and play, and grow together. Children love living in such close contact with their parents, and what an opportunity for parents to give themselves and their full attention to their children for those precious vacation days. Arguments can arise, of course, but most families learn to forgive and forget and how best to get along when they are camping together.

Siblings often correct the one that gets out of line, and parents have the opportunity to model the kind of love, patience, and affirmation that the hectic pace of their normal lives makes it sometimes hard to reflect. To paraphrase a familiar adage, the family that camps together stays together.

When to take your vacation is something else to think about. Again, if you are married, your spouse's needs or work schedule have to be taken into consideration, as well as your children's school schedules, if you have children. The church year is a determining factor. Most pastors take most of their vacation in the summer. Some like to space it out during the year, with periods of respite after busy seasons and holy days like Advent, Christmas, and Easter, which are extremely demanding times in the life of a pastor. Use a little imagination. There are usually more options than many pastors and congregations realize.[2]

Staying Fit Intellectually

Remembering that the Great Commandment is to love God with all our heart, soul, MIND, and strength (Matt. 22:37; Mark 12:30; Luke 10:27), it behooves us not to neglect the continual development of our intellect. Some pastors finish seminary and decide they are finished—finished reading, finished studying, finished growing! If they persist in that attitude, they probably *will* be finished! Seminary is not a finishing school. Pastoral ministry is an intellectual challenge as well as a spiritual one, especially for those who are called on to preach and teach regularly. Pastors who try to sustain years of preaching based solely on what they learned in seminary are pastors whose preaching becomes dated. If we stop fertilizing the subsoil, as one teacher of preachers has put it, pretty soon nothing new grows. To bring the analogy into the computer age, if we don't continue to upgrade the software, pretty soon the hardware won't do what we need it to do.

Your education should continue beyond seminary—for the rest of your life! Discipline yourself to learn something new every day—about the faith, about the Bible, about ministry, about the church. Take advantage of the continuing education time and whatever funds your congregation offers you. If they have made no such provision, talk to your church board and let them know that if they want to keep their pastor functioning well, they need to be sure you

2. For most married pastors vacations are a family affair. We do know of some couples, including a clergy couple or two, who prefer to take separate vacations. That's their prerogative, of course, but they are the exception, not the rule.

sharpen your intellectual saw regularly. Most church officers recognize and appreciate the importance of their pastor's continuing education.

Contact seminaries, your denomination, clergy journals, and other publications, and get on their mailing lists. You will receive a steady stream of continuing education and training offerings. Some pastors enter additional degree programs after seminary. This is not for everyone. Know your reasons. There are those whose main reason for getting a DMin degree is so that they can be called "the Rev. Dr. So-and-So"!

Consider the value of independent study and reading, as over against planned seminars. You may want to read or write in a subject area that is of particular interest or relevance to you. Also, seeking out a mentor can be one of the best ways of continuing your education as well as enhancing your spiritual development. Be judicious in choosing a mentor or spiritual director, to make sure you get someone who is right for you. Some who have never before served in that role may be better than others who are making a profession of it.

Clergy groups and pastors associations can also be sources of mutual learning and growth. Some groups discuss books, share ideas, talk theology, compare notes on ministry. This kind of exposure, dialogue, and sharing with one's colleagues and peers is very important, especially for those who are having a lonely hike somewhere out in the boondocks.

On a multiple staff, with other pastors around, you have (or should have) a built-in support group, with dialogue, feedback, and the weighing of ideas taking place all the time. There are some church staffs, however, that do not sense the need for this. That's when scheduling such sessions becomes important.

With regard to your personal study, keep reading! That's the best advice anyone can give you. Read all you can—newspapers, magazines, clergy journals, and other professional publications. Read church history and books about ministry. Read Bible commentaries and devotional literature. Keep stretching. Keep pushing the boundaries. If you have to, *pry open* your mind. If you close it, your people will know it, and your preaching will eventually show it.

It is helpful to do recreational and other reading, as well. A diet consisting of reading exclusively in one's own professional subject area is too limited. You might be surprised what you can learn about ministry or life by reading a good novel, or what you might learn about evangelism by reading a book about deep-sea fishing! In our pastoral work we've both discovered that *everything* we read, every book, every article, every journal, every magazine becomes grist for the ever-grinding sermon mill. You may be reading the sports page one day, or a home-remodeling magazine, when suddenly you see a perfect sermon illustration. It happens all the time to every preacher who thinks homiletically and keeps mentally alert. Wouldn't you agree?

Your Library

While we're thinking about reading, a word about your personal library is in order. Pastors collect many, many books. The mere process of completing seminary loads you up with many boxes of books. As you take up your ministry, buy more books, and are given books, your library grows. We hope you have built your library thoughtfully and wisely. There may not be a theological library within a hundred miles of your church, so make sure your personal library has what you need.

Whether or not you know what you have, or can find what you need, is another matter, one that needs your attention and some thoughtful planning. Otherwise you can waste a lot of time trying to find the books or articles you need when you need them, as on a Saturday night when you're caught with your sermon down. *Any* system for organizing your library is better than no system. That's up to you, but we have found it helpful to have our books arranged by major topics, with commentaries all in one section. The books we need most often are nearest to our desks. We keep within easy reach a modern dictionary and a grammatical style and reference book, our working Bibles, the hymnal our church uses, a good Bible dictionary, a concordance, a one-volume commentary of some sort, our church directory, our current devotional reading, our denominational directory, and any other books, manuals, or directories we use often. If your desktop is large enough, that's a good place for these kinds of books.

If you're like us, you often are lending books to your parishioners. It's a good idea to keep some kind of simple card file of the books you lend to others, as people are not always prompt in returning books. A particular book you are searching for may be one you loaned to a Sunday school teacher last year.

Another thing to think about is where to keep your books. It depends on what kind of facilities you have at the church and at home. If you have a den at home and a nice study at the church, where do you want which books to be located? Do you have computers at both places? Where will you be doing most of your creative work? Where will you receive most of your ministry-related e-mail or voice mail? We have found it helps to be set up in both places, if possible. Your own schedule and work habits determine what you should keep in which place. Wherever you do most of your pastoral writing and sermon preparation, that's the place you'll want most of your reference and resource books.

It is sometimes difficult to write or prepare sermons at church. People assume that if you're in your study, you're available to them. If you don't have a secretary to "guard" your creative times, you have to devise an approach you can live with and monitor it yourself. Some pastors set aside certain hours of the day, or certain days of the week, or certain parts of days when they are in their "sermon caves," or at their Bible-study desks, or in their devotional closets—some place where their solitude is to be protected.

Your church secretary, if you have one, can help implement this. But it takes real sensitivity and awareness on her or his part. Your secretary has to know when and under what circumstances you *want* to be interrupted. A good secretary will sense this after a while, but it calls for ongoing communication. Most pastors *want* to be interrupted for pastoral emergencies, crises in church members' lives or in the congregation, calls from their spouses or children, or particular calls (the dentist, the doctor's office) they may be expecting.

Using Your Computer

We mentioned computers above. We assume most pastors own or have access to at least one computer. Many have a desktop computer and a laptop. None of the disciples had computers. Paul didn't have a computer. For nearly twenty centuries the work of the kingdom has gone on without computers. The gospel has been preached, lives have been changed, the church has grown, and Christianity has been spread throughout the world long before there were computers.

But we now have this marvelous new tool at our disposal and we should make the best use of it. Some pastors seem to be joined at the hip with their computers, however. We all need to remember that our computer is a resource, not a way of life. It is not your ministry; it is a tool to be used in ministry. It's sad to hear of pastors so chained to their keyboards, or riveted to their video displays or indentured to the Internet, that they never spend time with people! Be wary! Check yourself once in a while. We know the time you spend in front of your computer can contribute enormously to your ministry. But if you're not careful, your computer can become a detractor from or a rival to your ministry.

Your computer's word-processing function can be one of your greatest aids to ministry. Pastors work with words, and computers help us handle words more easily and efficiently. Your computer can also be a marvelous source of information for your ministry. It is an almost unlimited source of information, a complete reference library at your constant and instant disposal. Most good clergy journals, pastors' conferences, and church supply catalogs will keep you advised of superb software to assist your study, teaching preparation, and sermon writing.

But once in a while you may need to force yourself to log off, turn off your computer, look up from your monitor and converse with a church member, a staff member, take a pastoral counseling appointment, or walk out to the parking lot, climb into your car, and go make a pastoral visit.

We need to add one final word of caution. The easy online access to pornography has been a real temptation to many adults, including, we regret to say, some pastors and staff members—perhaps to even more than we know! Take every precaution to use whatever screening and blocking programs you can find to prevent the misuse of church as well as personal computers. The use of computers should be carefully and strictly monitored, especially wherever and whenever they are accessible to children, and parents should be advised accordingly regarding their own children's use of their home computers.

The purveyors of pornography are aggressively seeking to corrupt the minds of young and old alike, and they are constantly using every legal means to justify their right (under the First Amendment) to peddle their filth. The courts will ultimately have to define what legally constitutes pornography, but any pastor can surely recognize it when she or he sees it. Beware lest some morbid curiosity or prurient desire, however masked, should tempt you into exploring or indulging what your conscience knows is obscene or unwholesome content. May our computers "lead us not into temptation"!

Pastoral Pointer

Keep your church bulletins and hard-bind them periodically (two or three years' worth). Do the same with your church newsletters, annual reports, and/or directories. They are a most useful record of your ministry. You will have occasion to refer to them often. Color code the books according to the churches you serve. They are part of your personal reference library.

Chapter 11

Reflecting on Work and Other Involvements

Work Habits

The late Dr. James I. McCord, former president of Princeton Theological Seminary, once told the story of a pastor who, when asked how he was able to survive in the same church for thirty years, replied, "I started off at a pace I could keep!"

Sometimes we pastors think that the work of the kingdom needs to be completed on our watch. We think that even though Rome wasn't built in a day, our church or our ministry *should* be! It's important for you to find a pace that *you* can sustain over the long haul in your ministry. That pace will be different for every pastor. It needs to be steady and responsible. It needs to be faithful. One wit has suggested that church leaders need to remember to eat the elephant one bite at a time. The job looks elephant-sized sometimes. That's because it is! But remember: you are building on the work of others, and others will come after you.

We are called to run with perseverance the race that is set before us (Heb. 12:1). Too many pastors, sadly, begin the race well but never manage to finish. Increasing numbers of pastors seem now to stumble or fall. They burn out, rust out, wear out. They leave the ministry. Sometimes it's because they have viewed the pastor's calling as an objective to be accomplished, rather than as a way of life. We need to keep a long view of our ministry.

In a sense we are always on the job as pastors. We are never off duty. When do we stop being pastors? Not on our days off. Not on our vacations. Not on Monday mornings. We are always on call. Much of what some people would call social (not work-related) activities will be pastoral *work* for you. Why? Because as a pastor you are always a pastor, no matter where you are or what you are doing. You can't escape that reality. You can't put it on and take it off like your robe on Sunday morning. The moment you are introduced to folks at a social gathering as a pastor, you will see the quick blink of people's eyes, the barely perceptible shift of their heads, as they adjust themselves (and sometimes their language!) to their image of what kind of person you must be. You're used to it by now.

You also realize that every encounter, for *every* Christian, is an opportunity to represent the One who calls you into his service. That's no less true for pastors. You are also representing the church you serve. You are, for example, always willing to listen, always available for counsel. At some point you stop being amazed and instead become grateful to find that, within minutes of meeting you, total strangers will reveal their deepest secrets to you. In a sense it is not you they are confiding in or reaching out to. It is the living God, of whom you are, in the words of Henri Nouwen, a "living reminder."[1]

Good living reminders have their own good memories. They remember at all times they are pastors. Contrary to what some may suppose, this *doesn't* take all the fun out of life. Rather it puts more fun, more challenge, more meaning, and more reward into it!

If you have a spouse who accompanies you on a speaking engagement, he or she will be surprised to discover how tiring it can be to be put up in somebody's home overnight. The need to respond to your hosts' personal problems or needs—for conversation invariably turns to such things—puts a subtle pressure on you, and on your spouse too. Yes, it's part of the ministry to which God called you. Yes, you sense God's pleasure and the presence of the Holy Spirit in these moments. Yes, it's part of the ministry you love so much. But it is tiring! It is not relaxing. It's work! In that sense, many pastors find themselves "working" eighty to a hundred hours a week. Even your reclining for a haircut often prompts the question from the person about to trim you, "What do you do for a living?" You say, "I'm a pastor," and suddenly you're back to work!

In other words, you're not working only when you happen to be in your office or at the hospital, or when you are making a pastoral call. You are working when you have lunch with a parishioner, or spend an evening with a group of church members in somebody's home. One minister, when asked what his fee was for speaking, would respond, "Two hundred dollars; four hundred, if I'm going to be housed in someone's home!" That was more than a facetious response.

People's work patterns depend on many things, such as their physical, mental, and emotional stamina, which varies with individuals, and whether they are at their best in the morning or evening. We two pastors are night persons, which prompted this poem:

1. Henri Nouwen, *The Living Reminder* (Seabury Press, 1981).

We put in just as long a day as early risers do.
The hours that we spend in bed are relatively few.
If early in the morning we are not a perky pup,
it's just because we go to bed when some are getting up![2]

And this one:

Hats off to those persons who rise before dawn
to study the Scriptures and pray.
They're doing what Jesus did long, long ago,
while I'm in bed snoring away.
In fact, they are doing much better than Christ,
for where, may I ask, does it say
in Matthew or Mark, or in Luke or in John,
that Jesus did that every day?[3]

That touch of humor notwithstanding, it helps to know what time of the day or night one's creative juices flow more readily. Our family responsibilities have a tremendous impact on our work habits. So does our sense of well-being about our ministry. When we don't like our work, it becomes a chore and we become less productive. Working under constant pressure also causes us to regard our work as a burden, not a privilege.

Our life's obligations also affect our work patterns. As a pastor you have obligations to yourself: to get adequate rest, to spend time in Bible study, prayer, professional reading, and sermon preparation. You have obligations to your family, if you have one: to spend time with them, to seek a respectable balance between what is being "at work" and what is being "at home." You have obligations to your colleagues, church staff members, and the lay leaders with whom you work. You have obligations to other pastors who turn to you for counsel or help. You have obligations to your community. You have civic, social, and professional involvements. You have obligations to your extended family, obligations to your friends. And you always have your fundamental obligation to God, who alone can help you prioritize all your other obligations, and who reminds you that Jesus Christ is head of the church, not you, and that the position of Lord and Savior has been filled.

If you are going to keep your sanity in the ministry, if you're going to thrive as a pastor, you have to learn how to live in the limbo land between all you have done and all you have yet to do. You will never be finished. There is

2. "In Defense of Night Persons," from *If I Do Say So Myself* by Richard Stoll Armstrong (CSS Publishing Co., 1997), p. 32.
3. "Rise-and-Shiners," ibid., p. 33.

always more work to be done. As long as you're in ministry, there will always be more church members needing your counseling, there will always be more unchurched persons to reach, more phone calls to make, more Sundays to get ready for, more books to read, more classes to teach, more baptisms, more weddings, more funerals, more whatever. Rejoice that only God will be able to finish the work God has started. Get used to the idea. Make friends with this affirmation, or your never-ending checklist will drive you crazy. The work of the parish minister will never be finished until Christ comes again. In the meantime, give thanks for the privilege and opportunity to serve!

Your Civic and Social Involvements: Four Rules

Nor is your work limited to your responsibilities in the parish. You are undoubtedly involved in other worthwhile activities outside the church. But watch your step! If you are not thoughtful and discerning, your civic and social involvements can consume more time than you can afford. We have found it useful to observe four simple rules when gauging our involvement in "extracurricular" affairs.

Rule 1: ***Be wary***, when you first arrive in a new church or community. It will seem as if every club, organization, and activity will be bidding for your time and commitment. Your phone will ring with calls to join this, join that. We have always found it prudent not to rush into things. It's better to wait till you get your feet on the ground at the church. You can say, "I really appreciate the invitation, but I'm still trying to get settled and to see how my schedule develops. A year from now I'll have a much better sense of things. May I call you back then?" If you don't need or want to wait a year, say "In a few months" or "In a few weeks." The point is: *wait* until you have a chance to get the lay of the land. The waiting period will give you a chance to learn much about the organizations and activities in your area.

Rule 2: ***Be selective***. A pastor's time is subject to innumerable demands. Free time is limited. Pick and choose the things you really *want* to do, the activities you truly want to get involved in. Look for activities where you can make a contribution, make a difference, find significant involvement, and truly enjoy the associations you will form. Don't join something just to join it. By the mere fact that you are a pastor, you will find yourself obligated to be involved in some things that do not inspire, engage, or challenge you. You should not duck those involvements. It isn't fair to do only those things that you want to do. So when you do have a chance to choose, choose those programs that really appeal to you. Look for organizations and causes that you really believe in. And once you get involved, continue asking the question, "Is my time being well used?" This is a question of good stewardship: "Am I investing my gifts and time wisely?"

Rule 3: ***Be consistent***. Your involvements should be consistent with your commitments. Why give time to any organization that does not conform to your basic purpose for being in ministry? It isn't fair, furthermore, or even ethical, to sign on with any group, activity, or organization if you are not interested or available enough to fulfill the commitment you have made. Some pastors like to join the local Rotary, Kiwanis, or some other service club. Others know they can't justify or guarantee the weekly commitment of time such involvements entail. It's not that these aren't outstanding organizations. It's just that some pastors know they can't commit themselves to that kind of time. Or, in some cases, they have known there were other activities, organizations, or causes they preferred to commit themselves to. Have a policy that enables you to be consistent in your involvements.

Rule 4: ***Be fair***. Take care to honor your commitment to your congregation. They expect and even need to see you involved in contributing to the good of the world beyond the walls of the church, but they also need to know your primary commitment is to them. They know you have obligations to your denomination, to your district, presbytery, or diocese, to the wider church, to the community, to your various alma maters, alumni associations, and so on. But you can't do everything. You have to distinguish between those involvements you accept out of duty and responsibility, and those which are worthy but nonobligatory. The congregation needs to know that these other commitments do not outweigh your commitment to them. Be fair to your flock.

Your Pastoral Ethics and Etiquette

Both your ethics and your etiquette will impact your witness and work—for good or for ill. If the latter, as is sometimes the case, you will not thrive in ministry. You may not even survive. Plagiarism, dishonesty, financial double-dealings will eventually derail any pastor's ministry. So will one's ill-mannered, or ill-tempered, treatment of people.

"Live your life in a manner worthy of the gospel of Christ," Paul enjoins the Philippians (Phil. 1:27). Timothy is exhorted to "Set the believers an example in speech and conduct, in love, in faith, in purity" (1 Tim. 4:12). And Peter echoes the charge: "Tend the flock of God that is in your charge, exercising the oversight, not under compulsion but willingly, as God would have you do it—not for sordid gain but eagerly. Do not lord it over those in your charge, but be examples to the flock" (1 Pet. 5:2–3).

These words can fill us with a sense of inadequacy, for we know our feet are made of clay. We thank God for putting God's treasure in earthen vessels, aware of what "cracked pots" we often are! But we need to take seriously our responsibility as pastors to be examples to the flock—not by our own strength or perfection, but by the grace of God!

We should show that we are aware, and be willing to admit to our flocks, that we are far from perfect. While we live with the scriptural injunction to be examples, we are also included in the biblical pronouncement that "all have sinned and fall short of the glory of God" (Rom. 3:23; cf. Rom. 11:32, Gal. 3:22) and that "there is no one who is righteous, not even one" (Rom. 3:10; cf. Ps. 14:2–3)! We ourselves are spiritual pilgrims, pressing on toward the goal of the upward call of God in Christ Jesus. We live and move and have our being in and by God's Spirit. We seek God's forgiveness. We rely on God's power and mercy. We're on the way, but we haven't arrived! Our sanctification is ongoing. Struggling at all times to be faithful, we are examples not of people who never stumble and fall, but of people who rejoice in God's goodness and depend on God's mercy and forgiveness.

We are sometimes to our parishioners as parents to children. We strive to set a good example, but are always aware of our failings and imperfections. Generally our congregations will be accepting and forgiving, if they believe in their hearts that we want for them what God wants, and that for their sake and for Christ's sake we are doing the best we can.

Some pastors resent the "double standard" imposed on the clergy. As a pastor you have the same right as anyone else to indulge whatever vices and human behaviors the law of the land allows. You can smoke to excess, you can drink to excess, you can flirt, you can gamble, you can speak profanely, you can buy pornography. You *can* do these things. The question is: Are you willing to give up those kinds of "rights" for Jesus' sake? That is, are you willing to give up a particular harmful habit as a pastoral responsibility and as a witness to others, out of gratitude and love for Jesus Christ and for the sake of the ministry to which he has called you? Or will you insist on indulging that habit simply because it is your right to do so?

Whenever we face a moral decision, it is our Christian calling and our great joy and privilege, indeed our *liberation,* to choose the way that best glorifies Christ and that achieves the greatest good for his kingdom. If one of two alternatives is less selfish and more altruistic than the other, less harmful and more beneficial to others, less demeaning and more glorifying of God, less destructive and more ennobling of human dignity, then that is the pathway to choose, the narrow road that leads to life. If we are ignoring the ethical dimension of faith in our own lives and decision making, how can we justify our right to preach to anyone else on any moral or ethical question? If we are not willing to make our own sacrifices for the living out of our faith, how can we expect anyone else to do so?

Christian ethics must be existential, not merely theoretical. Our ethical convictions must show in our behavior or they have no integrity. So the question is: How will you determine your lifestyle? How will you make decisions about the jewelry you wear, the clothing you buy, the kind of car you drive, the kind of movies you watch, the language you use, the jokes you listen to, the political choices you make, the company you keep? Do you see those decisions as integral to what you profess to believe, and to what you preach?

Nobody can forbid you to drive the most expensive car in your church, but what does that decision say about you and your priorities? You're kidding yourself if you think it says nothing. No one can forbid your having a home so full of "stuff" that there's hardly room to step in the front door. But your home will say something about who you are, and about your attitude toward possessions. Do you want your home to give the impression that you worship your possessions? Your furnishings should be tasteful. They may even be expensive. But they should not be overdone.

Smoking

Based on the principles stated above, and given what we now know about the harmful effects of tobacco, it is impossible to justify smoking as a better alternative than not smoking. It violates our stewardship of the gift of life.

> We sympathize with those who have the habit and can't shake it.
> We empathize with those with allergies who cannot take it.
> We recognize the ones whose tainted breath and clothes announce it.
> We eulogize the folks who used to smoke and now denounce it.
> We criticize those people who despite the risks still do it.
> We agonize with those who've lost a friend or loved one to it.
> We socialize with those who gave it up or never did it.
> We patronize those restaurants and places which forbid it.
> We chastise those who jeopardize the health of others by it.
> We scrutinize the ads designed to make young people try it.
> We minimize permission for those smokers who request it.
> We maximize the use of signs, and if none, we suggest it.
> We theorize no one would smoke who really understands it.
> We sermonize the stewardship of life clearly demands it.[4]

4. From a poem entitled "Smoking," ibid., p. 61. The first-person singular pronoun has been changed throughout to the first-person plural, since the authors have the same concerns about smoking.

Alcohol

With regard to the use of alcohol, most Christians agree that moderation is the key. Some insist on total abstinence. To those pastors who have no qualms about moderate social drinking, we would advise against flaunting that right. Awareness and sensitivity is called for here on the part of a pastor. You have church members who invite you into their homes and offer you a cocktail before dinner or a glass of wine with a meal. To accept, if you partake at all, can be a gracious and congenial gesture. To decline (graciously, of course) can be a witness, particularly if you or any of those present have problems with a pastor's consumption of alcohol. Let Christ and your conscience be your guide. But don't forget, others look at you as a pastor, and some will be quick to use you to justify their own drinking. How best can you set the believers an example: by drinking, or by giving up your right to drink?

Some Income Considerations

How you handle your income reflects on you as a Christian steward and as a pastor. In addition to your church salary, you may receive honoraria from weddings and speaking engagements, publishing royalties, and occasional income from other sources. Pastors need to decide what kinds of fees and honoraria they expect for their various services, what kinds of services they will not accept fees for, and their theological rationale for both. What working principles determine whether or not you will accept fees for baptisms, weddings, funerals, memorial services, guest preaching, conducting workshops at conferences, premarital and marriage counseling, and other services? How do you define "pastoral service"? As pastors, the two of us have always felt that weddings, baptisms, and funerals are part of our pastoral call. We have never required fees for these acts of ministry performed for our own church members. You may decide, as some pastors do, to treat weddings or funerals performed for nonmembers differently. But you can have a powerful and unforgettable witness to the love of God and the gracious acceptance of Christ and his church when you decline the honorarium the funeral director tries to hand you for doing the service of a nonmember.

Not all pastors are of the same mind on this. Pastors of high integrity and sincere commitment can often differ. *Your* feelings on this matter should relate to your personal stewardship, your attitude toward ministry and money, and to how you see yourself as a pastor-evangelist. What you decide to do may not be a "one-size-fits-all" approach. Our objective here is to challenge you to think and pray about this matter in the context of your own personal stewardship and your faith in the providence of God.

Funerals and weddings are occasions that provide a pastor with tremendous evangelistic opportunities. It's not merely what you say in the service—and those who attend *are* listening. It's how you relate to the people involved, how they perceive you as a representative of God and the church, whether you show a genuine interest in and concern for them, and whether they have sensed the love of Jesus Christ as you ministered to them.

As for speaking or preaching engagements outside their own churches, most pastors do not feel obliged to refuse an honorarium. Nor do we. There's a considerable amount of work involved, not to mention your valuable time, including travel time and the event itself. Sometimes we have had to drive several hours for an out-of-town speaking engagement, or have flown to a three-day conference in which we were invited to participate. Some of these occasions turn out to be "freebies." Both of us have preached and spoken on occasion without receiving an honorarium. Some churches do not even think to reimburse your mileage. Be sure your church is not one of those!

Like most pastors, you are probably uncomfortable when someone asks you, "What is your fee?" Most of us don't have an agent to negotiate for us, and we don't like to barter with churches about an honorarium. On the other hand, "The laborer deserves to be paid" (Luke 10:7), and churches should not impose on those whom they ask to speak or preach. Instead of asking, "What is your fee?" churches or groups inviting you to speak or preach should state their request and what honorarium, if any, they are offering. Then you can decide whether to accept or decline the invitation. Churches should also state whether or not they will cover your travel expenses, including car mileage reimbursement (so much per mile), particularly when the invitation is coming from far away. Then all the facts are known to you, as you consider their need in relation to your available time and other commitments. We'll have more to say about this in chapter 13.

All pastors receive requests for their services. Again, we urge you to think systematically and theologically about how you are going to handle them, so that you can be consistent in your practice. What will you say? How will your approach align with what you believe about your work and the call to serve Christ?

Tentmaking Ministries

The apostle Paul was a tentmaker. By working at his trade he was able to support himself while pursuing his missionary endeavors. He was proud of the fact that he earned his keep and did not have to burden those among whom he labored for Jesus Christ. Thus the term "tentmaking ministry" is aptly applied to the work of those pastors who are engaged in some sort of secular occupation while serving a church that cannot afford to pay them a sufficient wage to support them and their families.

There are many possibilities for those part-time pastors or any who need to supplement their meager church income in order to make ends meet financially. The purpose of the "tentmaking" is to enable the pastor's ministry. The tentmaking should not interfere with, compete with, or distract from that ministry; rather, it should facilitate it. Tentmaking should be a necessity, not a luxury.

Nor should you as a pastor decide to take up other employment without the full knowledge and blessing of the church board or those to whom you are accountable. Such employment should never be work that puts you in a compromising position or causes you any conflict of interest. The pastor who preaches on Sunday morning and stands behind a roulette table or tends bar on Monday night creates a contradictory image that will pose a problem for many. Your primary concern, attention, energy, commitment, and love should always be directed toward the church.

Tour Hosting

Many pastors of middle-class or more affluent congregations serve as tour hosts for groups composed largely of church members. Destinations may include the Holy Land and other areas rich in biblical history, such as Greece, Rome, Turkey, or Egypt; various European locations connected with church or denominational history; and spiritual pilgrimage sites, such as the Passion Play at Oberammergau, the Isle of Iona, or the Taizé Community in France.

These sorts of tours can be mountaintop experiences for those who participate and tremendous faith-building and teaching opportunities for the host pastor. They provide an extended period of in-depth fellowship and relationship building with your people. They yield a treasury of marvelous memories. They are exceptional learning experiences for you as well as for members of your congregation. Your church members grow spiritually, and so do you. Tour hosting can be one of your best vehicles for discipling people, if you go about it properly.

Don't overlook the fact that these trips and tours are very demanding and very tiring for the pastor who takes them seriously. Your work begins with the planning. Then follows the promoting, which must be very sensitively done. Before you leave you will probably find yourself conducting predeparture meetings, orientations, or briefings for those who have signed up. Throughout the trip you will be teaching and conducting worship services on the bus and at key spots along the way, encouraging the participation of the group and facilitating their sharing. As the host you are on duty from the moment you leave home to the moment you return and set down your suitcase. Even beyond that there will be follow-up work to do. Some groups organize reunions, share pictures, compile a tour scrapbook for the church.

One compensation for all this work is that for a specific number of persons in your group, you as the pastor may receive free passage. If the group is large enough, you can negotiate with the tour company for a lower price per person. By doing that you can allow some folks to have an incredibly enriching experience they could not otherwise afford. You are not doing this for money; you are doing it as a service to your people. The work is justifiable if you view it and treat it as part of your teaching and discipling ministry. Obviously it should not be allowed to distract from or interfere with your other pastoral duties. You must studiously avoid even the appearance of that. It is not a vacation for you, though it may be for the members of the tour group. For you it's work! It's a valid part of your ministry.

For these reasons we advise you to be very low key in terms of your promotion and advertising. The congregation must know that you view the tour you are offering as an extension of your ministry, as an opportunity for your people to grow in their faith and to deepen relationships and mutual caring.

Choose a good travel agency, a reputable one that will stand behind what they commit to and say. Check it out with other pastors. Ask for written letters of reference from other churches. Ask for the names of the last three pastors for whom they've organized trips. Call those pastors and talk with them.

No trip is without its occasional hitches. Something almost always arises that was unforeseen. Let your people know this in advance. Flexibility is the key. These unexpected occurrences are opportunities for the entire group to minister to one another. One thing is sure: whether or not the tour is a spiritually rewarding experience for the tour members will depend largely on your intentional efforts to make it so, relying, of course, on the Holy Spirit to honor your earnest efforts to be the teacher and spiritual leader you are called to be.

Pastoral Pointer

Make lists of things to do. Work lists keep things from rattling around in your brain. They help you remember what you have to do and make it easier to prioritize your time. As you check off the items, you can see the progress you are making and what still remains to be done. Making a list should help you to sleep better at night too, because instead of lying awake thinking about all the things you have to do, you transfer them to a sheet of paper and forget about them until the next morning. They'll be there when you wake up, so relax and get some sleep! If you are not already in the habit of making lists, we urge you to try it. It works!

Pastoral Pointer

If your tradition calls for the laying on of hands when ordaining ministers, elders, or deacons, remind the participants, for the sake of the ordinand, to do so LIGHTLY. The more persons taking part, the more important that rule becomes. Those hands can become pretty heavy on the bent head of the person kneeling!

Chapter 12

Following and Preceding Other Pastors

Your Predecessor

As pastors, every one of us stands on someone else's shoulders. Every one of us builds on a foundation that someone else has laid. None of us is writing the first page of the Acts of the Apostles. All of us are adding to an enterprise already under way. One plants, another waters, another prunes, another reaps. Your relationship to the pastors who precede and follow you can assist the work of Christ's kingdom or hinder it.

Eschew, therefore, odious comparisons. Resist the temptation to criticize or condemn any of the efforts of your predecessor. Don't encourage your church members when they want to catalog for you their problems with the previous pastor. Your people will soon learn whether or not you are the kind of person who will listen to that kind of talk. Take every opportunity you can, especially when you first arrive, to commend your predecessor publicly for the good things that he or she accomplished. But be sincere about it. Don't say anything you don't really believe. You shouldn't invent commendations.

If your predecessor was well loved by your congregation, and even if he or she was not, invite him or her back to preach sometime. Many will appreciate it. You will learn something about who they were as a church in the days or years before your arrival. It's possible that your predecessor, if you are open to it, can furnish you with background information and insights that you will find valuable as you get started.

Your predecessor should have enough sense and be sufficiently versed in church etiquette to stay out of your way, unless you specifically invite him or her to come back. If he or she doesn't know how to "let go," try not to let that upset you. Be gracious, magnanimous, supportive, generous, and secure. Don't be jealous or possessive of your pastoral relationships with your new flock. Don't be threatened by your predecessor's continued involvements with members of your new congregation. Some pastors do not recognize or understand the inappropriateness of continuing to do weddings, funerals, or baptisms, to lead Bible studies or conduct prayer groups, or even of continuing to worship in congregations they no longer serve without seeking and receiving the new pastor's permission. A thoroughly considerate former pastor wouldn't even be asking! It puts the new pastor in an awkward position. What new pastor, if asked by his or her predecessor, "Do you mind if I baptize the Lees' baby? They had counted on my doing that," feels comfortable saying, "I'm their pastor now. That's my responsibility"—knowing the couple and their friends might be offended or resentful?

While every member of every church understands the need for the old coach to be gone once a new coach is hired, for the former captain to clear the bridge once the new skipper has taken command, for the former president to leave the White House once the new president has taken office, for the former principal to stop walking the hallways once a new principal has been hired, sadly not every church member understands the need for pastors to respect one another's position in this same way. If *your* predecessor happens to be clumsy or unthinking in this regard, and doesn't know what it means to "decrease" (as John the Baptist said) so that your ministry can start to "increase," don't let it keep you up at night. Be publicly supportive. Be laudatory, be appreciative. Be complimentary whenever and wherever you can without being hypocritical. And, while you're at it, be thankful. Be thankful the offender is some *other* pastor and not *you* encroaching on *your* successor!

Your Successor

In relating to those who come after you, strive to be the kind of predecessor you would have preferred your own predecessor to be. The most reliable rule of pastoral etiquette is simple: When you leave a church, *leave!* Realize it's better for the church, even though a voice in your head may be whispering, "They still need me. I have to make sure this or that continues to be done the way I did it."

Realize that only by your clearing the decks will your congregation be able to (1) mourn your parting, (2) accept emotionally that you're gone, (3) begin to sift, make sense of, and catalog the memories and experiences they've shared with you, (4) begin to find out who they are about to become as a church, apart from who they were with you, (5) speak joyfully and gratefully of all that you did, and candidly of what you left undone, (6) undo anything you instituted to which you were too closely tied, or which never really worked for them, but which they knew meant a great deal to you, (7) begin to shift their allegiance from you to the new spiritual leader whom God has called to their church, and (8) be open in new ways to God's Spirit, without having to run every new idea past you!

And, it must be added, only when you really leave (emotionally as well as physically) will you be able to pour your heart into the new thing God has in store for *you*!

It is for these reasons and others that we believe you should not continue to worship in the church you have served. There are exceptions to every rule, of course. The new pastor may have a specific reason for inviting you to remain on the scene. At that point, it's your call. We don't believe you should make yourself available to conduct weddings, funerals, Bible studies, or other church functions without the expressed permission of the new pastor, and even under those circumstances be very judicious in accepting. Sensitivity and discretion are called for.

When you leave a church there will always be some folks left behind who, at some point in your ministry, became more to you than merely members of your church. They became personal friends to you and/or to your spouse. We believe it is appropriate to continue these friendships with some, but with the few, not with the many. And when you're with these special friends socially, you should take great care never to criticize or invite their criticism of their new pastor. Even if you disagree with what he or she may be endeavoring to do. If they want to share with you their misgivings about him or her (and chances are they will have some), change the subject tactfully. Talk about the concert you'll be seeing that night, or about what has been happening in your lives.

Once you have made the decision to leave the congregation you serve, believing in your heart that God has called you elsewhere or that your work where you are is finished, begin the *weaning process*. Help your parishioners to transfer their personal loyalty to and affection for you to the church and to the new person whom they will be calling to be their pastor. Help them especially to understand and to appreciate that their relationship is not with you, but with Jesus Christ, the Lord of the church. Prepare them to receive and accept their new pastor as an individual called by God for some special purpose at this point in the history of the church, with some unique contribution to make to the church's ongoing life and ministry. This is one of the most helpful things you can do for the pastor who will succeed you. It is one of the most helpful things you can do for the ongoing work of Christ's kingdom, and for the health and vitality of his church.

When Your Former Parishioners Ask for Your Services

What do you say to the parishioners who still call you, who still want you to baptize their new baby ("After all, you married us!"), or to perform their daughter's wedding ("You confirmed her; she wants you!"), or to conduct their father's funeral ("We don't even know the new pastor!")? You gently guide them toward their new shepherd, as you counted on your predecessor to do for you when you were new. You try to be firm and sensitive, tactful and pastoral. Sometimes you feel terrible about having to say no. You fear you may be hurting their feelings. You wish you could help them, but you know they should be turning to their new pastor. Their affection for you means much to you, and it would be a privilege and joy to accept their invitation. It's especially hard if you still live in the area, or are close enough at hand. But you have a *responsibility* to them still, as their former teacher and pastor, to help them understand that they now have a new pastor and they should not lock this pastor out of their lives. They must open the door to him or her from the very beginning.

If it is one of those infrequent cases when, for some special reason, it is appropriate for you to have a part in someone's memorial service or wedding, then we would suggest the following rules of pastoral etiquette:

1. ***Get the new pastor's consent***. Advise the church members calling you that they should ask their new pastor if it would be all right for you to have some part in their service. The reason for your participation on that particular occasion should be obvious, so that you don't give the impression that you are still available to every person in the congregation.

2. ***Their new pastor invites you***. If the new pastor says "Fine!" to their request, then the new pastor should contact you and invite you to take part in the service and indicate what he or she would like you to do. This private conversation between you and your successor will give you a chance to say, "Listen, if this presents any problem for you, I'll work even harder to discourage this sort of thing in the future."

3. ***Their new pastor should do the premarital counseling***. If it is a wedding you are being invited to take part in, it has to be decided who is going to do the premarital counseling. Normally this should be the new pastor. After all, he or she will be the one who will have future pastoral responsibility for this couple. It won't be you! You need to advise the couple to that effect.

4. ***Their new pastor conducts the wedding rehearsal***. As the invited guest, you take your cues from the pastor. If you have any suggestions, make them privately to him or her. Otherwise, do as you're told!

5. ***Their new pastor signs the certificate***. Normally it should be the new pastor who signs any official marriage, baptism, or other certificates for church members, unless you are the sole officiant. Death certificates should be given to the new pastor, although you may certainly ask for a copy.

6. ***Both pastors may sign the marriage booklet***. In shared weddings, both pastors should feel free to sign a couple's marriage booklet, their guest register, and the couple's personal copy of the license.

7. ***Their new pastor plans the service***. It is the responsibility and right of the new pastor to decide how he or she wants to divide the parts in the wedding or memorial service. A gracious pastor will invite the guest pastor's input, of course, and both will be sensitive to the wishes of the families involved.

Again, the pastoral Golden Rule applies: Treat those who follow you as you would like your predecessor to treat you. Or to put it negatively, Don't do to those who follow you what those who went before you may have done to you! Keep out of your successor's hair. Stay out of his or her way. Be gentle but firm with those who seek your continued pastoral services. It is part of the weaning process, and if you do it well, people will soon come to understand what is proper. Most will realize that this way is best for the church and for them. Some may never understand. All will be grateful for your support of their new pastor, and, in a very real sense, for the strengthening of their church. The number of requests will diminish and eventually cease, even though for very popular pastors it may take a while. We human beings don't shift our allegiances or our relationships easily! Change is hard!

Pastoral Pointer

If you invite another pastor to participate in a wedding, consider using a crisscross division rather than a "horizontal chop" in deciding who will do what. Alternate the reading of the vows, the blessings of the rings, and so on, instead of saying, "You take it down to here, and then I'll do the rest." A crisscross division divides the service more evenly and gives the impression of shared leadership, which the couple, the other members of the wedding party, and the congregation will appreciate, as well as the invited pastor.

Chapter 13

Wanting to Do What Is Right

Legal Issues

We believe most every pastor wants to do what is right. Unfortunately, in an increasingly litigious society, the right course of action is not always clear. That is why we want to begin this chapter with some thoughts about legal issues in ministry. There seem to be more of these every day!

Let us quickly say that we are not lawyers. What we are about to give you is not legal advice. It is pastoral advice from a legal perspective. If you want legal advice, talk to a lawyer. Perhaps your conference or presbytery or regional association has one who can help you. We try to know the law because we want to abide by it! But we are not attorneys. We are ministers. We try to be dutiful practitioners. Along the way, we have learned ministry is not impervious to legal issues. More than anything, we want to make sure *you* are aware of some issues that could affect your ministry and your congregation.

Your Church's Use of Music

Are you copying songs for use in your worship service? Are you printing song words in a bulletin? Are you projecting them onto a screen? If so, you should have permission from whoever holds the copyright to that music, unless it is in the public domain. One of the easiest ways to take care of this matter is to see that your church subscribes to a music copyright licensing service. For a reasonable annual fee your church gains the legal right to use music and lyrics from thousands of compositions, both traditional and modern.

Publishing Information about Your Church Members

Suppose someone calls your church, indicates he is new in town, and asks whether or not you have a men's Bible study. He says he has just moved into the community, and he would like to find a men's fellowship group to attend. You tell him that, indeed, your church has such a group. He asks if he might talk to the leader. He says, "I'd like to give him a call, just to introduce myself and find out about their meetings, and about what they're studying." The leader of your men's Bible study is a member of your church, a lay volunteer. You have his work number and home number in your church Rolodex. Do you give that information out to the caller? Note: This caller is a stranger, at least in the sense that neither you nor anyone in your congregation has met him.

One church that did, in a sincere effort to help and to provide a hospitable welcome, give out the information to a caller asking this very question, discovered the caller wasn't looking for Bible study at all. He wasn't looking for a men's group. He was looking for money. He was looking for a free room for the night. The volunteer leader of the men's Bible study who received his call was thrust, at least momentarily, into an uncertain position.

Do you publish your church members' birthdays? In an age of privacy concerns and identity theft, we would suggest that you get church members' permission before you do this. (We like the idea of publishing birthdays! It can draw people together and enrich their congregational fellowship.) One simple way to be sure you have your members' permission is to include a checkoff space on your church membership application form (or whatever information piece new members fill out for you), permitting them to say, "Yes, you may publish my birthday," or "No, I'd rather you didn't." You'll find most people will say yes. Some will want you to publish the day of their birth, but not the year. It's important to find out what a member will permit.

Do you post pictures or personal information about your church members on the Internet? Most churches today have a Web site. Do you display your members' faces and families there? Sometimes we forget that information put up on the Internet is available to anyone with a computer anywhere! This is not to say we should never post pictures. It *is* to say we should take care. We suggest that before you put information about your members (their photos, their children's names, their phone numbers, their health problems, their prayer concerns) on the World Wide Web, you get their permission to do so. Again, a simple checkoff space could be put on your new-member information form, or you could instruct your church's webmaster (if you have one) to check with folks before putting personal information where the whole world can see it.

Medical Privacy

In the wake of legislation governing medical privacy, regulating what information can be given out about whose health and to whom, we would advise you to take another look at how you are handling medical information about folks in your congregation.

If you announce from the pulpit that Mrs. Brown has just learned she has cancer, you had better be sure that Mrs. Brown is willing for that to be known! One church has developed a prayer-request card that allows church members and others to ask for prayer for medical or other personal needs. At the bottom of the card they ask church members to indicate whether their request may be shared with all, be added to the church's prayer letter, be announced from the pulpit, or be shared with the deacons, or whether it is for the exclusive information and use of the pastors.

For centuries, Christian congregations have engaged in a powerfully supportive ministry of care for the sick, and of intercessory prayer. We hope we never see that ministry end. We believe it's part of the calling of every church!! We simply want you to be aware of the fact that the law may affect what you can do in this regard. So make sure you are informed. As a pastor it takes you only a second to ask one of your flock, as you leave his or her hospital room, "May we pray for you at church? May we put you on the church prayer list?"

Sexual Misconduct

As one reads the newspapers one might get the impression that every church in America has had to contend with sexual misconduct. (One might get a similar impression reading the letters of the apostle Paul!) While not every church has had to deal with this, far too many have had to work through the misconduct of a pastor, a priest, a youth director, a Sunday school teacher, an organist or choir director, or some other formerly trusted church leader.

We advise you to make sure your church board has a policy aimed at the prevention of sexual misconduct. The people in your pews deserve your protection—especially the most vulnerable among them, the children. Perpetrators have learned that churches are especially vulnerable. Church members are trusting. Congregations are open. Too many lives have been devastated by sexual misconduct for churches today *not* to be preventive!!

No policy, of course, will be fail-safe. No form of prevention is ironclad. Even churches with preventive policies and measures in place are not exempt from misconduct cases. But it is far better to have preventive measures in place and not need them, than to have needed them and not to have had them!

Does your church have a policy delineating proper conduct for church workers and volunteers? If you don't know where to begin, contact your conference, diocese, presbytery, or other regional association, or your denominational headquarters. Whatever insurance company covers your church and its activities will also have suggestions and information. Pastors are busy. You always have too much to do and too many needs to meet. If your church has been slow to address this area and you don't have time to dig into it, then delegate this important matter to a church leader who will follow through!

Privileged Communication and Mandatory Reporting

Imagine the heartbreaking moment: A church member approaches you after worship. She pleads, "Pastor, can I talk to you for a minute in your office?"

No sooner have you found a quiet place away from the Sunday-morning bustle than she turns to you with an agonized expression on her face, and, sobbing, says to you, "My daughter told me this morning that my husband has been touching her in a sexual way. She has been afraid to tell me. She's only twelve years old! Please, please, will you to talk to her. And please, I want you to talk to my husband! I don't know what to do. I think he'll listen to you. But please don't call the authorities. *Please, don't tell anyone*! It would destroy him and our family. I know you can help us. Please, Pastor. I don't know where else to turn."

This is an awful moment in any pastor's life. There are so many issues to think about here, including legal issues, which are the present focus of our concern. Are you aware of them? If not, you could step into a snare. Perhaps the most urgent question from a legal standpoint (though, as pastors, we must confess both of us would be more concerned with the *pastoral* issues at a moment like this) would be: What is the law in your state? Currently, as we write these words, different laws pertain in different states!

In some states and jurisdictions, pastors are "mandatory reporters." They are included on the list of helping professionals who must, as required by law, report any incident or suspected incident of child abuse. The law demands it. If you are the pastor in the above situation and have that conversation in one of these states, the law requires you to pick up the phone and call the authorities. In a word, you must report it.

In other states and jurisdictions, we have learned, pastors are *not* mandatory reporters. The law exempts them, as clergy, from the requirement to report. These laws have attempted to preserve what has been termed "the sanctity of the confessional." In other words, pastors are prevented from reporting anything to the authorities that church members don't want them to report!

You will note in the above scenario, the church member said to her pastor, "Please, don't tell anyone!" From a legal standpoint, there are laws in every state governing what is known as "pastoral privilege" or "privileged communication." Generally speaking, those laws protect the confidentiality of privileged (confidential) communication between a person and a pastor, rabbi, priest, or clergyperson. The important thing to note about privileged communication is that the "privilege" is "owned" by the parishioner! The "secret information," as it were, is not owned by you as the pastor, but belongs to the person who told you.

If your conversation with this anguished mother took place in a state or jurisdiction like that, you could be sued by the parishioner for reporting the matter to anyone else without her permission. (You may be willing to run that risk if you are convinced it's for the good of a child.)

If your conversation took place in a state where you are a mandatory reporter, you could be sued for *not* calling the authorities. So could your church be sued also, from what we have been told, and so could your regional association or conference. There have been cases where pastors have chosen to go to jail in situations like this, rather than violate what they consider to be the sanctity of the confessional.

What's the bottom line? Be familiar with the law of your state! What is the law in the jurisdiction where you are serving as a pastor? If you don't know, contact your conference or talk to a lawyer. And you might also find out how the law affects other church workers on your staff, if you have any, as, for example, your church's nursery worker, children's choir director, or youth director.

Manner of Life of Your Church Employees

Suppose you open the newspaper one day and discover your church's paid nursery worker has been arrested for drunk driving. Or suppose you read that your church custodian has been given probation and a suspended sentence after a second arrest for disorderly conduct at a high school football game in your town.

Perhaps you or the head of your church's personnel committee would approach these employees about their off-duty behavior. Perhaps your church board would decide to put them on probation, or even to terminate them for conduct that undermines the effectiveness of their work and witness in the life of your church.

But what if those employees said to you, or to your personnel chairperson, or your church board, "What we do on our own time is our own business. We have never misbehaved in any way here in the course of our work. We have been dutiful, faithful church workers. We have never taken a drink or been disorderly here. We have never been reprimanded. We have done all we've been asked to do. We have received good reviews. We are not pastors, or youth directors, or choir leaders, or ministry types. We are a custodian, a nursery worker. Who cares about our life outside the church? You can't tell us how we spend our nonworking hours!"

The fact is, most pastors do care about the kind of person you are on or off duty. The fact is, most congregations also care. The fact is, the behavior of every worker on your church staff, on or off duty, has an impact, for good or ill, on your church's work and witness!

If you and your church board care about your church workers' conduct and witness away from the church, if you believe the way they live and behave when they are not on duty at the church impacts their effectiveness when they are, then you may want to be sure their written job descriptions say that. "Manner of life" clauses in the job descriptions of every church worker, we believe, are an idea whose time has come. Spelling it out is good for churches and good for church workers. It helps everyone know what is expected. AND it tells your church workers, from the custodian to the music director (and the pastor!), that their witness in and out of the church is vitally important, indeed, that *all* church workers are called to live their lives in a way that is glorifying to God and that seeks, with God's help, to be faithful.

Acknowledging Your Sources

Acknowledging your sources as a pastor is not only the right thing to do, it's mandated by the Eighth Commandment: "You shall not steal" (Ex. 20:15). You should always credit the person whose words, material, or ideas you use—especially in your writing. Here are some guidelines for giving credit where credit is due.

Remember that all the credit and the praise for everything you do go to God first. All that we have, all that we are, all of our abilities and, by extension, all that we are able to accomplish, are God's own gracious gifts to us. We are indebted to God for everything. We do not serve to our own glory. "Hallowed be *thy* name," we pray, not "*my* name." Nor should we be trying to build our own little kingdoms. We are *douloi* (slaves) of Christ, working for the kingdom of God. Pastors who forget that crucial distinction can be easily tempted to take credit for more than they should.

When it comes to crediting other human beings for the use of their material or ideas, pastors should bend over backward in acknowledging their sources. Give credit where credit is due. If you read something you agree with, digest the material, make it your own, and then restate the idea in your own words and format, you are on pretty safe ground. Even then, it would be proper to reference your original source in anything you submit for publication. A footnote might read, for example: "I'm indebted to So-and-So's article in the June 2004 issue of Such-and-Such journal, for starting me thinking along these lines."

Some things are in "the public domain." You may preface something by saying, "There's an amazing story going around right now," or "Someone told me an interesting story the other day," or "You have undoubtedly heard the story about the man who . . ."

If you quote directly from a commentary or any other publication in your preaching, your sermon manuscript or notes should footnote the source, as any written document would. From the pulpit, you might say, "Johnson says in her recent commentary on Romans . . ." Or you may acknowledge that what you're saying is not your original idea, by saying, "One commentator on this passage argues that . . ." The point is, if you are using someone else's material, you should make that fact known.

Most churches are aware by now of the need to pay a fee, and secure a commercially available license, if they want to use any music or lyrics not contained in their congregational hymnal or songbook. If your church is not aware of this, inform them. The fee is not prohibitive, and the usage rights gained are extensive.

If you copy, use, or reprint material designed or written by some other church, seek that church's permission before you do so. Permission is nearly always granted. Some churches subscribe to church newsletter services, church officer training programs, denominational mission update reports, and similar sources of information designed for use by the subscribing churches. Whether you are permitted to make copies of the material they send you—articles, quotes, cartoons, or other items—in your church newsletter, or reproduce their material for an officer-training event, is usually spelled out in the material you receive when you first subscribe, along with their requirements about acknowledgments.

When you get sermon *ideas* from others, or are inspired to preach on certain themes, from books, commentaries, clergy publications, newspapers, and other materials you've read, from conversations with teachers, church members, and others, from seminar speakers and lectionary or Bible discussion groups, or from the endless array of encounters and moments that inspire every pastor's preaching—generally you do *not* have to get up in front of your church and say, "This sermon idea comes from . . ." However, any time you use an actual title or quotation from material that has come from someone else, you should *always* acknowledge that; say, for example, "To quote the immortal lines of Alfred, Lord Tennyson, ''Tis better to have loved and lost than never to have loved at all.'" Then in a footnote in the distributed copies of your manuscript, you would indicate "From Tennyson's *In Memoriam*, pt. xxvii, st. 4."

If you do a lot of writing or speaking, you may find yourself in the unusual but not unheard-of situation of being accused of copying something from someone who originally copied it from *you*—without giving you credit!

Many pastors share jokes or funny stories they have heard. You can acknowledge these, if you use them, by simply saying, "You've probably heard the one about the woman who . . ." This lets people know you are not pretending to be the originator of something they may already have heard. An appropriate disclaimer avoids the risk of your being criticized on that score. It also lets them know that you realize the story is common knowledge or that the joke has been around for years, but you are using it for a purpose. It is always disconcerting, and even annoying, to hear a preacher tell a fifty-year-old joke as if she or he is the first one to tell it! If you use jokes or stories that *are* your own, you have no one else to credit—or, for that matter, to blame!

When You Invite a Guest Preacher or Speaker

We would not be including this section at all, or even commenting on this particular topic, if we hadn't personally been on the receiving end of invitations, time after time, that proved that many pastors do not know the proper way to invite a guest preacher or speaker. "What's to know?" you ask. "I can just pick up the phone, or send an e-mail or a letter."

You might be surprised how much more there is to it than this. In our experience we have both found the quality of the invitation reflects not only on the church but on the pastor doing the inviting. We hope this section will help you and your church to write the kind of letter the person you are inviting will really appreciate.

First, get the person's name and title right. As we pointed out in chapter 2, "Dear Rev." is incorrect. It's "Dear Dr. Jones" or "Dear Mr. Jones," or "Dear Ms. Jones," or "Dear Pastor Jones," or even "Dear Mary," or "Dear Tom," but not "Dear Rev." or "Dear Reverend Jones."

Let the person know why you're inviting him or her. Are you just looking for a warm body to fill your pulpit, or can you say something of a complimentary or personal nature? ("Our people enjoyed you so much the last time, they've asked me to invite you back again.")

Describe the event. The person you are inviting to preach needs to know how many services there are and whether or not they differ in style. For what other parts of each service will he or she be responsible—Scripture readings? A children's message? The pastoral prayer? The benediction? Will there be a liturgist or other persons helping to lead in worship? What is the normal attire for preachers at your church? Is there anything special going on that day (an anniversary celebration, the dedication of the new education wing)? Is there a special theme you would like her or him to preach on (stewardship, evangelism, the mission of the church)? How much time will there be for the sermon?

May your guest suggest the hymns that would be appropriate for the theme of the service? What hymnal or songbook does your church use? In addition to the sermon title, text, Scripture passages, and hymns, what other information do you need for the church bulletin (e.g., a prayer of confession)? What's the deadline for getting the information to you? It is very helpful if you can send your invited guest a recent sample of your church bulletin, so he or she can see how things normally proceed.

If you won't be there, who will act as the host of the guest preacher? How, when, and by whom will he or she be introduced in the service? By what time should the guest speaker arrive and who will be there to show him or her where to robe? Will he or she be gathering with the choir, the other worship leaders, the church officers, or anyone else for prayer before the service?

Do not neglect to spell out the financial arrangements. Indicate the amount of the honorarium and that you will be covering all travel expenses (food, lodging, airfare, mileage, etc.). If you offer a per diem, state the amount. It is proper to include travel days when figuring per diem expenses. Time is precious! If your church cannot afford to pay more than a token honorarium, or anything at all, say so! As we have already mentioned, most pastors don't like to be asked, "What is your fee?" Don't put your invitee on the spot. Decide what you can pay and state it. If that isn't sufficient, the speaker can decline, or accept anyway!

You should give the speaker a check before he or she leaves, if possible. And you should do it discreetly. Don't embarrass the person by handing him or her an envelope publicly.

Enclose directions to the church if your speaker has never been there. You don't want to force your guest to have to dig out a map, or look for your church on the Internet. Ask your guest to send you a bio and black-and-white head shot for publicity purposes. What does your guest want your congregation to know about his or her life and ministry? What would your guest like the person who introduces him or her to say?

We hope you'll keep these things in mind when you invite a guest speaker or preacher. You and your church will stand out in the mind of those you invite to preach or speak. They will also come better prepared! So you and your church will benefit too.

Your Sense of Humor

If you want to thrive and not just survive as a pastor, it helps, as we have said, to have a sense of humor. Oh, you may survive without one, but you surely won't have as much fun! And other people won't enjoy your company as much. It's important to take the work of the ministry seriously, but not to take *yourself* too seriously—in or out of the pulpit. You have to be able to laugh at yourself and to see the humor in any situation where there is humor to be seen. You have to look on the foibles and follies of your flock with amusement at times. You can do that, because, though you work as if it all depends on you, you can relax, knowing that it all depends on God. The church is in God's hands!

With that understanding, you can have fun in ministry. To be sure, there are pain and sorrow, dissension and conflict, disappointment and even bitterness at times, but what a joy, what a privilege to belong to the household of God! People are unpredictable, sometimes exasperating, but always interesting, always capable of surprising leaps of faith. So enjoy them. Set yourself a goal to have fun in your ministry. Tell yourself and God that you are going to enjoy it! For, believe it or not, ministry really can be fun! There are many laughs along the way. If you try to enjoy your people and love them, they will respond that way to you. Together you will be able to look on and enjoy the humorous side of day-to-day life in the church.

So if you find yourself having trouble smiling, or enjoying any aspect of your pastoral work, pull up for a moment, take a deep breath, and take a new look at things. Are you getting any time off, or are you working night and day? Don't say to yourself, "I don't have time to take a day off." Most of us don't have time, or strength, *not* to! Are you doing any physical exercise? Are you getting adequate sleep? Are you eating sensible food? Are you smoking or drinking too much? Do you have any interests or activities outside the life of the church that you would like to pursue? Are you spending most of your time with negative people, the chronic complainers, or do you have significant relationships with some positive people who brighten your life? If you score poorly on some or most of these questions, you may find yourself enjoying your work less and less. Don't settle for the status quo. If you can't figure out how to make needed changes, don't hesitate to seek help from someone you think might be able to advise you.

Wholesome humor is a tonic. As the writer of Proverbs said, "A cheerful heart is a good medicine, but a downcast spirit dries up the bones" (Prov. 17:22). We repeat: It helps to have a sense of humor!

Pastoral Pointer

A veteran pastor of a previous generation used to keep two special files, one labeled "Brickbats" and the other labeled "Bouquets." Whenever he felt himself getting too discouraged, almost ready to quit (not really!), he would pull out the Bouquet file and read a few of the letters he had received from people whose lives he had touched for good along the way. And, when he found himself becoming "too elated by the abundance of revelations," he would take out the Brickbat file to remind himself that he was only human. It takes only one or two brickbats to keep you humble! We have found this to be a useful practice.[1]

1. The veteran pastor referred to was the late Dr. James W. Clarke, who served for a time as professor of homiletics at Princeton Theological Seminary.

Chapter 14

Working with a Staff

The Burden of Administration

*I*t's often discouraging for solo pastors, for heads of staff, for interim pastors, for clergy couples, for anyone who finds himself or herself in the pastor's chair in a Christian church, to discover how much time must be spent on administration. While they envision themselves writing sermons, preaching to the flock, tending the sick, baptizing babies and new believers, inspiring Bible-study classes with compelling insights, the truth is that many if not most pastors find themselves having to devote much of their time and energy to their inglorious, often daunting administrative chores. Let's face it: there's a church to be run, and the buck stops with the pastor.

No one who has not done it has any real idea how much thought, work, and day-to-day attention are required to keep the average church running smoothly. Churches do not run themselves! Anyone who has ever lived in a family with just two or three other persons knows how hard it can often be to keep even that small group of folks "in the know" and functioning efficiently. Coordinating schedules, dealing with conflict, planning for upcoming events, making sure various duties are covered, paying the bills, keeping the family calendar straight, maintaining the family dwelling, hosting visitors, keeping rooms picked up, celebrating holidays and special occasions, reenacting family traditions, staying in touch with the extended family and close friends, keeping family documents and other important papers and records in order, to name only a few of the necessary functions, are a challenge to any family.

Churches are just like families, except that there are a hundred, or two hundred, or five hundred, or a thousand or more family members! The responsibility of keeping things running smoothly in most churches falls to the pastor. It would surprise, even shock, many church members to know that pastors may have to spend far more time on this crucial, often overlooked facet of pastoral work than they do on the teaching of Scripture or the preparation of sermons!

The devil, it has been said, is often in the details. A poorly run, carelessly administered church can often seem to be bedeviled! So how can such a heavily burdened pastor thrive and not just survive as an administrator?

Staff Relationships

Let's start with staff relationships. You may now or someday find yourself working with one or more other paid church workers, some ordained and/or some not ordained, such as youth directors, musicians, organists, pianists, choir directors, nursery workers, bookkeepers, office workers, receptionists, church administrators, Christian education directors, parish nurses, and pastoral counselors. If you are the pastor, and especially if your church polity considers you to be the head of staff, the cooperative functioning of this group of people will be largely up to you. In churches with large staffs this task can take huge amounts of the pastor's time, energy, and attention.

It is our observation, after visiting hundreds of churches and speaking with many hundreds of pastors, that poor staff relationships are the number-one problem afflicting churches with more than one pastor. Again, this statement would surprise most laypeople. Studies have found that pastors are more likely to leave their churches as a result of difficulties with other pastors on their staffs than because of problems with their congregations. Too many associate pastors are not happy with the senior pastors they work with, and too many senior pastors are not happy with their associate pastors.

Why? It seems to be one of the perils of the profession. At least we know it's biblical. Jesus' disciples argued about which of them was the greatest. Paul and Barnabas had to go their separate ways because they couldn't settle their disagreements. Paul and Peter were at odds in the early days of the church over the role and place of Gentile believers.

Why is it hard for pastors to get along? Maybe it's because in some ways pastoring is like parenting, or coaching, or teaching. Each person comes at it in his or her own unique way. It's an intensely personal activity, based on very deep beliefs and convictions, and on very personal experiences and philosophies. It is more of an art than a science.

It is not like making widgets. It is *not* the case that there is only one way to do it and to do it well. There may be many ways, all of them different but all of them effective to varying degrees. Put two human beings together and ask them to parent the same child, and they do not always agree, even if they are already in love with each other and are already married! Even if they have "preselected" one another and have spent several years living together, they may not always agree. So when two human beings are brought together and asked to be pastors to the same group of people, they will not always agree.

Their disagreements, furthermore, will in some ways be sharper and harder to reconcile than disagreements between a mother and father about raising their children. Why? Because pastors' differences are based not only on their personal qualities, gifts, and philosophies, but also on what each one believes about God and how they interpret God's word. One's beliefs are convictionally determinative. Thus two equally sincere persons can find themselves differing on some moral issue, for example, based on their respective interpretations of God's will. Each one's allegiance to God supersedes their allegiance to each other, or to the church board, or to the congregation. The stronger the convictions, the harder it is to be reconciled.

That's why it's rare to find two pastors working together seamlessly and harmoniously. It's sometimes hard to find pastors working even *cooperatively.* Having two very different pastors in the same church is all too often like having two different artists painting the same landscape, or two different coaches running the offense for the same football team. Sure, both pastors are Christians, but, sad to say, that's no guarantee of their ability to get along. To assume as much would be like assuming that two chefs will work well together merely because they are both vegetarians.

More often than not, pastors have little or no say in choosing their colleagues. Pastors are often placed by bishops, bureaucracies, or committees who would never trust themselves to be matchmakers, but who are perfectly content to try to "marry" two different pastors together! It is less than successful much of the time.

Pastors have difficulty working together because they encounter differences in theologies, goals, and priorities, differences in leadership styles and in their understanding of worship, differences in approaches, backgrounds, and beliefs. They may find they don't share the same philosophy of staff management. One thinks preaching is the most important calling; the other thinks a social-justice ministry is primary. One is a workaholic. The other thinks a fifty-hour workweek is more than enough time to devote to ministry. One would never think of using a manuscript in the pulpit. The other thinks a preacher without a manuscript is unprepared. A retiring bishop used the same metaphor we quoted on page 15: "Trying to get pastors to work together is like trying to herd cats." Most pastors insist on doing things their own way.

You might say, "Someone has to be in charge. If someone simply calls the shots, wouldn't that get pastors working together, and help them to pull in the same direction?" It would if senior pastors were willing to call the shots, and if associate pastors were willing to heed them. But typically neither is willing. Why? Senior pastors do not want to appear dictatorial, authoritarian, or in any way autocratic. They want to be seen as respecting the differences in style and approach of their colleagues. They recognize the futility, often, of trying to tell someone to approach worship or teach the Bible in certain ways. They're uncertain that it can even be done. They want to respect diversity.

Associate pastors, meanwhile, often feel very little accountability to the pastor who ostensibly is head of the church staff. They reason, "My first responsibility is to God, to carry out my ministry as God directs me. Next, I am accountable to the bishop who placed me here [or the church board, or committee that called me]. Third, I am called to serve this congregation as it seems best and right to me. Only last do I answer to the one they call 'the Pastor.'"

Often associate pastors believe that senior pastors have little or no authority to affect their tenure, their position, or their salaries. They reason they will continue to do what they think is right regardless of what the pastor thinks. They do not realize the need for every ship to have one captain, every organization to have someone in charge.

If you are an associate pastor on the staff of a church, and find that you cannot get along with the pastor and cannot work out your differences, we believe it is better for you to leave than to stay and be critical of your colleague, or foment rebellion, or maneuver for the ouster of the pastor, as associates are sometimes known to do.

If you are an associate pastor having problems or disagreements with the pastor of the church, the proper place to air them first is with him or her; the next is with the church's personnel committee. If you are the pastor having problems with an associate, the same sequence should be observed.

Church members, of course, are always free to talk about what they like or what they don't like about their pastor. If you are an associate pastor and find them saying good things about your colleague, feel free to affirm them in their opinion. If they are speaking negatively, however, you should tactfully defend your colleague, or, if you can't in good conscience do that, then opt out of the conversation. To do otherwise would be unseemly, and what the British would call "in poor form."

Someone has noted, "The hardest instrument to play in the church orchestra is second fiddle." If you are the second or third pastor on the staff of a church, you may find yourself biting your lip on occasion, wondering if you should say something to someone about things you observe that cause you concern. We believe any church staff member who has strong disagreements with the pastor, or the head of that church's staff, should express those disagreements to the pastor behind closed doors, but they should present a united front to the congregation. If that staff member cannot do so, he or she should start looking for another church. This same principle should also apply to what is said in staff meetings and church board meetings. Disagree, if you need to, behind closed doors. Present a united front to the congregation.

Sometimes there are professional jealousies. Don't forget that God selects every church pastor from a group of creatures called human beings. These creatures are all quite imperfect, and sadly flawed in a number of ways. Even after they have become pastors, they are still subject to the same temptations and insecurities as all mortals are. Sometimes they look at the pastor down the hall and think, "He or she is no better than I am, and maybe not as good. How come he's the pastor and I'm the associate?" Or they wonder about a classmate: "How come she is called to that plush suburban congregation and I'm stuck out here in East Podunk?" The green-eyed monster is ever lurking in the shadows of one's mind.

This attitude is what afflicted Jesus' disciples—the desire to be first, the need to be number one. Jesus had to intervene when his disciples argued about this. Public figures are always prone to ego involvement. That is no less true of pastors, who are also public figures. The unfortunate tendency of people to make comparisons, often in less than tactful ways, makes pastors all the more vulnerable to the temptation of pride. How many times does an associate pastor have to be told by his or her special friends, "I'd rather listen to you than to Pastor Henry. Why doesn't he let you preach more often?" before he or she begins to think that way too? Most church members do not realize how the subtle and not-so-subtle things they say can prick a pastor's ego and stir up unhealthy thoughts and emotions.

If God has placed you at the head of a church staff, you have to try very hard to keep everyone working together, particularly if there are other pastors on board. It will not always be easy, unless you have managed somehow to handpick the people you are working with. Even then you will have challenging moments, and keeping a happy and smooth functioning staff will take much of your time and energy. The members of your flock may see you less than the members of your church staff, and get less of your time. But the end result will be good for the church if you can keep things running smoothly. And it will be good for the ministry of Jesus Christ.

It will not happen automatically. Staff members have to work hard to help each other find fulfillment, satisfaction, and joy in their various ministries. What motivates, what excites each person? If they could define or map out their own ministries in the life of the church, what would they want to do?

What would be the "dream role" for each one? To the extent that you are able, to the extent that it serves the church and the mission of Christ, try to help your colleagues realize their dreams.

As head of staff you want to follow the rule of "public praise and private reprimand" in relating to the members of your church staff. Commend them publicly whenever possible. Correct them when necessary, but do it constructively, lovingly, and privately. It is appropriate in any organization, but especially in the church, to affirm your colleagues. Don't damn them with faint praise. Let the members of your staff know what you most appreciate about them. Help them and others to see their good points. Try to affirm and point out their gifts. Defend them when others criticize them. If they are criticized for legitimate reasons, respond to the critic with the good things you can say about the particular staff member. Defend him or her tactfully but firmly. Be up front with staff members when you are aware of a problem, and affirm your commitment to work with them to make them successful and to resolve the particular problem in question.

Your goal as pastor should be the best possible "care and feeding" of the persons who make up your church staff. Why should not the church of Jesus Christ be one of the best places for someone to work in our society, as opposed to being the last place someone would want to work? Help your church staff members to feel energized in their work, motivated, adequately recognized, compensated, and appreciated for the good work they do. At the same time, challenge them to keep on learning. You hope they *enjoy* coming to work, instead of dreading or resenting it. You want them to feel that their gifts are being put to good use, that their ideas are appreciated and their efforts valued, and that their contributions are making an important difference in the work of the kingdom.

Job Descriptions

For staff members to feel that way, they need to have a clear sense of what their areas of responsibility are and a clear understanding of what is expected of them. Written job descriptions can be a great help here, if they are written properly and updated regularly. Churches are notorious for overloading their staff members and volunteers, for expecting more of a person than is reasonable, given the time and support allotted. Job descriptions must be doable, and not prescriptions for burnout, frustration, or martyrdom. Goals must be conceivable, believable, and achievable. As you look out for your colleagues, be sure that you or some committee, group, or individual in the church (in addition to your spouse) is keeping a similar eye on you.

A word about salaries: Your church will never regret hiring the best people it can, and paying them as well as it can in relation to comparable positions. Trying to cut corners or to save money by skimping on the compensation of its professional staff can cost the church more in other ways, perhaps in higher turnover, more money and time spent on recruiting and training, more "down time" as various staff positions remain unfilled. The church, like any other organization, should strive to hire good people, treat them well, and keep them!

The Church Secretary[1]

Speaking of hiring good people, you are truly blessed if your church can afford to hire a good church secretary, who also functions as your secretary. Many people jokingly say that the real power behind the pastoral throne is the church secretary. Who really runs the church? Many pastors would answer, perhaps only half jokingly, "The church secretary!"

There's more truth than humor in those statements. In small churches especially, the church secretary's office is the information center, the communications center, the operations center, and the production center of the church. The buck may stop at the pastor's desk, but it usually has to go across the church secretary's desk to get there.

It's hard for a busy pastor to survive, let alone thrive, without any secretarial help. If the only paid employee is a church secretary, you need to have a clear understanding that she or he is also and primarily *your personal secretary*. You are the head of staff, and you are the one who determines her or his duties. That point must be absolutely clear to everyone concerned—the board, the congregation, the other employees (if any), and above all to the person in that role. It is crucial to your ministry, because your secretary, more than anyone else, is in a position to help you to thrive and not just survive as a pastor.

What kind of person makes a good secretary? Ideally it should be a mature Christian person, someone who is pleasant, caring, teachable, dependable, conscientious, discreet, understanding, patient, able to work under pressure, comfortable with deadlines, and loyal to you. A pleasant telephone personality is an indispensable requirement. Those are the *qualities* we would look for.

1. We acknowledge that the word "secretary" is falling out of favor as a job title in some settings. It is still being widely used, however, and for both of us the title of "Church Secretary" refers to an honorable and dignified position, one that is critical to the smooth functioning of any church, but especially to smaller churches. We have decided, therefore, to use the traditional term with appreciation and respect for all that it still signifies to countless congregations.

As for skills, the person must definitely be very computer-literate, with excellent word processing and keyboard skills. He or she should have good writing ability, and sufficient layout, design, and desktop publishing skills to do the church bulletins, annual reports, and other in-house publications like the church newsletter. Every secretary should have workable systems for filing and record keeping.

Given these qualities and skills, what should be his or her duties? Three premises underlie the job description for your secretary. First, to a large degree the job description has to be tailored to fit the person, since people are usually stronger in some areas than in others. You will want to discover his or her special talents, assets, and gifts and utilize them in the most efficient and effective ways. Second, the job description has to be flexible enough to allow room for growth and development. You will give your secretary greater responsibility as he or she improves under your tutelage. Third, you have the right to ask him or her to do whatever is most helpful to you in the performance of your ministry. Your secretary's main role is to free you to do what you have been uniquely trained and called to do.

Based on those three premises, his or her duties would minimally include typing your letters, sermons, articles, and anything else that you need typed; maintaining a filing system that you can understand and access in his or her absence; answering and routing telephone calls or supervising telephone volunteers (recording and dating messages, appropriately responding to needs and requests, and tactfully protecting your privacy when asked by you to do so); collecting the information for and producing the Sunday church bulletin and other church publications and/or congregational mailings; providing backup support for committees; maintaining the church calendar and various church records; keeping the membership roll and the church directory up to date; ordering office supplies; dealing with salespersons and other visitors to the church; and dealing with emergencies, semiemergencies, and countless other things that come up day after day, week after week.

How many of these duties your church secretary can handle will depend, of course, on the size of your congregation and the number of hours she or he is able to work. If it is a part-time position (and there is no money to hire additional staff), you will have to determine your order of priorities. Whatever the person is unable to do, you will either have to do yourself, or enlist volunteers. Part-time or full-time, your church secretary is your chief ally in your battle for survival. She or he helps you manage your time, reminds you of what you have to do and where and when you have to do it, protects your privacy, defends you against your critics, supports your efforts to be all things to all people.

Your secretary is sometimes your confidante, often your adviser, occasionally your savior, always your friend. Treat your secretary well. Mutual loyalty, respect, and trust define the relationship. Train your secretary to do things the way you like them done, and give her or him opportunities to improve her or his skills. She or he will appreciate your compliments, expressions of gratitude, and public praise for work well done. Convince the church board of the secretary's importance to the church and to you, and pay him or her a decent salary, with comparable benefits, days off, and vacation time. In other words, do all you can to make your secretary's working conditions as pleasant and enjoyable as possible, for everyone's sake—including yours!

Performance Reviews

No church staff members, including your church secretary, should have to wonder about what you expect of them and whether or not they are doing good work. Regular evaluation and performance reviews are extremely important. The latter should be done at least annually, more frequently when needed. They should not be seen as opportunities to pounce on church workers. Nor should there ever be unpleasant "surprises." If a staff member's performance needs constructive adjustment or a course correction of some kind, that staff member should be advised and worked with when the problem is first noted, and not clobbered with an unfavorable report at annual review time. Any ongoing problems or areas for improvement can be noted during the annual review, but should not be sprung on staff members without warning. Focus on specific job description items. Never take aim at the totality of the person. Any particular skills that need to be worked on should be put into a positive context. Don't hesitate to adjust or revise job descriptions if necessary. They should never be encased in concrete. Given that they have to cover the needs of the church, remember that job descriptions are made for people, not people for job descriptions.

At annual review time staff members can discuss their goals for the past year, set new goals for the coming year, comment on their own sense of completion and progress. Any special needs they may have can be addressed. Comments of their specific supervisor should be noted. Their special achievements can be recognized. Job descriptions can be updated to reflect new skills, abilities, or responsibilities. Staff members should know whether they are performing their duties in a generally satisfactory way or not. They should be queried about the adequacy of the compensation they are receiving, and any needs or deficiencies noted. Well-cared-for staff members will generally take better care of the church and their assignments than workers who feel neglected, underappreciated, overwhelmed, or undercompensated.

Your Filing System

We mentioned the need for the church secretary to establish a workable filing system. In addition to the files maintained and kept in the church office, you will have your own personal files, which as the years go by will become more and more unwieldy unless you set up and stick to a good system. A good system is one that enables you to find what you want when you need it. You can waste too much precious time looking for things you can't find! Wasting time is exasperating and stress producing. It hinders your thrivability. Because of the importance and prevalence of this problem, we'd like to suggest a simple filing system, which can save you countless hours if you don't already have a system that works for you. If you do have one, stay with it.

First, there are some things you need to decide concerning both the church files and your personal files. By what criteria will you decide what to keep and what to throw away? Who will have access to the files? If you have an office both at home and at the church, what files will you keep in which office? What do you consider to be confidential and where will it be filed? How long will you keep various kinds of correspondence, and how often will you clean out your files? These are questions each person must decide for herself or himself.

As for the filing system, we recommend your using a straight alphabetical rather than a digital system, using three-cut manila folders. Set up three indexes: a primary index on the left, using left-tab folders; a secondary index in the center, using center-tab folders; and a tertiary index on the right, using right-tab folders. The categories in each index are arranged alphabetically, with as few categories as possible on the left, more in the center, and as many as needed on the right. Color-code each folder according to its index; for example, green on the left, red in the center, and black on the right. That way working folders can easily be put back in their proper place. If a file is to be removed for more than a day, put a slip of paper in its place, indicating when the file was removed and who has it. Cross-index as necessary (e.g., "See also under 'Recommendation, Letters of'"). Have a "Miscellaneous" folder behind every secondary tab. As a Miscellaneous folder grows, reduce its contents by adding new tertiary folders.

It is very helpful if your secretary maintains a chronological file of all the nonconfidential letters he or she types, in addition to the copies you have in your personal files. As your files grow, you will have to keep rearranging the contents of your file drawers. You may need separate drawers for particular categories. With regard to your correspondence files, you can anticipate your drawer space requirements by remembering that slightly more than half of all correspondence will be under six letters: S, B, M, H, W, C. You can make up your own acrostic for remembering those letters. Here's one possibility: "*S*mall *B*oys *M*ust *H*ave *W*hite *C*andy."[2]

The system we have suggested will help you bring order out of chaos and save you bundles of time in the long run.

When an Employee Has to Be Dismissed

Sometimes it is the case that a certain staff member needs to be dismissed. That can be stressful. In fairness to the employee, as well as for legal reasons, several conditions should have been met: (a) the worker has had a clear and fair job description; (b) there has been no confusion about what was required or expected; (c) the employee has been given the tools, resources, and support needed to accomplish his or her mission; (d) he or she has been counseled and advised on successive occasions—first by his or her immediate supervisor, then by the head of staff, then with the input and involvement of the personnel committee chair, then with the involvement of the entire committee, if he or she so desires—that his or her work has been substandard or unsatisfactory, and in what ways and in what specific areas; (e) these detailed deficiencies and the sort of counseling sessions described above have been noted and documented; (f) clear recommendations have been made and adequate time given for the worker to demonstrate improvement; (g) good faith efforts toward, or signs of, improvement have not materialized; and (h) a reasonable person would not see any age-related, gender-related, disability-related, race-related, or other discriminatory forces at work in the individual's unsatisfactory reviews.

We believe a church should always look for a person's strengths and try in every possible way to utilize them—even if it means a revision in the job description, a reduction in responsibilities, a shift in duties—before deciding to terminate that person's employment. If the person is uncooperative, incompetent, or totally nonresponsive, and if there's no other place for him or her in the organizational structure, then the best thing for the church and for that individual is for him or her to move on to some new place of service. Where or what could it be? You might help the person to find it, and not summarily dismiss someone who has been a faithful, if ineffective, employee.

But, if the person's attitude is negative, or if he or she is disloyal, is noncooperative, doesn't share the church's goals and objectives, is not comfort-

2. We are indebted to Mr. Richard Boyd, a former executive with a large office supply company, for this statistic and the accompanying acrostic. Our simplified filing system is an adaptation of some of his suggestions to customers.

able with your leadership, is nonsupportive, is not a team player, or does not represent what the church and its ministry should be (i.e., he or she is rude, impolite, insensitive to people, profane, unreliable, uncaring), and if there is no evidence of change or attitudinal improvement, then that particular employee should be let go. It's difficult, almost always unpleasant, but necessary. It's for the good of the church, and usually it's for the good of the person as well. Employees who are being terminated should be so advised in a face-to-face meeting with two or more church leaders, including the chair of the personnel committee, the head of staff, and, if there is one, the person's immediate supervisor. This will help protect both the employee and the church from any later misunderstanding about what transpired.

Church Member Employees

As you can imagine, if a church needs to terminate an employee who is a *member* of the church, special problems can develop. You run the risk of losing not only the employee, but the employee's family too. Sometimes it is an *extended* family, with years of involvement in the church. These situations are extremely delicate. You and your board will agonize and not find any good solution. There *is* no good solution! You will end up making what is always a painful decision, but because the employee is a member of the church, there will be lots of additional pain. You may see the person lose a job, coworkers, a pastor, and also his or her church—simultaneously! It may have been their family's church for several generations.

For the protection of their own people, therefore, and as a safety measure, some church boards decide never to employ church members. For most churches, however, this is not a hard-and-fast rule—many congregations make exceptions. But besides risking the person's relationship with his or her church, there is also the pastoral care issue: every church member is entitled to the pastoral care and concern of the pastor, or one of the pastors if there are more than one. What happens when the pastor happens to be that person's "boss"? In many cases, the person in effect loses his or her pastor. There's a world of difference between being somebody's boss and being somebody's pastor. The roles are not identical. In some instances, they are mutually exclusive.

There can also be legal complications involved in the hiring of church members. The law protects what a person says to his or her pastor. Those conversations are generally privileged, deemed confidential under the law. The law treats differently what a person says to his or her boss in a work-related situation, however. If your church bookkeeper, a member of your flock, says to you, "I took some money. I was desperate. I didn't know what else to do"; or if your youth director, a church member, says, "I crossed the line; I think I did something I shouldn't have done"; are you listening to employees asking you for help, or the secret confessions of parishioners? How you respond to the one differs greatly from how you respond to the other.

And if your parishioners ever need someone to listen to their confessions or to their spiritual struggles, or to hear about all of their problems at *work*, will they want to talk with a pastor who also happens to be their supervisor? You are never "not a pastor" (double negative intended)! You need to remember that the responsibilities of an employer are sometimes distinctly counter to those of a pastor.

Church members on the payroll also find that they sometimes lose their sense of "church." The church secretary who works in the office all week, answers phone calls, types the bulletin, prepares announcements, keeps the calendar straight, and responds to countless requests, may arrive for worship on Sunday morning only to find that his or her fellow church members continue to badger him or her with lists of things they need—before, during, and after the service! So going to "church" on Sunday morning is going not to a place of spiritual respite, renewal, and ongoing spiritual growth, but to a place of work, where the list of things to do gets longer and longer! Many church members who work for their own congregations find themselves searching, eventually, for someplace else to *worship*!

It is for the *spiritual welfare* of their own members that some churches are reluctant to turn these folks into employees. Many well-meaning pastors and church boards have hired their own church members, not aware of the risks and pitfalls they are exposing them to. At the very least, they should be practicing full disclosure, which calls for saying something like this to the prospective employee: "You should know, if you take this job, that the church will probably in some ways feel different to you, and so will your relationship with me as your pastor. Also, if this job ever fails to work out for you or for the church, it quite possibly may adversely affect your feelings or your family's feelings toward the church. Do you understand?" If you are up front like this, a church member would at least become a church employee with his or her eyes wide open, having been made aware of the potential awkwardness should the relationship have to be terminated.

To be sure, some churches have employed church members for years with few if any problems. You and your church board will continue to weigh the pros and cons, based on your own experience. We recommend that you come up with a policy that is flexible enough for you and your church to live with.

Learning to Delegate

When it comes to administering a church or a staff, you will be more likely to thrive in your ministry if you learn to delegate. Good delegation requires knowing when you've reached what we'll call the "Exodus 18:18" point, which records Jethro's advice to Moses: "What you are doing is not good. You will surely wear yourself out, both you and these people with you. For the task is too heavy for you; you cannot do it alone." Many pastors can identify with Moses. But too many do not recognize it, or they don't know what to do if and when they do reach that point.

It is not always easy to delegate. Many pastors and lay leaders show by their actions that they think it is easier to do everything themselves than to share the responsibilities of ministry with others. In a way they are right. It takes time to delegate. It takes effort. It takes planning. The one to whom you delegate the task may not do it the way you want it done.

In a more profound way, however, pastors are wrong in believing that doing it all themselves is easier. If Moses had continued to do everything himself, he would have become increasingly ineffective. The needs of his people would not have been met. The work of the Lord would have been limited. Eventually Moses would have worn himself out, and there would have been no one ready to take over. He would never even have *seen* the Promised Land!

Some pastors delegate responsibility but not authority. They put someone in charge of the church mission dinner but expect every decision to have the pastor's own final stamp of approval. When you delegate, you must delegate authority commensurate with responsibility. You must allow people the freedom to use their own initiative, even to make mistakes. The best delegators paint a vivid picture of the desired outcome and the destination, but they give others the freedom and authority to decide how they will get there. Accountability is essential. It must always be clear who is in charge of any particular effort or project. Where does the buck stop? Who makes the decisions? If the answer in every case is "the Pastor," then you are not delegating effectively and your people are not growing as they could be—in confidence, in experience, or in designing and carrying out the tasks of ministry.

While responsibility and authority can and should be delegated, leadership is a quality that cannot be delegated. It is a gift of God. It can be cultivated and developed, however. Leadership development is an important part of your pastoral ministry.

Communication is crucial in any organization, including the church. As head of staff you have the right to expect to be kept informed. But you should not think that means you have the right to micromanage everyone else. Those to whom you delegate must know where they can turn for help. They must feel your support and encouragement from start to finish, but they don't want to feel as if you are always breathing down their neck.

Delegation is risky. It means giving up some degree of control. It means trusting others to carry out their ministry. You don't always know in advance what they're going to do, or how they will go about the task. Delegation means learning and practicing the spiritual discipline of "letting go and letting God." It also means being willing to accept the possibility of failure. People need the freedom to fail, or they will never be willing to try anything new. Even when people fail, you want to express your appreciation to them for their effort, and celebrate with them what they learned from their mistakes. Earnest effort deserves commendation. Coaches appreciate players who are always hustling, always giving it their best shot. In every failure there's a lesson to be learned, and the good news is that nothing that happens in or to your church is beyond the bounds of God's redeeming love and power.

One of the blessings you receive from delegating is the great satisfaction and joy of watching others spread their wings and begin to fly. And you will be humbled by the realization time after time that things can be done more creatively, more effectively, and more thoroughly if others are involved than if you are trying to do everything yourself.

"Equip[ping] the saints for the work of ministry" (Eph. 4:12) requires thoughtful delegation. As pastor, you set the tone and the example for this in the life of your congregation.

Pastoral Pointer

When you first arrive at your new pastorate, have a volunteer or your secretary go through past bulletins as far back as they are available (five or even ten years, if possible) and record the number of times every hymn has been sung in that period. List just the numbers on a couple of sheets of paper and put a slash mark beside each number every time it's sung. You will be surprised how many of the hymns have never been sung, and how a relatively few of them have been sung fairly often! Introduce one of those unsung hymns every month as the "Hymn of the Month." Introduce it on the first Sunday, giving a brief history of the hymn and/or anecdotes about the author and/or composer. Ask the choir director to have it sung as an anthem on the first Sunday, and sing it as a fourth hymn the next Sunday, and as one of the three hymns on at least one of the remaining Sundays of the month.

In addition, record in your personal copy of the hymnbook the dates that every hymn is sung. This will encourage you to choose more hymns and avoid repeating some hymns too often. It is also useful information in responding to requests for or complaints from the congregation about the hymns. So when someone says to you, "Why don't we ever sing the good old favorites?" you can reply, "Which ones did you have in mind? Are they still in our hymnal? If so, I can tell you *when* we sang them—and *how often* we've sung them. And I can tell you which ones we'll be singing in the coming Sundays." You may also want to say something like this: "I try to select at least two hymns that most of the congregation will know every Sunday. But what's familiar to some is not necessarily familiar to others. And how can any hymn become familiar if it's never sung? That's why we have a hymn of the month. I want the congregation to become familiar with some of the other great hymns in our hymnbook."

If you explain what you are trying to accomplish and how you are going about it, the congregation will go along with you and will even applaud your effort to help them grow in their understanding and appreciation of Christian hymnody.

Chapter 15

Trying to "Run" a Church

Communicate! Communicate! Communicate!

We have already mentioned the importance of communication. Just as family life rises and falls on the effectiveness of its communication, so good communication is a cornerstone of good church administration and of congregational life. Some would say communication is all-important. With it you can handle just about anything; without it, everything is complicated.

Good communication is two-way communication. As pastor you must keep your associates (if you have them), professional staff members, church leaders, and church members informed about what you are thinking and planning and doing. It is demoralizing and even embarrassing for your colleagues on the staff or church leaders to be asked about something in the life of the church and not to have any idea of what's going on.

Similarly, as pastor you must be kept informed of what others are planning and doing. Don't assume you always know what's going on or what your people are thinking or feeling. Such an assumption is a mistake many leaders unconsciously make. You may know what's *happening*, but do you know what's *going on*? There's a difference! Be sure you have ways to get feedback, either formally or informally, from your congregation. You need to know what's going on and whether what you *think* about what's going on is accurate.

The most obvious way to keep informed is to get around. That means talking with and listening to people. It means asking the right questions, questions that invite helpful information and insights. For example: "What are the kinds of things people in our congregation are concerned about these days?" "Do you know of any problems we need to be dealing with?" "What are people excited about?" Or more specific questions, such as: "Do you have any ideas on how we might improve our adult education program?" "How can we get people interested in forming home Bible-study groups?" "What would you think about our hiring a full-time youth director?" "Can you think of anything we can do to attract more people to our worship services?" A visit to your church's summer Bible school, if you are not involved in it, will give you a better sense of that ministry than reading about it in your church's newsletter!

Staff Meetings

Staff meetings can contribute greatly to the communication flow. Make them *meetings that matter*! That includes opening with prayer, of course, and possibly a brief devotion. These responsibilities can be shared among the staff members. Sharing personal joys, needs, concerns, and sorrows helps people to bond. It is important to take some time for intercessory prayer. In planning future events and hammering out the church calendar, make sure everybody is on board. Allowing the members of your staff to share their hopes and dreams for their ministries helps ensure their commitment and cooperation. So does acknowledging their various contributions to the life and work of the church. Being sensitive to opportunities for faith sharing helps people connect and reminds them of their common bond in and allegiance to Christ. As time permits, sharing memories and past experiences also strengthens relationships and helps foster a good climate for communication. "How did you spend Christmas as a child?" "How did you come to believe in Jesus Christ?" "What has God done for you lately?"

Heads of staff need to develop the habit of thanking people and commending them in front of their colleagues, and including everyone. For instance, "Alice really worked hard on the newsletter and I appreciate what she did—and what all of you do around here every day. You're a great group!" It should be so easy to give praise, and it means so much! Why can't we learn to do it more often?

To reiterate, it is especially good and uplifting to talk about faith and one another's spiritual journeys at staff meetings. This can be very bonding for a church staff, and it points up the importance of their being theologically and spiritually compatible with one another.

Caring for One Another

The church staff that prays together and plays together usually stays together. Pastors should encourage the members of the church staff to spend time with and to care for one another. That entails being intentional about getting together socially or enjoying a meal together. Staff members need to encourage each other to fulfill and cherish family time and responsibilities. They should cover for one another when they can, and keep one another from working to excess. That calls for flexibility in scheduling. Balance is the rule! The head of staff should call to account anyone who is not taking any time off, and should make sure everybody is using his or her vacation time, study time, and opportunities for continuing education and ongoing training.

It is to be hoped that physical exercise is something the church validates and supports for all staff members and is not seen as "down time" or as shirking their work. Church workers who never exercise, eat the wrong food, do not get enough sleep, and otherwise misuse or abuse their bodies become vulnerable in ministry: they are prone to fatigue, exhaustion, possibly even to burnout, and to temptation, carelessness, and neglect. The effectiveness of their witness is diminished. Staff members, including pastors themselves, need to be cautioned or admonished tactfully and privately when necessary. They have to support and help each other when someone is under unusual strain or pressure.

And they need to defend a colleague who is unjustly criticized! As we have pointed out earlier, pastors owe this to, and they should expect it from, their fellow staff members. Staff loyalty demands it. A good rule is: defend your colleagues, not yourself. As a pastor you have to learn, and help your colleagues to learn, how to absorb negative criticism, which is never easy to take, especially when it's ill founded and takes the form of a general condemnation. You also have to absorb misplaced credit; that is, hearing others' being given and, what's worse, *accepting* credit for something good you have done. Conversely, there are times when you have to absorb publicly the blame for someone else's mistake, because the buck stops with you, even though you can reprove or admonish the other person privately.

Not as unpleasant but almost as exasperating is what might be called people's delayed understanding; they finally "get it," without acknowledging that what they now understand is what you have been preaching and teaching all along! As pastor you often have to live without the satisfaction of having been granted a point. Finally, what is probably the toughest criticism of all is the "cheap shot" that occurs after you've gone, but that too must be absorbed. You must simply hold to your conviction that God is the ultimate Vindicator.

Remember Your Two Hats

The distinction has been made between a leader and a manager, between a visionary and an administrator. Managers figure out the right way to do things;

leaders figure out the right things to do. Managers see that things happen. Leaders decide what things should be happening. Managers ask, "What needs to get done today? Who should do what? How should it be done?" Leaders ask, "Why are we here? Who are we? Where are going?"

As a pastor you are both a leader and a manager. As a leader you help to define reality in any given situation. It's amazing how your attitude helps shape the attitudes of your people regarding the church's goals, challenges, and successes. If you are the pastor of a church, the shepherd of a flock, you can rest assured that your people will look to you for leadership. Many will also hold you primarily responsible for the overall management and operation of the church. As a manager, you should have a complete and thorough understanding of your church's budgeting and stewardship. You must be a good planner, organizer, and facilitator, one who knows how to allocate resources to accomplish objectives. You need to work well with committees and be comfortable with process.

Planning is all-important. It is the task of both leadership and management to outline a course of action so as to optimize the use of resources to achieve your church's mission objectives. There are needs for one-time plans, single-project plans, ongoing plans, contingency plans, midrange plans, long-range plans, and other plans in the life of a church. Make time for planning! Plan your planning sessions. If you or your church never do any planning, your ministry will be less than it could be, and your church will find it difficult ever to gather a sense of direction, purpose, or momentum. To paraphrase the Cheshire Cat's point to Alice, if you don't know where you're going, you'll never get anywhere. A pinch of planning is worth a pound of patchwork. But plans should never be encased in cement. They should be flexible enough to allow for changing circumstances—even that flexibility is part of the planning process!

An Important Distinction

Good administrators are mindful of an important distinction that is easily lost amid the pressures and demands of a pastor's life: the distinction between what is urgent and what is important. Pastoral visitation, we feel, is important. It is not always urgent. Incoming faxes and cellular phone calls are not always important, but they will almost always feel urgent. The leaky fixture in the women's restroom at the church may be neither urgent nor especially important compared to the telephone call you just received from a church member whose teenaged daughter attempted suicide. But that leaky fixture suddenly *becomes* both urgent and important when the leader of the "Mom's Morning Out" Bible-study group knocks on your door, pleading that something be done about it immediately, because she's expecting a group of twenty or more who will be needing to use that restroom!

Day and night you are presented with unexpected situations in which you have to make quick decisions about what is urgent, what is important, what is both, and what is neither. Nearly every day of your ministry people are presenting you with needs that to them are either urgent or important. If they didn't think so, they would not call you. If it is not a personal need, it may be something they feel is important for you to do, or something you need to know. They are trying to be faithful church members. They are trying to help. You should be grateful for their concern. They keep you informed. They care about you. They care about the church. "Pastor, I haven't seen Mrs. Smith in church in a few weeks now. Don't you think someone should call her?" It may not have occurred to the concerned member that he or she might go ahead and make the call, and then let you know what he or she finds out. Or, "Pastor, I noticed your microphone wasn't working right last Sunday morning in church." Or, "Pastor, are you aware of the fact that next week is Tom and Mabel Smith's fortieth wedding anniversary?"

These folks all have your best interests at heart, and the interests of the church. The trouble is, there are so many of these kinds of calls that it's hard to know how to prioritize them. Not only that, there are always some urgent as well as important things awaiting your attention. The church secretary is waiting (patiently?) for the bulletin information for this coming Sunday, and you may not even have decided what your sermon topic will be. And here it is Thursday! There's a special staff meeting this morning, you have someone coming to see you for counseling, and you just received word that one of your church leaders has been in a serious automobile accident.

So you have to sort out what is truly urgent, what is truly important, and what other things just seem to be one or the other but in reality aren't either. What really has to be done now, what can wait until later, and how can you keep yourself focused and centered? Pastoral emergencies and needs are almost always urgent and important. Responding to the needs and requests of church leaders and staff is almost always important, but not always urgent. Practicing the elemental disciplines of your devotional life—devotional reading, study, prayer, reflection, meditation—never seems urgent but should be seen as the most important aspects of your ministry. They never demand your attention, but always deserve it. Sermon preparation is always important, and its urgency increases as the week progresses. If you come to Saturday night and your sermon isn't prepared, urgency has reached the point of desperation!

Both of us have always chosen to treat calls from our spouses or children as top priorities. Other phone calls, e-mail, faxes, pages, and beeps defy advance categorization. Remain attentive to them all, but learn to differentiate them quickly—that is, if you want to thrive in ministry, and not just survive.

So the rule is, *do the important* and *urgent* things first! Save the unimportant and not urgent for last. Don't hesitate to ask yourself, "Which is this?" many times each day.

Church Volunteers

The volunteers of your church are the very corpuscles that animate and activate the body of Christ. Some churches list their pastor's name(s) on their letterhead, but list as *"Ministers: every church member"!* Some of the principles that apply to the "care and feeding" of staff members apply also to the "care and feeding" of church volunteers. They require and deserve thorough instruction and training. They deserve to be praised and recognized publicly, not because they're doing what they're doing to be seen, but because acknowledging their efforts is the right thing to do. Public praise is a kind of seal, a ratification, a sign that their work is important and has been well done. Besides, recognizing and thanking volunteers encourages others to use *their* gifts in ministry.

With volunteers, as with the staff, the rule is public praise, private reprimand. Any correction that is needed should always be done pastorally, which means caringly and sensitively. And as with staff members, clear communication with volunteers is essential, as are clear lines of accountability. Know who is responsible for what, and to whom.

As pastor you don't have the same sanctions in dealing with volunteers that you have with respect to staff members. If a volunteer fails three weeks in a row to show up at the church to help answer the phone in the office, you are not in a position to penalize the person or to dock his or her pay. Volunteers must be motivated somewhat differently. They are not working *in any sense* for the money. They have to see their work as important. They have to know that they're making a difference. They have to believe that they are serving the cause of Christ and, if only in some small way, that they are helping the church to accomplish its overall mission.

Another prime motivator for many volunteers is the expectation of *fellowship*. Many volunteers serve because they're looking forward to meeting and getting to know other church members. In the increasingly fragmented society in which we live, many people are seeking ways to overcome their sense of loneliness, disconnectedness, and isolation. For such people fellowship is a reward for service. Indeed, it is one of the prime compensations. You should be looking for ways, therefore, to provide opportunities for your church volunteers to get to know one another!

It is important not to overwork your volunteers. There will always be more to do than you can possibly handle. There will always be more to do than the members of your church staff can handle. There will also be more to do than your elders, or deacons, or congregational leaders can handle. But don't be tempted to overwork your volunteers. It is a temptation, for they will seem willing and the work is important. Pastors and church leaders sometimes have a way of imposing on willing people. All of us pastors have probably been guilty of it at some time or other, not because we're bad pastors or uncaring, but because we *care so much* about the work of the kingdom!

If we don't watch it, however, we can burn out our people, just as *they* can burn *us* out if they don't watch it! It is a sure signal of impending burnout when someone feels overwhelmed and exhausted, with no hope of relief in sight, and is thinking, "This isn't fun anymore!" Check with your key volunteers once in a while, the ones you know are expending the most energy. Ask them if they are still enjoying their work, or if they are feeling overwhelmed. In most cases they will let you know. They will tell you the truth. And even if they are reluctant to say, they will be glad that you asked them! Some volunteers will never cry "uncle," no matter how much is loaded on them! It may be a matter of personal pride. They may think saying "Help!" is a sign of weakness. They may even believe it's "unchristian." After all, didn't the apostle Paul tell the Corinthians, "I will most gladly spend and be spent for you" (2 Cor. 12:15) ?

Volunteers should never be appointed for life. Nor should they feel deserted after being appointed. To say to someone, "God has laid it on our hearts to ask you to head up our stewardship campaign. Will you do it?" is to pose a question that can sound pretty scary! Starting when? With whose help? *Until* when? It would be much better to say to someone, "We have a very important leadership assignment we'd like you to consider. We'd like you to serve as vice-chair of the stewardship campaign this coming year. We have been praying about this, and we believe you are the one. Phyllis Park has agreed to serve as chair this year, with the understanding that you will take over as chair the following year, at which time we'll appoint a new vice-chair to assist you. In other words, it's a two-year commitment, starting in September. Will you pray about it? I'll be glad to answer any questions you have about the work. You'll have plenty of support from me and the rest of the staff, as well as from your committee."

Try to see that requests for the key lay ministries in your church are all fairly well "bookended." Church members should not be asked to commit themselves to tasks without starting and ending dates attached to them.

"Would you be willing to serve as a senior high adviser for this school year?" This also helps prevent your having the wrong person end up in the wrong spot and homesteading on that spot forever!

If you use any type of "time and talent survey" in your church to determine the gifts and interests of church members, do what you can to allow your people to serve in their areas of interest and giftedness. People are annoyed, and rightly so, when they indicate their willingness or desire to help and are never called or asked to do what they said they would like to do for the church. Don't ask your people to fill out a survey if you're never going to ask them to serve. Or if you're not going to use them right away but may use them later, then let them know that.

Church members should always be *trained* for whatever role they have accepted. They should be told what to do, and shown how to do it, not because they are not intelligent, clever, thoughtful, capable people, but because chances are they have never done the thing the church is asking them to do. Ushering in church on Sunday mornings may look simple, but it's more involved than it appears! There are things an usher needs to know, such as how to escort people down the aisles and how and where to seat them; when and where to seat latecomers; what to do if someone faints or gets sick; what to do in case of a fire, or a boiler explosion, or some other catastrophe; how to handle the offering (when to come forward, where to stand, how to move down the aisles, when and how to bring the offering plates forward). Ushers need to know where everything is (first-aid kit, a stretcher, temperature and lighting controls, extra chairs), and how everything works in the sanctuary. They need to be able to answer people's questions, or know what to say when they don't have the answers. Greeters and ushers give visitors their first impressions of the church. They need to be trained so that the impression is positive!

Many churches have volunteers who answer the phone or serve as receptionists. It is dismaying how unhelpful and even unfriendly some "front desk" people can be—even in churches! Careful training can help these volunteers immensely. How do you want them to answer the church telephone? What do you want them to say? What do they need to know about worship service times, the church calendar, the availability of church staff members, your whereabouts? What should they say to drop-in transients asking for money from the church, or to church members calling for pastoral help? If someone calls to speak with the pastor, should they ask for that person's name or not? (Some people calling for pastoral counseling prefer not to be identified by name. They will insist on speaking directly with the pastor.)

The point is, don't ask anyone to take on a responsibility or task in the church without equipping him or her for that task! It takes work. It takes time and attention. You shouldn't have to do all the training. You train people to train others. But someone should be training every volunteer in every area. That's the way to develop confident, enthusiastic volunteers. It's amazing how much more they will take pride in what they're doing, and how much better they'll do it! The cause of Jesus will be better served. Training volunteers is worth the effort!

As pastor you are typically perceived by your people to be both the spiritual leader of the flock *and* the administrator or manager of the church's program. How they perceive you has a large bearing on how they perceive themselves in relationship to the program of the church. Are you someone they would like to work with and for? Can you interpret the needs of the church in such a way that they will want to respond and become involved?

Their perception of the elders, deacons, or other lay leaders of your congregation has the same kind of impact on the members' willingness to serve, to help, to become involved. Their perception of staff members running highly visible programs can have a big impact too. If church members lack confidence in the Sunday school superintendent or Christian education director, or in the *volunteer leader* in charge of that area of the church's life and work, they are less likely to want to get involved than they would be if they were inspired by the example of their leaders or peers.

But the pastor sets the overall tone. If the people sense that you love and care for them, they will more than return that love. Just as you must win the right to be heard, you must also earn the right to be followed! After all, they *are* volunteers! You can't force them to do anything, but God can use you to inspire them to do wonders.

Pastoral Pointer

Inexperienced lay readers, especially young ones, tend to speed up when they read Scripture in worship, even when you have coached them beforehand. The more inexperienced they are, the faster they go! Also, many get softer when they lead unison prayers or readings, instead of speaking so the congregation can hear and follow them. They need to keep up their volume, even with the Lord's Prayer. It's a good idea, therefore, to put a little sign on the lectern, where the reader is sure to see it:

"SLOW AND LOUD!"

Chapter 16

Working with Committees

Committee Structure

Committee and organizational structures vary from congregation to congregation. As pastor you have opportunities to affect and adjust, and in some cases even to create, the committee structures in your church. Our strongest recommendation to you is to let need determine mission, mission determine program, and program determine structure. And let faithful service to Jesus Christ be the goal of all.

Continue to reflect on the structure of your church. Is it doing what you need it to do? Is it enabling you to move forward in ministry, or is it an obstacle? Every church works best if certain duties are assigned to specific persons. An effective organizational structure is an asset to your congregation. The number and types of the committees you have depends on the size of your church, the availability and willingness of people to serve, the particular mission and ministry of your church, and even on your pastoral style. Whatever it looks like, the committee structure of your church needs to accommodate at least the following minimal functions:

Christian Education

That's the total program, including recruiting, training, and resourcing teachers: setting up classes for all age levels; selecting or at least recommending curriculum materials to the church board; nurturing faith at all levels of the congregation, "from the cradle to the grave"; special educational programs, like daily vacation Bible school, weekday educational programs, and Lenten studies; family devotionals; the scouting program; and resourcing and supporting small groups. In many churches the youth program will fall under Christian education, as will the confirmation or commissioning program. Other churches will lodge these responsibilities with a committee devoted to youth ministries.

Church Membership

That would include the initial contact, cultivation, assimilation, and nurture of new church members; membership preparation, orientation, and new member reception. The membership committee may also have responsibility for special fellowship programs to foster relationships among church members. Specific evangelism programs and activities of the congregation are often included in this area of ministry if there is not a standing committee for evangelism.

Stewardship and Finance

The preparation of the budget and the management of the church's financial affairs may be delegated to a board of trustees, if there is such a board.[1] In larger churches these responsibilities may be shared among two or more committees. They include the receiving and disbursing of funds; keeping the church's financial records and receiving financial reports from all the organizations and committees of the church; conducting the every-member canvass, or whatever the annual fund-raising effort is called; teaching the congregation about Christian stewardship and making it a year-round, ongoing emphasis, not just a once-a-year "campaign." Usually a subcommittee or a separate committee is responsible for the management and investment of the church's endowment funds and memorial gifts. Another subcommittee or separate committee (if not the mission and outreach committee) might be responsible for the church's benevolent giving.

Worship and Music

Because music is such an integral part of worship, we feel it is better if the church's worship and music ministries are the responsibility of the same committee, rather than separate committees. It reduces the peril of the adult choir's becoming the war department of the church! The members of this committee work with the pastor in planning the worship schedule, including special services and musical programs; preparing the elements for Communion; training and working with the acolytes (if you have them), ushers, and greeters; arranging for members of the congregation to serve as liturgists and worship assistants; helping to host guest preachers and artists; and overseeing or assisting with many other duties relating to corporate worship.

1. Many churches have unicameral boards including the trustee function, instead of assigning those duties to a separate board of trustees. The civil laws of each state determine whether a church may be incorporated. However, a congregation may select persons to serve as trustees, whether or not the church is incorporated.

Mission, Outreach, Church and Society

These are the outward-looking functions of the church. Whoever is charged with these responsibilities brings to the church board information and recommendations concerning local, national, and worldwide issues that impact the church and its members, as well as problems and needs that call for the church's attention, involvement, response, or assistance. This committee serves as the church's liaison with community action groups, social-service agencies, mission bodies, and other organizations and churches, and as the church's recruiter of volunteers from the congregation to serve on various worthwhile community projects and organizations. It can make recommendations to the appropriate committee regarding benevolent grants to worthy mission causes.

Public Relations, Publicity

This ongoing function needs to be lodged with one or more individuals with the writing, layout, publicity, and promotional skills, media know-how, computer expertise, and creativity to handle everything from the church's newsletter to promotional displays, press releases, printed programs and reports, Lenten study programs, and other forms of internal and external publicity. If there is a public-relations committee, its members can suggest policies and programs regarding the various publics to which the church relates.

Building and Grounds, Property

Whoever has this responsibility is always one of the busiest individuals or committees in the church. The cleaning and maintenance of the church's building(s) and grounds, the upkeep and replacement of its facilities and equipment, the care of its utilities, the establishment of operating procedures and safety and security measures, overseeing the use of church facilities—there is all this and much more to attend to. The appearance and condition of the building and grounds is a reflection of the church's corporate stewardship.

Some churches own other properties, such as a cemetery. Often these properties are income producing. Depending on the value and complexity of the property, there may be a separate committee or board of trustees responsible for its management, for the necessary record keeping, and for reporting regularly to the official board of the church. If not to a separate board, the responsibility may be assigned to a subcommittee of the property committee. In the case of a church-owned cemetery, rules regarding who may be buried there and the costs involved, if any, must be clearly defined, updated as necessary and permissible by the original deed or grant, and communicated regularly to the congregation through the newsletter and other church literature.

Planning

We have already discussed the importance of planning. Here we simply want to stress the necessity of incorporating the planning function in the committee structure. We recommend that there be a representative planning committee to see that the various organizations and committees of the church do their own planning and to keep the church looking ahead. As the legendary Gordie Howe, the former National Hockey League star, once said, "You don't skate to where the puck is now; you skate to where it's *headed*!" Church planning involves short-range, intermediate, and long-range planning. Those who plan are the "dream team." They're continually studying the community, projecting population trends, tracking membership trends, noting who's joining the church and why and where they're coming from, and considering implications of all this for the future. They consider the church's program, facility, and staffing needs in relation to community demographics and religious trends. Do the stated goals and objectives need to be refined, amended, or discarded? Is the church program consistent with its mission statement?

Personnel

There needs to be some committee evaluating the performance of the members of the church staff and looking out for their needs. Every employee, from the pastor to the part-time sexton, is entitled to an annual review, the proceedings of which are strictly confidential. The personnel committee helps with the recruiting, hiring, and retention of lay personnel, and with the development of job descriptions. It is concerned with such matters as salary scales, benefit plans, vacation policies, continuing education, and staff morale, and with the overall optimal functioning and satisfaction of every member of the church staff. The committee's work contributes to the health and vitality of the entire congregation and to the accomplishment of the church's mission.

All these functional areas report ultimately to the deacons, the session, the vestry, the church council, or whatever the official board is called in your denomination or religious tradition. In addition to its own standing committees, the church board will probably have other organizations reporting to it, such as a women's organization, a men's organization, a small-groups coordinating council, and others to which specific functions can be delegated, such as food services and the operation of the kitchen, the annual church picnic, the prison ministry, the soup kitchen, the tutoring program, the hospital equipment loan service, the scouting program, ecumenical relations, and so on. They may have their separate budgets, but they are responsible to the church board.

The areas we've outlined above do not represent a precise pattern or structure. They are areas of ministry, responsibility, and function that we believe should be covered by whatever organizational structure your congregation chooses. The deciding question is not, "What does it look like?" but rather "Does it work?" Does the organizational structure of your church propel and sustain your ministries, or does it encumber and impede them?

Working with Your Church Board and Committees

As pastor you don't chair or convene every meeting in the life of your church, but you know the people who do. You have access to them. You have opportunities to offer suggestions. Church leaders, moreover, can learn how to run their meetings by watching how you run yours.

Wherever there are groups with differing, sometimes conflicting, needs and agendas, tensions inevitably arise within any organization. Some seem to be built into the functional divisions of the church, tensions that can become a source of friction, if not controversy: for example, the tension between stewardship principles and financial practice, between budgeting needs and benevolences, between the music department and the worship committee, between the property committee and the Boy Scouts, between the youth and the adults, between the trustees and the church board.

You have chaired enough meetings to know that you have to allow adequate time for discussion, without letting the meeting drag on too long. It's good parliamentary procedure and saves considerable time to have a motion or recommendation on the floor before discussion. Too many church boards do it the other way around, with the result that discussions run on forever. You don't want people to get home so late that they'll wish they hadn't come at all. Church members who have worked long days, or who have families and obligations at home, or early commitments the next day, should not be kept at the church past 9:30 p.m. or so, and 9:00 p.m. is a preferable limit for night meetings.

Grant enough time for discussion, so that folks feel they can *participate*! Don't let one or two people dominate every meeting. Watch the body language and facial expressions of those who haven't spoken, and solicit their ideas, making sure that both sides of any debate have equal opportunity to be heard.

But try to keep the meeting moving along. Few people have much free time to waste in meetings that are going nowhere and accomplishing nothing. A good moderator or chair knows when and how to summarize, how to capture the sense of a meeting, incorporating various points of view, and always seeking consensus, if possible. Pastors have to cultivate the art of reconciling different opinions, even though most church polities require only a simple majority for decision making.

Occasionally you will have to clarify or explain the implications of a vote that is about to be taken. You sometimes have to be the teacher. If so, do it graciously, not condescendingly. At times you will even need to be the prophet, and call people to greater obedience, to repentance, and to faith. Occasionally you may want to vacate the chair in order to enter into the debate.

Set the example of running the meeting and not allowing the meeting to run you. Be gracious and good-humored, but be in charge! If your church follows any form of *Robert's Rules of Order*, by all means be acquainted with them, so that you don't get entangled in parliamentary procedure. Run your meetings by the book, but don't let it get in the way. Always leave room for the Holy Spirit to work. Parliamentary rules were made to facilitate meetings—meetings weren't made for the sake of the rules.

Help those present to keep things in perspective. Give them a sense of history. Make them mindful of their relationship to the wider church and to the role and mission of the church throughout the ages. Point out the lessons to be learned from their grappling with contemporary issues, and lift up what is important. Help them to see their committee's work in the light of Christian history and tradition and the scope of modern contemporary witness.

To lead a meeting without dominating it, to guide discussion without stifling others' initiatives, creativity, or contributions, takes sensitivity and tact. It's an art, not a science. This is a fine line to walk, and any pastor can misstep on occasion. It is a the narrow path that leads to life. No one wants to be part of a meeting that doesn't go anywhere, where the wheels spin endlessly. But nobody wants to be steamrolled, either, by a meeting that gives them no chance to think, or act, or speak!

Be sure the church board keeps the congregation informed of what it's doing and of the actions it takes. That's part of the communication process we talked about in chapter 15. Church members deserve to know what's going on. Without their prayerful support and involvement, no program can succeed. Keep them informed and you will have their support, or at the very least you can answer their honest, thoughtful questions.

One of the best ways to keep your church members informed is to publish digests of board minutes or important actions in the church newsletter. Writing these should be the responsibility of the board secretary, but as moderator you may want to edit them.

Minute taking is an essential function and a most important responsibility, particularly at the board level of any congregation. Not everyone can take good minutes. You need to find someone who can. Good minute takers can capture the sense of a meeting and the decisions that were taken without reflecting their personal bias or coloring the facts. They should have a sense of history, a sense of what needs to be preserved. What will be important to future generations? They should be able to write clearly and correctly. They should know how much information to include in the minutes—not *everything* that's said, but not *just* the actions. They should include enough to give historians or anyone looking back from some future point a true sense of the meeting. They must conform with denominational requirements, if any, regarding format and content, and of course they must attach all necessary documents, appendixes, records, and anything else that will give future readers a full sense of the meeting and of the actions taken.

Making Meetings Matter

Church meetings should always occur in a context of prayer. One of the pastor's and church leaders' responsibilities is to help church members to keep the work of the church in proper perspective. That means helping them to see the "big picture," so that they serve with a sense that the task at hand, be it planning a retreat, or deciding whether to renovate the sanctuary, or approving the budget, or receiving new members, has a purpose and place in the kingdom of God. If you are going to spend as much of your time on administrative matters as everyone says you have to, then you want to make that part of your ministry as meaningful and important as possible. Every meeting can be a teaching opportunity, a learning experience, a source of renewal and inspiration, a chance to talk about what Christians believe. As pastor you are always a teacher, always a spiritual guide. Don't ever abrogate that responsibility. But a teacher is also a learner, so let your style reflect that too. To that end, you want to make meetings as instructive and as interesting as possible, especially congregational meetings, where you can use drama, testimony, role plays, music, PowerPoint, and other audiovisual aids to enliven the agenda. Be creative!

You will have regular opportunities to engage the church board in these ways. Normally you are present at all their meetings, which in most religious traditions call for the pastor to be the moderator, or chair. You can't attend the meetings of every committee or task group in your church, nor do you need to. You have to decide where and when your presence will be most needed or most helpful. Where you show up and how often you decide to attend will say a lot to your congregation about what you consider to be important. Therefore, you want to make sure that your absence is never interpreted as a lack of interest on your part in the work of a particular committee, or as a measure of that committee's importance. You can communicate this in a number of ways: for example, by letting the chairperson know you won't be there; by showing up now and then (but not always); by appearing, giving your input, and then heading out to whatever other pastoral duty you may have at that time; by a personal note indicating your interest and offering your ideas or suggestions; by public and private affirmation of those involved in that area of ministry; and above all, by *genuinely caring* about that aspect of the church's work. If you do, most people will know it.

More and more, wise pastors are endeavoring to make their church board and committee meetings more than mere gatherings for business as usual. They are trying to ensure that these gatherings have a spiritual aspect, that they are more than routine journeys through arid agendas. We encourage you to work toward this end in the life of your church. A church's meetings that are not for business only, but are also times when people can share their lives, their stories, their faith, have an enormous impact on the spiritual temperature of your congregation.

It goes without saying that every church meeting should be opened with prayer. Not all who chair your church's meetings may feel up to this. You can help them by providing them with simple prayers they can use, devotional readings that would be appropriate. If the chair of a meeting is not comfortable praying aloud, he or she can ask (beforehand!) another member of the committee to offer the opening prayer or devotion. (It is to be hoped that your church officers and members, as they grow in their discipleship, will overcome their fears about praying aloud and leading others in prayer. See chapter 20, under "Teaching and Discipling.")

There are other ways the committees and boards of your church can begin to evolve from mere task-oriented groups into genuine fellowships of faith. Instead of beginning meetings with the typical obligatory, brief opening prayer and diving right into business, set aside a little more time and invite those present to connect as human beings for a few moments. Encourage the committee members to "check in," to relate something that is happening in their lives, to share what one pastor colleague, Norman Parsons, has called some of their "happies" or "heavies." At first some may seem reluctant, but they will be the few and not the many. After a time, if your boards and committees are a reasonable size, their members will begin to know and trust one another. Allow a few moments for quiet prayer after this time of "connecting" is done. Take some time for intercessory prayer for one another. Some will be led by the Spirit to pray aloud.

The primary board of the church can set the example for this, and model it for other church organizations and committees. Yes, it takes a bit more time to get to the business at hand. Yes, the committees don't get to their agendas quite as quickly. But how often someone shows up for a meeting, sits down at the table, picks up an agenda, and looks over the business at hand while hiding a hurt or a worry of which no one else is aware! Maybe he or she lost a job that day, or came away from a medical examination with a grave diagnosis, or received word of his or her child's suspension from school. Offering even a brief opportunity for sharing and prayer at the start of church meetings can make all the difference. Maybe the committee doesn't get to its business as quickly, but church meetings go more smoothly and lives may be changed in the process! Is there any business more important than that?

The church of Jesus Christ is called to be an active community, so we meet for business. The church of Christ is also called to be a community of faith, hope, and love, where we "bear one another's burdens, and so fulfil the law of Christ" (Gal. 6:2 RSV).

Congregational Meetings

We have mentioned the need to enliven congregational meetings. Why shouldn't they be interesting and enjoyable? They need not be and should never be dull and boring, nor should they feel like endurance contests. Some churches have a dinner beforehand. The program is spiced with entertainment, group singing, and humor. Maybe you are already doing that. If not, talk with your church leaders about how they can make their presentations lively and creative. You want people to have fun, even as you try, through it all, to help your people to see the big picture. How does a particular activity fit into the mission of the church? How does the mission of your church fit into the work of Christ's kingdom? People need to understand the importance of what they're doing—in every area. What may seem obvious to you may not be obvious to everyone else.

Involve as many people as possible in planning and presenting the program. The more the merrier. Also, the more people involved, the more people will show up for the meeting! Support from the pulpit is important. People need to be reminded of the privileges of church membership, of their right to participate in the life of the church, and of the significance of this particular event. It is always important to stress the family aspect of the church, and to help people to feel close to one another. Do everything you can to encourage their sense of belonging—young and old, married and single, men and women, boys and girls. If the annual meeting is seen only as a time for transacting business, it probably will be. If it is seen as a time for experiencing Christian fellowship and the joy of belonging to a family of faith, it certainly *can* be!

Pastoral Pointer

Moderators and punctual committee members wonder why meetings never start on time. There is a simple solution to that problem: START ON TIME! If you don't, they won't. If you do, they will. It's as simple as that. You're the one who can make it happen. Maybe this poem can help you remember:

> Some pastors and chairpersons have legitimate complaints
>   about the frequently encountered lateness of the saints.
> Committee meetings often don't get started when they should,
>   for people just assume you're starting late, and that's no good.
> Rehearsals, weddings, classes, meals, and funerals as well—
>   if nothing ever starts on time, then why obey the bell?
> Those who arrive there promptly have a reason to complain.
>   To punish punctuality is awkward to explain.
> The level of frustration of those there is very high.
>   A late beginning is a dreadful waste of time, that's why.
> So here's our rule for those who wonder how to start on time.
>   It's very simple, but it works. The rule is: "Start on time!"[2]

2. From *Enough, Already! And Other Church Rhymes* by Richard Stoll Armstrong (Fairway Press, 1993), p. 56.

Chapter 17

Welcoming New Members

*H*aving stressed the importance of encouraging a sense of belonging, we need to think about assimilating new members into the life of the church. You and the church board have undoubtedly discussed this. Even so, you may want to take another look at how you are preparing people for membership in your congregation. Some congregations have virtually no preparation for new members. Others offer some, but limited, orientation. Others have a very substantial program to prepare people for membership. We believe your church, your ministry, and your new members will all be more likely to thrive if you follow the third course of action. The specific circumstances, the nature and ethos of your church, and your own theology and ecclesiology will help to determine the program you need. Whatever you decide to do requires continual consideration and periodic reevaluation.

At some point in their preparation for church membership, prospective new members should have an opportunity to learn about your dreams and your vision for the life of the church. What excites you about the church and your ministry there? What are the possibilities for the future? What are you and the church board dreaming about? What are some potential directions for the church to go in the future? Make sure new members know what you stand for, where you're "coming from," what your priorities are in ministry, what you're trying to accomplish in your preaching/teaching ministry. Help them to see how they can fit right in. This is a time in their spiritual journeys when people are usually extremely interested in "connecting."

The inquirers class, orientation class, explorers class, or whatever you call your membership preparation class, provides a wonderful opportunity to deal with current or potential issues. It calls for full disclosure. It is not fair for a person to be led into membership in a church only to find out later that the church or denomination stands for something he or she cannot accept or live with. The class gives prospective members a chance to ask questions and to express themselves, and to hear you express yourself. In the process they see that it's possible to disagree in love!

We believe people should be advised not to join the church if they can't join with enthusiasm. Attending the new-member classes should never obligate someone to join your church. For some, the orientation class will help them to discover your church is *not* the right spiritual home for them. Because of the obsessive consumer society in which we live, you will often find "church shoppers" in your new-member classes. These are individuals who are looking for a "better product," a "new and improved" version of something they have had before, rather than looking for a church they can make a commitment to, one they will stick with through thick and thin. If they are fleeing an imperfect church in search of a "perfect" one, let them know your church does not qualify as the latter. Again, full disclosure is called for. What church can claim to be perfect? Maybe the best thing for them to do would be to go back to their former church and work to make it better! If they are fleeing an imperfect pastor, maybe they should seek to be reconciled. Failing that, they need to know that if they spend any amount of time as members of your church, they will discover how human *you* are!

Above all, make sure people know what's expected of *them* if they become members of your congregation. Some folks join a church not to serve, but to be served. They're not interested in being equipped to serve others. Too many churches cater to that mentality!

The orientation and training your prospective new members receive is an introduction not merely to the life of your church and to its various committees, organizations, activities, staff, programs, and emphases. Make sure it's also an introduction to *Jesus*, and to the basic affirmations of the Christian faith! You can't assume, just because a group of folks have decided to join your church, that they understand what it means to commit one's life to Jesus Christ. Nor can you assume that they understand the meaning of words like grace, salvation, redemption, faith. They need to be able to take their vows with integrity.

As they join, having taken seriously the membership vows that underscore their new commitment to Christ and the church, your new members are pouring needed hot water into your congregational teacup! If you have prepared them properly, new members are usually very serious about their commitment, including their financial stewardship. They have thought and prayed about their financial contribution to the church, and in our experience their level of giving is invariably higher than that of the members who were never properly prepared for membership, often including some of the church officers! If you have followed a pastor who took this responsibility seriously, you are fortunate indeed.

In any case, those who attend your preparation classes and decide to join the church are almost always enthusiastic, eager for challenge, and ready to serve. They are uniformly positive about the church, and as they begin to move into positions of leadership they bring new life to all the ministries of the church, and a renewal of faith and enthusiasm among all the church's members.

Once again, we remind you that it is not our purpose to prescribe a curriculum for a membership preparation class. We are throwing lifelines, not how-to books on every aspect of ministry. As we stated in chapter 1, we want to help those who are battling the daunting waves of pastoral ministry not only to keep afloat but to enjoy the swim.

Pastoral Pointer

Every church should have a pictorial directory! It helps you and the members to put names and faces together. New members (and new pastors!) especially appreciate it. Members of the family of faith need to be able to call one another by name. There are reputable companies who produce pictorial directories for any size church *at no charge to the church or to the members*. "What's the catch?" some skeptical trustee might ask. There is no catch! These companies know that enough members will order copies of their photos to enable them to make a good profit. They supply a free directory to every family or individual member who poses for a photo, plus a number of extra copies for the church office. Depending on the size of the congregation, they also include photos of the staff and scenes of life in the church. Volunteers from the congregation schedule the appointments, remind people of their dates and times, and make sure people are properly identified as they check in. Other than that, and publicizing the project and encouraging people to participate, there's little else for the church to do. The company produces and delivers the books. It's a great deal for all concerned.

Chapter 18

Worrying about the Church's Finances

*I*n a very real sense this is not your worry, fundamentally, that is, because as pastors do we not believe that it is God who provides for the work of his church? If we don't believe that, how can we expect our people to rely on God's power to provide when it comes to their own stewardship and personal giving? How can we be joyous and free in our own giving? How can we ascribe glory and honor to God for the fact that the church of Jesus Christ continues to stand after more than two thousand years? The gates of hell have not prevailed against it!

Furthermore, how can we keep our priorities straight and concern ourselves with our preaching, teaching, and pastoral care if we are relentlessly eyeballing the church's bottom line? If you are more concerned about money and the church's finances than anything or anyone else, your ministry will suffer. Congregations generally do not respond well to pastors who view everything through green-colored glasses.

The Importance of Church Finances

In another sense, however, the church's finances *are* your concern—at least tangentially. Finances are a matter of tremendous importance to any organization, including the church. A pastor has to keep abreast of the church's financial situation. If you know nothing about your church's financial picture, if you have no knowledge of the budget, no understanding of the church's "cash flow," you can hardly participate intelligently in matters relating to the church's corporate stewardship, let alone give leadership to that crucial aspect of the church's ministry and mission. Nor can you expect to thrive as a pastor. The members, and particularly the leaders, of your church expect you to know about this fundamental aspect of church administration.

If you feel inadequate in these areas, find someone who can explain the basics to you. Minimally, you need to understand the budgeting process and how church funds are allocated. You have to be able to interpret the church's financial reports, including both the income side and the expense side of the operating budget. You don't have to be an expert on investment strategies, but you need to understand the basic concepts of planned giving so that you can encourage average working people to include the church in their estate planning. You don't have to be a certified public accountant, but you have to be able to interpret a balance sheet.

It is important for your church to be able to estimate its income with some degree of accuracy. The church undertakes all its work by faith, of course, but that doesn't obviate the need for realistic income projections. The main source of income for healthy churches is the members' regular giving, which can be fairly accurately estimated on the basis of their pledges. It is to be hoped that the anticipated shortfall resulting from deaths, membership transfers, and members' income reverses will be more than matched by the income from new members and occasional midyear increases from members.

Plate income from the worship services, which is mostly cash contributed by visitors and nonpledging members, can also be projected, based on past experience. If your church has any unrestricted endowment funds, a percentage of the estimated endowment income can be included, based on the church's investment policies. You may also have income from the use of the church's facilities for weddings, meetings of outside groups, and other approved purposes. There should be a line item for "miscellaneous income" to cover any sources not included in the above. Designated gifts for specific items not covered in the operating budget can be footnoted and included as "wash" items as the money is expended.

Generally, your church treasurer and/or finance committee should have a pretty good handle on income projections. The same holds true for expenses, which are easier to predict, based on past experience. The finance committee or budget planning team should be able to present reasonable figures for the board's approval, including a line item on the expense side for contingencies.

The church is not a business. It does not exist to make a profit. The church with the biggest bank balance is not by any means the most successful or faithful. You do not need a church treasurer who thinks his or her job is to amass or protect a hefty bank balance. The church's purpose is to *expend* itself—in worship, service, and ministry. To say the church is not a business does not mean, however, that it should not do things in a businesslike manner. That means doing things responsibly, carefully, systematically, and never haphazardly or slovenly. Faith is always the prime factor, of course.

The financial life of a congregation should be as subject to prayer as any other aspect of ministry.

The responsible management of its resources is the hallmark of a church's faithful corporate stewardship. The church's funds should always be managed in ways that ensure accountability. The use of payment or request vouchers is important, particularly in larger churches. Funds should never be spent without the written authorization of some responsible person. Make sure there are adequate controls for doing this. There is no room for shoddiness or sloppiness in this area! Some churches require two signatures on every check over a certain amount. Find out how other churches in your area are doing things. Decide which one you think sounds most responsible, and drive over with your church treasurer for a look at their system.

Faithful church boards will at times be led by God's Spirit to go forward with special initiatives or ministries without necessarily knowing where every dime will come from. We have found that congregations usually understand and support such an action when they believe their boards operate in faithful, responsible, and trustworthy ways.

Those who handle the funds in your church should be bonded. Is money being properly handled in your church? What happens to the Sunday morning offering? Where, and how, and by whom is it counted and recorded? Any practice that could invite trouble should be corrected immediately. For example, money should never be counted by fewer than two, preferably three, persons. Nor should it ever be counted where it is visible to passersby. Funds should be deposited as soon as possible after they are collected, even if you need to use a night depository. Cash or checks should not be left at the church or in somebody's home while awaiting deposit. It is prudent not to keep more than a minimal amount of cash at the church. It is also a good idea to rotate the money counters.

If the church's business affairs are being managed properly and things are running smoothly, you have much less to worry about, and you have cleared a huge stress hurdle that keeps many pastors struggling to survive instead of thriving.

The Stewardship "Campaign"

Since their giving is a measure of where people are spiritually, pastors worry about their congregation's financial stewardship. Churches have many ways of encouraging and increasing their members' giving. Some churches have annual or periodic stewardship "campaigns," based on the principles of Christian stewardship. Other churches put the focus on their budget needs. Those campaigns should more properly be called fund-raising campaigns. In recent years, however, churches are doing a better job of teaching a more holistic understanding of stewardship, of which a person's financial stewardship is a very important part. We have already made the distinction between fund-raising and stewardship (see chapter 8). Properly understood and managed, your stewardship campaign or program can be an exceptionally fruitful, meaningful, and even life-changing opportunity for ministry and spiritual growth. Remember, nothing happens to a person's giving until something happens to the person's heart. Spiritual growth leads to greater personal stewardship, and it can also work the other way!

As we have said, Christian giving is *motivated by grateful obligation.* Therefore, as stewards we don't give grudgingly, or under compulsion. We give our *firstfruits*—right off the top of what God gives us and in *proportion* to what we have. Those who have been given much should thus be giving more. Whether rich or poor, Christian stewards give *sacrificially.* We're not just tipping God. We have to feel it. And Christian giving is also *systematic,* not sporadic. We have to cultivate the habit of giving.

We cannot overstress the importance of the pastor's involvement in the stewardship life of his or her church. We urge you to make it a major emphasis in your preaching and teaching ministry, *not* because the church needs money, but because you can help your parishioners to experience the wonderful joy of growing spiritually. It is part of your discipling ministry. Any time you spend working closely with the person or group responsible for stewardship in your congregation is time extremely well spent. Your demonstrated interest in and, as much as possible, your personal involvement in the organizing and planning of the campaign, in recruiting volunteers, in training and motivating the campaign workers, in educating the congregation, in giving inspirational encouragement during the actual campaign, in tracking the results, following up on nonresponders, and maintaining a year-round emphasis on stewardship—all will help you and your flock become more faithful stewards.

Should the Pastor Know?

One question pastors have to answer is whether or not they should look at the pledge cards. Some churches publish the figures for *everyone* to see. In other churches only those who need to know for record keeping and budgeting purposes are privy to the information. One reality is that in no church is the information completely private, since some members are willing or even eager to discuss their pledges with stewardship callers and/or with the pastor. Another reality is that many people *assume* the pastor knows what they give, and they have no problem with that. So the prior question is, Do you want to know? That is: Do you feel you *need* to know?

There are definitely two ways of looking at this. On the one hand, some would say that most pastors, human nature being what it is, might be inappropriately influenced by that information. They could begin to favor some members. They might lean in the direction of the "big givers," play to those with the deep pockets. The temptation, say those who hold this opinion, would be to overvalue the opinions of the church's "heavy hitters," while discounting the opinions of those who give little. Pastors would be disappointed by some and amazed by others when they find out what people give, and that knowledge couldn't help coloring their relationships with some people. And even if they are not tempted that way, their people might *suspect* that big givers are treated differently from other members.

In addition, holders of this view maintain that giving should be motivated by gratitude to God, and not by a desire to impress or please other people, including one's pastor. The best safeguard, according to this view, is for everyone's giving to be kept confidential, between God and each giver. At the same time, this approach affirms the importance of talking about the principles of giving and stewardship, of sharing stewardship stories and personal testimonies, and of regarding a person's giving as a barometer of his or her walk with God.

Other pastors feel they not only *should* know but *have to know* what their members give, in order to disciple people as stewards and to track their spiritual growth. Who are the "big givers"? they ask. Percentagewise it is not the wealthy. What the records reveal would be a surprise to those pastors who never look at them! And even more so to the congregation, who assume that one's position and possessions are the index of one's giving. Not so! The "biggest givers" are those whose giving represents the greatest sacrifice. And even the amount they give may exceed that of many who have far more than they of this world's goods. Some of the wealthiest members would be shocked to discover that!

Most pastors are honest enough to admit that they can sometimes be influenced by people who throw their weight around. Knowing what people give, these pastors say, makes them actually less likely to be *unduly* (i.e., sinfully) influenced by the wealthy, who need to be challenged in their stewardship.[1]

1. John Galloway Jr. puts the point bluntly in his book *Ministry Loves Company: A Survival Guide for Pastors* (Westminster John Knox Press, 2003): "I can be influenced by money. I admit it. That is why I need to know what people give, so I can be influenced biblically rather than fall into the trap of being influenced unbiblically. I want to be influenced by people whose giving shows they are serious about their faith. I do not want to be influenced by people whose giving shows little to no commitment at all" (p. 140). For Galloway's full discussion of this topic, see his chap. 19, "Knowing What People Give."

That information in no way affects how they relate pastorally or minister to people, these pastors would say.

They argue, furthermore, that people should not be secretive about their giving. Faithful stewards should *want* to discuss this important aspect of the Christian life. These pastors want the traditional privacy around members' giving to give way to a different paradigm, where church members talk about Christian stewardship, share their struggles to become more faithful stewards, and help each other to grow in this important area of Christian discipleship. They consider it not to be idle curiosity or nosy prying, but to be as appropriate to the sharing of faith as discussing each other's prayer life. (Others consider that to be a private matter too!)

Pastors who feel they have to know what people give make the distinction between what is *personal* and what is *private*. Faith is indeed a personal matter, they would say, but it should never be private. As Christian stewards we can't keep our faith to ourselves. We have to share it. We have to grow in it. We have to live it. It's not a private affair. Neither is stewardship, which is such an important dimension of Christian faith and life. To say, "It's nobody's business what I give to the church! That's between me and God!" is making stewardship a private affair.

Holders of this view admit that discipling people takes time. One does not arrive overnight at the kind of openness they are appealing for. It's an educational process. As the congregation matures spiritually the members reach the point where their Christian giving is a topic to be shared openly and joyfully. For the apostle Paul, the grace of liberality was the crowning mark of a Christlike character. Instead of scolding the Corinthian Christians for what they hadn't done, he told them of what the Macedonians had done, as an inspiring example of the grace of God at work. The Macedonians had been so inspired to give that they gave to others before taking care of their *own* needs!

It is important to note that holders of these differing views concur on the basic principles of personal stewardship that we have discussed (see chapter 8), especially the principle that people's giving is a measure of their spiritual health. Every pastor has to choose his or her own approach to stewardship, of course, but in doing so, one should have considered carefully the issues we have identified. You know your own heart and your congregation better than anyone else. Still, it might help for you to get the perspectives of some other pastors on this issue. As you think and pray about it, God will honor your sincere efforts to do his will in this regard. Your decision will impact how you go about discipling people to be faithful stewards, which is indeed one of the most important aspects of your preaching, teaching, and pastoral ministry. Once again, we all need to remind ourselves that our own stewardship house must be in order before we can disciple others to be good stewards.

The Stewardship Committee

Assuming that is the case, here are a few practical things to think about. Be sure that you and your church board (or nominating committee) select the right person to head up your congregation's stewardship program. The person should be a committed Christian steward, a faithful giver. You need someone who is spiritually mature, enthusiastic about the church, committed to the work and mission of Jesus Christ. Pray about who that person should be, one who can make a difference in the life of your congregation. Ask God to raise up the right person for this crucial position. When you or others approach the person whom God has laid on your hearts, tell him or her how important a role this is and why you are asking him or her to fill it. It is a key invitation to service. Answer the person's questions. Assure the person of your support and the board's support. Pray with the person, and if she or he needs more time, suggest you talk about it again, after both of you have continued to pray about it. Incidentally, we feel that it's the way you and your church should approach every potential leader, for whatever role. God has to be involved in the team-building process. After all, it's his church![2]

Depending on the size of your church, the stewardship committee should be a standing committee of the church board, and not a spontaneously gathered or abruptly delegated entity. The task is too important, too vital to the life of the church. All the members of the committee should themselves be good stewards. Impress this on them when they are asked to serve. Let them know the great significance of their ministry. At the meetings take time for them to share stewardship stories that remind one another how God provides and how one cannot "outgive" God.

2. A footnote from KWM: Here's an idea worth considering: For a number of years we have elected church leaders in the church I serve using an approach that has had an amazing effect on all aspects of our congregational life. In late summer each year, the nominating committee of our church prayerfully considers and nominates leaders not just to seats on the board, but to *specific areas of ministry,* i.e., to specific leadership roles in the life of the church. For example, the committee nominates a church member not just to serve as an "elder," but to serve as the "stewardship elder," or the "building and grounds elder," or "Christian education elder." The nominating committee looks for church members with specific gifts and passion for a particular aspect of the church's life. Thus, when these leader-nominees are elected they have the vote and full support of the whole congregation for their particular leadership role. They come in with authority, enthusiasm, and a full head of steam! It has been a wonderful process for our congregation.

The Pastor's Role

Part of your role as pastor is to keep reminding the committee and the congregation that stewardship is what we do with what we have, with all that God has given us. There are all kinds of stewardship materials available through your denominational headquarters. Pastors' Web sites, church-related publications, and many books and articles provide excellent help in the area of stewardship. Make them available to your committee.

You may not be a professional fund-raiser. You are, or should be, a faithful steward. You have to be, in order to set a good example. You can't preach with integrity what you don't practice. You can't preach tithing if you don't tithe. Part of your calling as a spiritual teacher and example to the flock is to share your own desire and struggle to be a faithful steward.

One of the most important things you can teach your people is that Christian stewardship is not based on need. We have talked about this in chapter 8, but it bears repeating in our present context. Stewardship, we have pointed out, is based on our obligation to give something back to God in gratitude for what God has done for us. It is our way of acknowledging that *everything* belongs to God. We own nothing; we manage everything. Our Christian giving is not based on what our particular church needs this year, but on what we have been given! An extremely important corollary to this concept is that we do not give to the *church*. We give to God *through* the church. We do not give to meet a budget. We give to a budget to meet human needs. We do not give because a pastor or a stewardship chair asks us. We give out of grateful obligation to God! That's true Christian giving. We place our gifts in God's hands and dedicate every dollar, every penny, to God. We ask God to use our gifts for his work, however and wherever that may be. How the church uses the money entrusted to it is a matter of its corporate stewardship.

These concepts are still foreign to many church members, even to some who have been faithful attenders for most of their lives. Take advantage of every opportunity you have to educate your flock. Help them know what true Christian giving really is. Remind them of the basic principles of Christian stewardship (grateful obligation, priority, sacrifice, proportionality, regularity). Help your people understand what it means to be a faithful Christian steward, and how to reflect that understanding in their giving. Jesus said, "It is more blessed to give than to receive" (Acts 20:35). Even today his followers marvel to discover how true his words are!

As part of their overall stewardship education, you will want to see that your people learn about the opportunity and need to continue supporting Christ's work even after their days on "terra firma" are over. Church members should be told about deferred gifts and bequests. You might consider a "wills emphasis" Sunday. A surprising number of church members have never made a will. Most have never thought of making a "Christian" will. There are plenty of materials available to help people find out about these things. You don't have to be rich to make a will. Every husband and wife, every parent, should have one and keep it up to date.

A Memorial Gifts Fund

A memorial gifts fund is another practical way to expand your flock's financial stewardship. If your church doesn't have one, the sooner you establish one the better. The church board or some designated committee or group needs to administer the fund, which over the years can become sizable. They keep the congregation informed of the church's needs. When a friend or a loved one dies, relatives and friends can, if they choose, give a gift to the church in that person's memory, even if he or she was not a member of your church.

You and the memorial gifts committee should acknowledge every gift with letters to the giver and to the family members of the deceased. Every gift should be recorded in a permanent record of the church. The church board needs to establish a clear policy on how the money may be spent and with whose approval.

Experience has shown that it is usually best if people's gifts are put into a single memorial gifts fund to be administered by a very responsible committee, rather than to have individual memorial funds. The latter approach results in a constantly growing number of individual little funds that become harder and harder to administer and account for. The policy of having everything go into one fund can be modified to say if the money given in memory of a particular individual is of a certain amount (for example, $1,000 or more), you can then select something appropriate as a memorial to the person, in consultation with the family. Often the family will want to add to the fund in order that a particular item might be purchased or a special interest of their loved one may be represented in the item selected (new robes for the choir, new carpeting for the church parlor, a new portable lectern for the assembly room, e.g.). Occasionally a memorial gift may be large enough to warrant establishing a separate fund; for example, a family gives $150,000 to establish in memory of their son a revolving educational fund, the income from which is to help members of the congregation who are studying for the ministry.

With bequests, as with any special gift, the wishes of the donor must be respected and followed, unless they are in conflict with church policy or practice. The committee may even want to decline a gift if they deem it inappropriate or one that would encumber the church financially or otherwise. The gift of an undesirable property with a huge lien attached would be an example of the latter.

The Church's Mission Giving

We have made the distinction between personal and corporate stewardship. You must help your church officers and members to understand that distinction. Just as they grow in their Christian stewardship by giving back to God a portion of what God has given them, so the church gives away a percentage of its income in grateful recognition that all the church has is by the grace of God and as a sign that Christ is indeed Lord of the church. The basic principles we have stated apply to the church's corporate stewardship as well as to an individual's personal stewardship.

Some churches strive to give a dollar to mission beyond their walls for every dollar they spend on themselves. Others modify that formula to make it a dollar to mission for every dollar given by their members. Some churches put themselves under great stress trying to maintain even a one-for-two ratio. The pastor and the church officers have guilty consciences because they can't keep their mission giving at the same level as their operating expenses increase. If they anticipate a 10 percent increase in expenses, they appeal to the congregation to increase their pledges by 10 percent, and when the members respond accordingly, they wonder why the percentage of mission giving goes down. They have overlooked two important factors: first, that in order to maintain the same ratio, they have to increase *both* sides of the budget by 10 percent. That means the members will have to increase their pledges by *more* than 10 percent! The second factor most churches overlook is that while their members' giving is probably the major portion, it is not their total income. So to increase the *total income* by 10 percent, the members would have to increase their giving by an even higher percentage! Depending on how much of your income is from other sources, your members may have to increase their personal giving by 20 percent or more, and that for many people might be too much to ask. Get out your pencil and do the arithmetic, and you'll see for yourself .

Regardless of what percentage you decide on, it is surely the case that your church will make some funds available to give to mission causes. You can ease the stress of the decision-making process for everyone by adopting a policy and a formula for determining how best to distribute your mission funds. Here's a way of doing that: Divide your giving according to several major categories and determine what percentage of your giving will go to each category. You may decide that 20 percent of your giving next year will go toward educational ministries. Your mission budget is $40,000, so you will have $8,000 to divide among the requests you receive from theological seminaries and other educational ministries. Along with other categories (e.g., evangelism ministries, social-justice ministries, human services) you have a miscellaneous category to accommodate late requests you deem to be worthy of your church's support.

In considering the scope of your mission giving, you can also factor into your formula percentages for local, regional, national, and international giving. Let's say you decide that 30 percent of your mission giving should go to local causes or ministries, 10 percent to regional ministries, 25 percent to national ministries, and 35 percent to overseas ministries. Still another factor for some churches is the division between their own denomination's ministries and those that are not denominationally affiliated or approved.

You and your church board should keep all these factors in mind, in formulating your mission giving policy, which should clearly state the principles and guidelines by which you choose which requests to honor. For instance, under educational ministries you might want to support those seminaries where members of your congregation are studying. Under human services and social-justice ministries your policy might be to give priority to those worthy causes in which members of your congregation are involved. In other words, "Follow people with dollars." Having such guidelines makes it much easier to sort out the causes you want to support. When you have exhausted the funds allotted for a given category, you can have a nicely worded form letter explaining your policy to those organizations whose requests you have to decline. In some instances you may want to leave room for hope, in case there should be extra funds at the end of the year.

For the sake of those organizations, institutions, and causes that are dependent on the support they receive from churches and individuals, it should be your policy to make your grants as soon as possible. Don't wait until the end of the year. The organizations you support need money throughout the year. Priority giving means giving to mission *off the top*. Systematic giving for the church means giving both to current expenses and to mission on a regular basis.

Pastoral Pointer

In lieu of property taxes, which the church does not have to pay, consider making a voluntary contribution from the church to the township or city budget for the services the church receives, such as police protection, fire protection, and trash collection. It is fair return for services rendered and a gesture that will earn the appreciation, goodwill, and respect of the community. It is good to make friends, furthermore, with the local police and fire departments.

Pastoral Pointer

Are you uncomfortable about confronting someone whose behavior or attitude needs to be challenged? There are two rules that can help in such situations. First, always be up front with your feelings, or with whatever it is that is bothering you. Second, you can say the hard thing if your face and body language communicates an accepting, nonjudgmental attitude and a caring, sympathetic heart. It's speaking the truth in love (Eph. 4:15).[3]

3. For a fuller discussion of this and other aspects of faith sharing, see *The Pastor-Evangelist in the Parish* (Westminster/John Knox Press, 1990), pp. 34–37. See also *Faithful Witnesses*, Participant's Book (Geneva Press, 1987), pp. 44–46.

Chapter 19

Wrestling with Conflict

*W*hat causes pastors more stress than anything else? Most pastors would probably agree that conflict is the biggest stress producer. It can make life miserable, especially if you are the focus of it. And as we keep saying, the buck stops at the pastor's desk. Although we have alluded to conflict in the preceding chapters, we feel the subject is important enough to warrant a separate chapter, in the hope that we can toss a lifeline to those who may be close to drowning in it or who may one day be plunged into it. We are not talking about healthy disagreements here, but about stressful conflict in which you are personally involved, perhaps even as the issue.

Conflict Is Almost Inevitable

Let's assume you are a solo pastor. (Multistaff situations only compound the problems!) Speaking from a purely human standpoint, you can assume conflict. Why? Because you know the congregation isn't where it ought to be (is any?), and because you understand your role as a leader is to try to help it get there. That will involve change—personal and corporate, moral and spiritual, behavioral and relational. Such change is threatening to some, and being threatened leads to conflict, because you and they are human, not divine. You and they are fallible, not infallible. You and they are not perfect. Even Jesus had conflict, and as one irate parishioner reminded his pastor, "You ain't Jesus!"

Ergo, you can assume conflict. According to the Duke University National Clergy Survey, "Two-thirds of the clergy report that their congregation has experienced some form of conflict over the past two years, and over 20 percent report that the conflict was 'significant' or 'major'—the latter leading to members leaving the congregation. We asked what these conflicts were about, and the issues listed are interesting for several reasons. First, what congregations fight about are not the same issues as those that trouble national denominations and that are often in the news. The survey responses indicate that congregational conflict most often is about pastoral leadership styles, interpersonal relationships, building maintenance and use, church finances, and changes in worship and music styles."[1]

You can also assume, therefore, that you are sometimes, if not often, going to be the object of conflict, and in some people's minds the *cause* of it! Perhaps it's something you said in the pulpit, so that now they object to just about everything you say in the pulpit. It could be that they are threatened just by what you represent as a minister. Your very lifestyle is an indictment of their own behavior. You are a goad to their conscience and they defend themselves by attacking you wherever they can. They instinctively know that in church fights the best defense is a good offense!

Or it could be your style of leadership that irritates them, or what they perceive to be your failures as a human being. Whatever it is, their antagonism and rejection is hard to take, especially when your attempts to be reconciled are rebuffed. It's hard enough to survive, let alone thrive, when you are the target of hostility and unfriendly opposition.

If you are functioning adequately, doing the best you can, and if you have not made any major, obvious mistakes that would warrant such criticism, you can assume that on any given congregational issue, of those who were there when you arrived on the scene: (a) some will be supportive; (b) some will be critical; and (c) some will be neutral. The critical folks may include supporters of your predecessor, whose image you don't fit, and those whom you may have offended by something you did or didn't do, or something you said or didn't say. These negative folks are always more vocal (louder) than your supporters. The vocal critics almost always *sound* as if they are more representative than they actually are. They are the most talkative at congregational meetings. They are the vocal minority!

Time Is Your Ally

The neutral folks don't have much to say. They're on the fence, or uninvolved. They can be swayed one way or the other, but it is usually not personal with them. You don't know where they stand on an issue until the vote is taken. Time is in your favor, usually. That is, some of your critics will get used to

1. The National Clergy Survey was a major component of "Pulpit and Pew." See chap. 1, n. 1.

your style, learn to trust you, even like you. You will win them because of your pastoral services. They will see that you don't avoid calling on them when they need you, as when there is a sickness or death in the family, or some other calamity.

You will also win some with your preaching, if it's biblical, broad-based, relevant, well prepared, and persuasive. You will win those who begin to recognize your earnest desire to be fair, to listen to all sides, and to take their comments seriously. You will win them because of your lack of rancor. They see that you don't hold their opposition against them. You will win them because of your very humanity. You don't pretend to be perfect. You admit your mistakes. You keep your sense of humor.

Through it all, your supporters will also be helping to win over your critics. Those who have benefited from your pastoral care, from your preaching and teaching, will help people to see you from their positive perspective. So will your former critics, who now see you differently.

So time is your ally in conflict situations. It's best to avoid knee-jerk reactions. Of course, you may also make some new enemies (critics). "You can't win 'em all," as losing sports teams like to say. If you're preaching prophetically, you're bound to step on a few toes. And you can't *do* it all! You probably have been criticized for your sins of *omission* more than for your sins of *commission*. In the life of a busy pastor, some things are going to fall through the cracks.

You will also be criticized for things beyond your control. You may be totally blameless for something that happened, but you become the focal point for the criticism simply because you are the pastor. You know where the buck stops! You may have to absorb the blame publicly for a colleague's mistake, even though you have reprimanded your colleague privately.

So conflict is inevitable. If it happens, you are in a normal situation. That's the bad news. Here's the good news: through it all, back in the church parlor you've been conducting orientation classes. New people have been joining the church. They've joined having heard your vision of the church and its mission. They've been made aware of the issues—all sides!—and they know where you stand on them. They've had ample opportunity to express themselves, and have learned that it is possible to disagree in love. As they become involved in the life and leadership of the congregation, you are adding to the roster of active players new team members who are supportive, positive, and enthusiastic. When the vote on a controversial issue is taken, you'll find, if you have been faithful, honest, sincere, and fair, that the church will follow your leadership. They'll go your way. Just make sure it is Jesus' way!

Some Precautions

The preceding paragraph leads us to make the following cautionary points:

1. Be careful in your assessments of people. You can be wrong! People can surprise you—both ways. Some who can most easily use Christian jargon may be the first to run when push comes to shove. They may punctuate every statement with an "Amen!" or a "Praise the Lord!" but be the first to desert when they think the ship is sinking. Others who are too timid to lead in silent prayer take their stand when the chips are down. They stay with the ship!
2. Make sure *you* are faithful. That really is your main, if not your only real, worry. You've got to try to do what you believe in your heart is right. Some readers might be thinking, Don't pastors always think what they're doing is right? Not by any means! They know in their heart of hearts when there is an element of doubt! They may not admit it, but they know!
3. Assessing our actions, attitudes, and opinions requires honest self-examination. When we're wrong we have to admit it. And we have to do what we can to make amends, always seeking to be reconciled, but always moving ahead "toward the goal for the prize of the heavenly call of God in Christ Jesus" (Phil. 3:14).
4. But not too fast! You don't want to go charging up the hill on your own personal crusade and get so far out in front of the troops that you're mistaken for the enemy. You may wind up being shot in the back!
5. Nor should you harangue the congregation from the pulpit. That never works. It only makes the people you're trying to win angrier! And even your supporters don't like it.
6. Do most of your "hard-selling" in one-on-one conversations, or in small-group discussions, where people have a chance to express themselves and feel that they've been heard.
7. Don't overestimate the power of your preaching to change people's attitudes, but at the same time don't underestimate the power of the Holy Spirit to *use* your preaching for the cause of Christ. Preaching is a unique and powerful medium of communication, as well as a fantastic privilege and awesome responsibility.
8. Preaching is also a wonderful medium for relating to people. Your congregation can really get to know you, *if* you are an authentic person. People will know how you feel about things, what excites you, what your values are, what you believe and why you believe it—about God, about Christ, about the church, about everything. If they come regularly they will know you better than almost anyone else.
9. Being authentic means being the same person in the pulpit that you are out of the pulpit. It means *being* what you preach, and preaching what you

are. To be inconsistent is to destroy your credibility. It's hypocritical, dishonest, insincere.

10. At the same time, you don't want to come across as a holier-than-thou person. You have to share your struggles, as well as your convictions, and you have to do it dialogically, so that you are dealing with their struggles too.
11. Your people need to understand that what you believe in is more important than what you know. You want them to know *that* you believe in Jesus Christ, not just what you know *about* him. People are moved more by someone who really believes what she or he is preaching than they are by a clever pulpit orator who doesn't know the Christ he or she is talking about.

All of this is to say that although conflict happens sooner or later, it does not have to be totally destructive. It can even be healthful to you and to the opposition, if it is properly dealt with. No one should revel in conflict, but rather see it as an opportunity for reconciliation, renewal, and personal growth. Seen that way, it does not have to be the stress-producing experience it can so easily become for those who ignore the kinds of things we have been saying. We have not tried to present an outline of a conflict management seminar. As we said at the beginning of this chapter, we are simply tossing you another lifeline that we hope will keep you from drowning in the sea of conflict.

P.S. We feel we must add a postscript to this chapter to mention something that seems to fit better here than anywhere else in this book. It can be personally devastating when one of the active leaders pulls out of the church in anger. It is hard enough when a faithful, supportive member dies or moves out of town, especially when you have a small congregation and that person was one of the key contributors and a strong leader whose counsel, example, and support you have always counted on. It's like losing a member of your family. It's even harder when someone who has been in that role leaves mad, despite your efforts to smooth his or her ruffled feathers and to be reconciled. It is painful indeed when that happens, and the scars remain long after your wounded heart has healed.

Why is it that those who leave mad are often persons who have been recipients of your pastoral ministry, people with whom you may even have spent more time than with most other members of your congregation? We have no solution to this problem, nor an antidote for the pain, but perhaps the following thoughts will help a little.

1. Don't panic. Jesus Christ is still Lord of the church. God knows what's going on.
2. You are not the only one this happens to. Most pastors, especially those who are strong leaders, have had folks "leave mad." It often happens when

a church is about to move forward. The only boat that doesn't make any waves is the one that is dead in the water. Building campaigns, for example, can threaten some folks, because of the money involved. People can argue about bricks-and-mortar issues with impunity, they think, because "it has nothing to do with one's faith in Christ." The plausible reasons for their anger blind them to the underlying stewardship issues. Whatever the reasons, some folks often get angry enough to leave the church. The saying is true: you can't please everyone.

3. Try to respond with patience and love to anyone who is agitated. It is best to deal with such persons face to face. Be prepared to eat humble pie. Don't argue. *Listen*. Your willingness to do so may be all that is needed to bring the disgruntled person around. He or she may never have felt "heard" before. If your sincere efforts fail, you will have the satisfaction of knowing that at least you tried.
4. Grieve the departure with your church leaders and with the congregation tactfully. Do not celebrate the loss of anyone, no matter how difficult that person may have been.
5. Ask: What is God teaching us in this situation? What does God want *me* to learn from this experience? What can I do better the next time? Some of your leaders and other members can be helpful in this process.
6. Don't underestimate the reconciling power of the Holy Spirit. Leave the door open for the departed person to return. Teach and encourage forgiveness, and set the believers an example.
7. Pray for and encourage others to pray for those who leave your church that they will join some other Christian congregation and continue to be active in the work of Christ's kingdom.
8. Try to look ahead, not back. Follow where you believe the Lord is leading you and the congregation, and pray that you can be faithful.

Pastoral Pointer

It is helpful to use "planning calendars" in preparing the master church calendar. Distribute pages to each member of the staff, a page for each month of the year, with seven squares across for the days of the week, dated appropriately, according to the number of days in each month. Every member of the staff fills in his or her program events for the entire year. These are then coordinated into one large master calendar. Other known church events, special worship services, seasonal activities, meetings not already included, deadlines for publications and reports, and anything involving the use of church space or in which the church is involved, are added to the master calendar. Conflicting events and other glitches are worked out. The master calendar is then reviewed, approved, reproduced, and copies distributed to all concerned persons. The master calendar is prominently posted in the church office, and upcoming events are published in the church bulletin and the monthly newsletter. The calendar can be amended as necessary throughout the year. It is amazing how much more smoothly, easily, and efficiently the master calendar can be produced using the process we have briefly outlined here.

Chapter 20

Fulfilling Other Roles

*I*n addition to being an administrator you have other roles to fulfill as a pastor. You are a preacher. You are a worship leader. You are a teacher. You are a counselor. You are a discipler. And precisely because you are pastor, you are a public figure; you have visibility in the community.

Each of these roles has its own satisfactions, and each has its unique stress factors. Having to keep up with the demands of all these professional roles is a test of your survivability; your enjoyment and sense of fulfillment in each of these roles is a measure of your thrivability. Here are a few lifelines to help you do both.[1]

Preaching and Worship Leadership

Most pastors like to preach. The hard part is deciding *what* to preach, and then writing the sermon. One pressure point is the deadline for the Sunday church bulletin. When the church secretary is bugging you for the bulletin information

1. A footnote from RSA: You are, or should be, also an evangelist. How do you fulfill the apostle's exhortation to "do the work of an evangelist" (2 Tim. 4:5)? I have long argued that for a pastor it is not a matter of "doing evangelism," but of doing everything with evangelistic sensitivity. With that as my premise, I have attempted in other writings to answer the question, first, by examining the pastor's evangelistic ministry in terms of personal relationships and the various factors that determine the context and shape the style of that ministry. (See *The Pastor as Evangelist*, Westminster Press, 1984; this book presents a theology and style of evangelism and a thorough discussion of the nature and role of faith in the process.) In a second book (*The Pastor-Evangelist in Worship*, Westminster Press, 1986), I looked at two of the pastor's professional roles through evangelistic glasses. The first half of the book is devoted to the pastor-evangelist as worship leader, the second half to the pastor-evangelist as preacher. The third book in the series (*The Pastor-Evangelist in the Parish*, Westminster/John Knox Press, 1990) looks at how the pastor-evangelist fulfills her or his ministry as a visitor, counselor, teacher, discipler, administrator, and public figure. The professional roles of a pastor are covered much more thoroughly in the latter two books than we can do here. Many of the ideas in those books would certainly help a pastor to thrive and not just survive.

and you have neither a text nor a topic because you've had two funerals, a board meeting, and several emergency hospital calls, that's when you feel the stress. But then comes Friday and you haven't started writing yet, and the stress builds.[2] Whenever you begin to be anxious about finishing your sermon and worrying because you know you haven't had time to give it your best shot, that's a pressure point. And when your anxiety turns to desperation, you are struggling for survival, not thriving.

We have one suggestion: **plan ahead**! Many pastors use the lectionary. That helps, but it doesn't solve the problem. You still have to plan ahead. It's very hard and stressful to work Sunday by Sunday. Not only that, it's inefficient. You will save yourself hours, even days, of time if you work out your sermon schedule for the entire year, or at least for several months. Applying in a carefully thought-out way the various criteria by which you determine what aspects of the many-faceted jewel we call the gospel you want to focus on in a given year, you plan your Lenten, Advent, and other series, your themes for special Sundays, and for every Sunday of the year that you will be preaching Think in terms of your *preaching ministry*. You are not just preaching isolated sermons week by week. Where do you want to lead your congregation?

Use the Common Lectionary if you must. If you do, we urge you nevertheless to plan ahead. There is much leeway in choosing texts from the lectionary passages. We much prefer, however, to make our own lectionary, and we recommend that you do the same. After all, you know your congregation better than those who plan the Common Lectionary, and they are far from infallible. In fact, the Common Lectionary omits many passages of the Bible and repeats others disproportionately. In planning your own preaching schedule, you can force yourself to tackle difficult passages never covered in the Common Lectionary, and—what's even more important—you can choose passages that relate more relevantly and accurately to your congregation.

Our point here, however, is not whether to use the Common Lectionary or one of your own making. Our point is: plan ahead! To do that you will need quality time by yourself. Some use their continuing education time for independent study, during which time they plan their preaching and worship schedule for the next year. Others use part of their vacation time.

In planning your sermon schedule you will draw on the countless ideas that you have already collected and stored in your "Sermon Ideas" files, to which you are constantly adding new ideas that come to you from your devotional

2. We strongly recommend you discipline yourself to write out your sermons, even if you don't use a manuscript in the pulpit. You owe your congregation your clearest thinking, your most careful research, your best effort.

reading of the Bible and other reading you do, from your personal prayer life, from events and conversations in your day-to-day ministry, from the news media and current events, from parishioners' requests for you to preach on particular topics, from ideas that pop into your mind "out of the blue," and from many other sources, as the Holy Spirit hones your homiletical instincts. Indeed, by the time you finish planning your sermon schedule for one year you'll have so many ideas for future sermons and series of sermons you will have already started thinking about the following year.

You will already have thought of many good titles for the budding sermons in your files, and as you choose your themes and topics ideas for other sermon titles will come to you. You may be thinking topically, but you will, of course, approach your topic biblically, using the texts that inspired the idea in the first place, or other parallel or compatible texts that have shed further light on the topic as you do your preparatory research. Having chosen the Old and New Testament passages and your text (if there is one) for every sermon, you add these to your master schedule, along with appropriate responsive readings if your liturgy calls for such, and the hymns for each Sunday.

By selecting your hymns far in advance, you will save a huge amount of time, while assuring a much wider use of your hymnbook, and you can make sure that you have selected the hymns that tie in best with your theme for each Sunday. You can't do that when you work from Sunday to Sunday. How much time you could spend preparing for a single worship service, as you thumb through the hymnbook looking for just the right hymn and in the process discover that it would have fit better with last week's sermon! There are enough good hymns in most hymnals to avoid having to repeat any hymn too often. In discipling your people as worshipers, you want them to become familiar with far more hymns than the average church member now knows. If you are working a year ahead, you will be selecting hymns for services throughout the year as you come across them. You will often discover that a hymn you have chosen for one Sunday would fit better with your sermon on another Sunday, and you're free to make such switches. You can't do that when you're working one Sunday at a time.

Your master schedule also indicates all special Sundays, Communion services (if you do not observe the sacrament every Sunday), baptism Sundays (if these are regularly scheduled), Holy Week services, Christmas Eve, Thanksgiving Day, and, of course, all other evening and/or weekday services you have. If you are the pastor of a multistaff church, the schedule should also show who is preaching and who is the liturgist for each service.

Having completed your master schedule, you then make copies available on a need-to-know basis to your associates and staff members, including most importantly the organist and choir director, to the church secretary, of course, and to whoever is responsible for producing the church newsletter. You want your congregation to know about your forthcoming sermon series, and to be intrigued by your sermon titles. You can't do that if you don't plan ahead! Some pastors also encourage their congregation to read and reflect on the corresponding Scripture passages before coming to church each Sunday, as part of their preparation for worship. They will appreciate your sermons much more if they do, and you will find them more interested and receptive to your preaching.

Planning ahead is actually fun! Your creative juices will be flowing freely as you explode with ideas all over the pages. Another benefit of knowing what you will be preaching about down the line is that you will be collecting sermon illustrations and jotting down thoughts as they come to you and sticking them in your sermon files. You can't do that when you don't plan ahead. You may collect plenty of sermon illustrations, but you'll have to sort through them each Sunday, looking for appropriate ones to use. And sometimes, as with the hymns, you may use an illustration that would have fit much better with a later sermon. You don't need a separate file for each sermon, but you might want to have a separate file for each series and one catch-all file into which you put all other illustrations, indicating on each item with which sermon you may want to use it. Your file will often include brief and very preliminary outlines of sermons, thoughts you had when the idea first came to you, perhaps as you were reading the Scripture passage. Sometimes the outline leaps out at you as you read.

Having a sermon schedule eliminates the anxiety of wondering what you're going to preach about next Sunday. But you still have to write the sermon! And you still have to give the church secretary whatever liturgical information she or he needs for the church bulletin, such as the call to worship and a prayer of confession. Having planned ahead, you can write each sermon more easily and earlier, because you have chosen the Scripture passages and the hymns, and you know what you will be preaching about. In other words, you've given yourself a running start!

Even though you have planned your sermons for the entire year, you can make every worship service, including the sermon itself, as relevant as the daily news by the illustrations you use. The gospel is always relevant! And if not in the sermon, you can do so by what you say in your pastoral prayers and in the announcements, which in our view are a very important part of the worship service. The fact that you have planned your sermon topic in advance does not prevent you from changing it at the very last minute on any given Sunday, in order to address some local uproar or national catastrophe such as a terrorist attack or the death of a president. Planning ahead allows as much flexibility as you want. A sermon schedule is not a straitjacket.

This is not a book on homiletics. We have no intention of discussing the content or delivery of your sermons or the style of your worship leadership. We are, as we have repeatedly stated, tossing you a lifeline to help you thrive and not just survive as a preacher struggling to produce a sermon and prepare a worship service every week. By the way, if you are an associate pastor and preach only once a month or occasionally, you should still plan ahead. Coordinate with the pastor in planning your own sermon schedule, but determine what you want to accomplish in your own preaching ministry, limited though your opportunities may be.

If you are already planning ahead, then look on what we have said above as a confirmation of what you are doing, and keep up the good work. You are a thriver, not just a survivor!

You Choose the Hymns!

We have pointed out some of the many advantages of planning ahead, not the least of which is the immense amount of time it saves. If you are called to a church where the music director, or the organist, or the church secretary, or anyone else has been selecting the hymns for worship, you may have another stress point to deal with. As the worship leader and the one whose sermon determines the unifying theme of any particular worship service, you are the one who should select the hymns to be sung. Your assumption of that responsibility can be a source of friction with the person who formerly performed that function. Let's hope the transfer can be effected amiably, without your having to pull rank. In any case, you will assure the organist of your desire to work closely with her or him in preparing all the music for worship. Explain your practice of planning ahead and the criteria you use in selecting the hymns for worship. Our own criteria would include at least the following:[3]

a. *Is it related to the theme of your message?* The text or part of the text of each hymn should enhance the unity of the worship service by tying in with some aspect of the general theme, if possible.

b. *Is it seasonal?* Take advantage of the opportunities to sing hymns that are especially appropriate for particular seasons or days of the church year (Advent, Christmas, Palm Sunday, Easter, Pentecost, etc.).

3. Adapted from *The Pastor-Evangelist in Worship*, pp. 30–34.

c. *Is it familiar?* One of the most common complaints of the saints is, "Why don't we sing hymns that are familiar?" Of course, what is familiar to some is not familiar to others. And hymns that may have been sung frequently by some congregations may not be known to others, even if they use the same hymnbook! If you can find at least two familiar hymns that tie in with the theme, great! The saints will not object to singing an unfamiliar hymn once in a while, if they realize that you are always trying to choose hymns that most of them know, and if you explain that you have chosen it because it ties in so well with your message.

d. *Is it singable?* If the tune is not familiar, it should at least be singable. The melody line, range, rhythm, or intervals may be too difficult for the average person, who doesn't read music. If sometime you feel you have to use such a hymn, ask the organist to stress the melody, and perhaps have the choir sing one stanza first. Sometimes the hymnbook will include more than one tune for the same text, in which case we would opt for the more-familiar tune, unless we deliberately wanted to introduce the congregation to the less-familiar tune. In the latter case, a word of explanation is always in order.

e. *When was it last sung?* There are enough good hymns and spiritual songs not to have to repeat the same one over and over again, unless you are introducing it as a new "hymn of the month." Keep a record of the hymns that are used, showing when and how often each hymn is used. If four different hymns suit the purpose equally well, choose the one least recently sung.

f. *Is it appropriate to the order of service?* If there are three hymns, the first is traditionally a hymn of praise, but it can still be related to the theme. If the service ends with the sermon followed by a closing hymn, the hymn should reinforce, punctuate, or reiterate the theme and mood of the sermon. If the sermon comes earlier in the service, followed by a hymn, that hymn should do the same. A hymn preceding the sermon would be more preparatory, but still theme-related.

g. *Is it theologically appropriate for worship?* Your denominational and cultural traditions will determine that. Some hymns are dated theologically or by their noninclusive language. Some would be more fitting around a campfire, or at a Sunday school assembly, or even at a "praise service."[4]

4. Midweek evening praise services are very popular in Korea, and many churches in America have adopted the practice of having such services, where congregational singing is featured and the music is much more contemporary, with appropriate accompaniment.

h. *Do you want to elevate,or accommodate?* On the one hand, you want to increase their appreciation of Christian hymnody, improve their understanding of what constitutes good hymnology, and whet their appetite for the great hymns of the church that have stood the test of time. On the other hand, you take into account where they are now. You don't want to go too fast. There has to be a sensitive balance between your desire to elevate and your need to accommodate your congregation's musical tastes.

i. *Is there a special reason for selecting a particular hymn?* Maybe you are introducing it as the hymn of the month. Or maybe you promised to select one of the top ten winners of your recent "favorite hymn survey." Maybe it is being sung in recognition of the anniversary of some important event when the same hymn was sung. Or maybe a family in the church asked if it could be sung, and you decided there was good reason to honor their request.

In selecting hymns for worship you have to decide which criteria take precedence on any given Sunday. Sometimes the season of the year will be the primary consideration. So you choose Advent hymns and Christmas carols during Advent, and passion hymns on Good Friday, and resurrection hymns on Easter. On other Sundays it's sometimes a juggling act, as you try to find hymns that meet as many criteria as possible. When you find a hymn that does, Eureka! As we have been saying, the task is much easier if you plan ahead.

Your organist will appreciate having the schedule and the care with which you have selected the hymns. Having the schedule will help him or her to understand why you need to select the hymns, thus reducing that potential source of stress. It will also enable the organist and choir director to choose anthems, preludes, postludes, offertories, and other special music that will tie in with the theme of the service—and to plan ahead! What a pleasure and privilege it is to work with a talented musician who is both a compatible and a cooperative partner in the planning process and in the leadership of worship. You will both be thrivers and not just survivors as worship leaders.

Teaching and Discipling

Teaching and discipling are related but they are not the same. Teachers impart information; disciplers change lives. Teachers relate information about Christ; disciplers relate people *to* Christ. Teachers can change lives too, and they can bring people to Christ. But when they do that, they are also disciplers. Jesus was certainly both. He was called "Rabbi," which means "teacher," but he spent three years discipling twelve handpicked men. Discipling includes teaching, as Matthew's version of the Great Commission illustrates: "Go therefore and make disciples of all nations," said Jesus, "baptizing them . . . and *teaching* them to obey everything that I have commanded you" (Matt. 28:19–20a, emphasis ours).

As a pastor you have many opportunities to teach. How goes the discipling? The stress factor here, once again, is time. It takes time to disciple people. You have to spend lots of time with them, teaching by word and by example. Ironically, however, if you spend more time discipling, you will have more time to teach. You have to disciple others, who disciple others, who disciple others, who disciple others, who. . . . That is one way to describe the mission of the church. It is fulfilling the Great Commission on the home front.

It helps if you think of five areas of discipleship. You want to disciple people as stewards, as servants, as worshipers, as witnesses, and as leaders.[5] There is much to be said about each of these topics. Suffice it to say here that because you can't do it all yourself, you have to train other people to share the load with you, people who will in turn train others, to train others. It's a duplicating process. It's not that everyone will become a preacher like you, but that you will disciple a few who will disciple others to become true worshipers, committed servants of Christ, faithful stewards, effective witnesses, and leaders in the church. The key to your thriving as a pastor lies in building a strong team of colaborers in Christ. When you are confident that Elder Sanchez can train the evangelism callers as well as you can, or that Deacon Kim, who was trained by Deacon Park, can supervise the hospital calling team as well as her predecessor did, you are close to if not already thriving.

When you can call on any member of the church board to offer prayer and know that he or she is totally comfortable with being asked, as evidenced by the beautiful spontaneous prayer he or she offers, you are making real progress as a discipler. When church members can see and describe their occupation as their Christian *vocation*, when they know how to be Christians on the job, and when they are striving to live their faith and serve Christ every day of the week, they are becoming true disciples. When their spiritual growth is reflected in their giving to the church, you know they are growing as disciples. Yes, it takes time to disciple people, but oh, the returns! What satisfaction it brings and how much time it saves in the long run! Team building is an indispensable key to your survival as a pastor, and discipling disciples who disciple disciples is the secret to your thriving as a pastor. Indeed, it is the secret of a thriving church—along with prayer, of course!

5. The role of the pastor as discipler is covered in *The Pastor-Evangelist in the Parish*, pt. 4, pp. 141–171.

Counseling[6]

As a pastor you know that your counseling ministry can be very time-consuming. The secret of survival is knowing when and to whom to refer people. While pastoral counseling is a valuable part of your ministry, you need to recognize your professional limitations. People who are psychologically disturbed or who have serious emotional problems should be referred to those who are qualified to help such people. If they are mentally sick, they need to see a doctor, not a pastor.

If you have not already done so, you should establish relationships with some reputable psychiatrists, psychotherapists, clinical psychologists, and other professionals who are more qualified than you to deal with addicted people, or people who need marriage and/or divorce counseling or family counseling or financial or legal advice.

Not only should you be able to discern when someone ought to be referred, but you also need to develop tactful ways of doing that, so that a parishioner doesn't feel as if you are refusing to help. You are not refusing to help; on the contrary, you are giving a person the very best help when you refer him or her to someone who can do more for the person than you can. Also, you are assuring the person of your continuing concern and availability when your spiritual counseling is needed. The confidential relationships you establish with those to whom you have referred people are both helpful and reassuring in your continuing ministry to those whom you have referred. They themselves may often voluntarily tell you how things are going. What a relief it is to know they are receiving the proper kind of help!

So the lifeline we want to toss you for surviving and, we hope, thriving as a counseling pastor is knowing when and how to refer.

Your Role as a Public Figure[7]

As the pastor of a local church, you are a public figure. You are visible in the community. If people don't know you personally, they know about you. They know the church you serve. Your presence is felt at PTA meetings and other school events. You are invited to serve on the boards of various civic and social organizations. You are asked to speak at graduations and dedications and meetings of the local service clubs. Indeed, your involvements in the community

6. See *The Pastor-Evangelist in the Parish*, pt. 2, pp. 69–109.
7. Ibid., pt. 6, pp. 195–220.

can begin to consume more and more of your time, and pretty soon they are adding more stress to your already overcrowded life. "Help! I'm still a pastor! Can you toss me a lifeline?"

Yes, we can: Learn to say NO! You don't have to accept every invitation to speak, every request to give an invocation, every entreaty to serve on a board or join this organization or help with this cause. As we said in chapter 11, be selective in choosing your "extracurricular" involvements. Weigh the commitment carefully before you make it. Know what's involved, how much time it will take now and in the future. Remember, your church has first priority on your professional time. You have a right, indeed an obligation, to engage in some outside activities. Your ministry is not restricted by the walls of your church or to the families of the church. As a public figure you are always an ambassador for Jesus Christ, always a witness, always a servant. Nor do you ever stop being a pastor. Your involvements outside the church are part of your ministry, but not to the extent that they interfere with or detract from your obligations to your own congregation.

Once again, it's a balancing act. If you find your stress level building because of your nonchurch involvements, then the scale is tipping in the wrong direction. So learn to say no. And learn when enough is enough, or maybe too much! It's time to pull out and pull back, and refocus on the congregation you were called to serve. They're your first—not your only, but your first—professional priority, and they deserve to be served by a pastor who is not stressed out by extracurricular activities. You're not thriving just because you're high-fiving with the Rotarians! Learn how to say no, and when to say no, and to whom to say no. That's the lifeline for someone who is always in demand.

Pastoral Pointer

If there are any ministers, elders, or deacons in your new-members class, consider inviting one or more of them to participate in leading worship on the Sunday the members are publicly recognized. They could give the call to worship, read a Scripture lesson, lead the responsive reading or a special litany, or perhaps give a brief testimony about their experience in the new-members class and why they joined this church.

A Concluding Word

"Unless the LORD builds the house, those who build it labor in vain" (Ps. 127:1a). No one knows that better than a pastor, and no one needs to be reminded of that more than a pastor who is struggling to survive. The most comforting, the most freeing lifeline, is the knowledge that it all does not depend on you! "Apart from me you can do nothing," said Jesus (John 15:5).

"My grace is sufficient for you, for power is made perfect in weakness," he told the tormented apostle Paul (2 Cor. 12:9), who declared in his letter to the Philippians, "I can do all things through him who strengthens me" (Phil. 4:13). And so can we!

The ultimate lifeline, the one indispensable lifeline, is not one we can throw you. It is the one that connects you with the Lord of the church, without whose presence and power no one can thrive as a pastor, but with whose help and by whose grace all things are possible.

Implicitly and explicitly throughout this book we have emphasized the importance of prayer and the devotional life. Prayer is the lifeline that connects you to the Lifesaver, the power line that connects you to the Power Source.

We are well aware, and so are you, that all the ideas we have shared in this book, all our suggestions and comments, are worthless apart from your faith in and dependence on the God who called you into ministry, whose Son you are striving faithfully to serve, and who in and through the Holy Spirit is with you every step of the way.

So do the best you can and leave the rest to God. Trust in God's promises, pray for God's wisdom, and rely on God's strength. And believe the good news you have been declaring to your congregation Sunday by Sunday: "In Jesus Christ we are forgiven!"

May God bless you mightily, and may the grace of our Lord Jesus Christ be with you and empower you to thrive and not just survive in all your worthy labors for his kingdom.

We hope you will join us in this closing prayer:

> Almighty God, renew each day that faith I once could claim,
> when from the depths within my soul I heard you speak my name.
> O wondrous thought that you should call a sinner such as I!
> Grant me in Christ the strength to serve in this your calling high.
> Embolden me by your own will to play the prophet's part,
> to speak your word with fearless tongue yet meek and humble heart.
> Instill me with a holy zeal; pour out your grace on me;
> and let your Spirit fill my life, that I your priest may be.
> A patient heart I pray to own, an attitude of love,
> a scornless eye that ne'er disdains but rests on you above.
> Yet gird me now to meet the world, to wield the two-edged sword,
> and witness to the truth divine that Jesus Christ is Lord![1]

Amen.

1. "An Ordination Prayer," from *Now, THAT'S a Miracle!* by Richard Stoll Armstrong (CSS Publishing Co., 1996), p. 60.

Appendix A

Parish Nursing

The Rev. Dr. Granger Westburg, a Lutheran hospital chaplain, is the person credited with the idea of enlisting registered nurses as paid or volunteer members of church staffs. From the handful of persons he enlisted in the mid-1980s, the number of parish nurses has rapidly multiplied, so that now there are many hundreds serving in churches throughout the United States, Canada, and other countries.

In an article entitled "Linking Faith and Health," Donna Coffman, executive director of Caring Congregations, writes: "Registered nurses by the hundreds are answering God's call to serve in churches. . . . They are strengthening the capacities of individuals, families, congregations, and communities to connect what they believe with how they care for themselves. They are empowering members to take responsibility for healthy lifestyles based on faith."[1]

Parish nurses serve in a variety of ways. "Using the nursing process of assessment, planning, implementation, and evaluation," explains nurse Coffman, "a particular ministry of a particular congregation in a particular location is created based on the assessed needs of the congregation and the community surrounding it, along with the gifts and skills of the parish nurse."[2]

The American Nurses Association recognized parish nursing as a specialty practice in 1997 and approved the "Scope and Standards of Practice for Parish Nurses" in 1998. Parish nurses must be licensed in the states where they practice.

We hope this brief introduction to parish nursing is sufficient to help our readers understand why we wanted to include a practicing parish nurse's

1. From "Linking Faith and Health," by Donna Coffman, published in 2002 by Union Theological Seminary, Richmond, Va. Coffman, a registered nurse and ordained Presbyterian minister, is executive director of the Caring Congregations program, which provides training and support for parish nurses and others who work in congregational health ministries.

2. Ibid.

perspective on the health problems and needs of pastors. The following comments are from the letter we received from Michelle Arya, RN:

> As a Parish Nurse, I have seen firsthand how hard it is for pastors to live balanced lives. I've spent a lot of time with pastors at the three churches where I now work. I've learned much about what church life and ministry are like in the other twenty-five or so churches in the metropolitan area where my fellow parish nurses work.
>
> Every Wednesday I meet with the other twelve parish nurses in my area. We share problems, stories, and inspirations. We also pray for the congregations we serve, and for the pastors who lead and serve those congregations. I have learned that pastors face unique problems and challenges they do not readily share, because of the expectations others place on them and because of the expectations they place on themselves.
>
> Every time I take a pastor's blood pressure, I'm reminded of the same thing: pastors are human! They are made of real flesh and blood. I see many pastors in therapists' offices. Most of their problems have to do with the stress they're under, the continuous care and concern they bear for the crises and griefs of others, the "never-off-duty" nature of their work, the expectations placed on their families, the demand to be all things to all people, and their general lack of attention to caring for themselves.
>
> Depression is common among clergy—as it is among all kinds of people. The experts have described depression as "the common cold of emotional illness." Pastors are not immune to colds—either the physical or emotional kind. I have discovered that even the deepest religious faith does not vaccinate people from becoming depressed or cure them when they are depressed.
>
> The common symptoms of depression include a persistent, sad, or anxious mood; profound feelings of emptiness, hopelessness; loss of interest or pleasure in ordinary things that used to make a person smile; feelings of worthlessness, low self-esteem, despair ("things will never get better"). Depression often brings with it sleeplessness, insomnia, oversleeping, or early-morning waking. It can cause either a decrease or an increase in appetite, sexual problems, anxiety, neck or chest or lower back pain, and more. Some of these symptoms are easily recognized; some are less obvious.
>
> The good news is that depression is treatable! There are medications with few side effects. There are support groups. Exercise and good nutrition can really make a difference, too. I think some pastors are afraid to look at the possibility that they may have any kind of illness, emotional or physical, because they think it would make them appear weak, or because they think their faith should be strong enough to keep them healthy, or to heal them. I look upon medicine as a gift of God. I also believe God calls people to be doctors and nurses! I believe ALL healing comes from God, whether God

uses a vaccine, a splint, a support group, or a prescription. I believe prayer is essential in healing, but that it is not a substitute for sensible treatment. Let's pray for healing, but let's also pray for wisdom for doctors and nurses. Let's pray for medicines that work and for treatments that help heal God's people of things that afflict them. Pastors can be great role models for their congregation by taking care of their own health. That takes both prayer and healthful, balanced living.

Another health problem I see in too many pastors is high blood pressure. This is a tough one, because the most common symptom is death. No exaggeration! The only way to know you have high blood pressure is to have it monitored regularly. Making lifestyle changes, such as exercising regularly and eating the right foods, can help you and others avoid the need for medications to lower blood pressure later. These lifestyle changes help with all of the stress-related disorders I've mentioned. They can also help you avoid a stroke or other debilitating heart disease. I have seen too many pastors develop heart trouble in their forties and fifties.

Some of the other common health problems I see in pastors are weight problems resulting from lack of exercise, overbusy schedules, improper eating, gastrointestinal disorders like ulcers and reflux disease, migraine headaches, and a lot of neck pain and back trouble. My fellow parish nurses and I have also discovered that some pastors struggle with substance abuse (mostly alcohol) and eating disorders, as well. These can be attributed to stress, and they can be prevented by minimizing bad habits and their destructive effects.

To any pastor who wants to have a life in ministry that is fulfilling, satisfying, and sustainable, one that is less likely to lead to "burnout" or some other serious health problem, I would say what any doctor or nurse would undoubtedly say: Eat right and exercise regularly! Eat as many fruits and vegetables as possible. Drink large amounts of water. Avoid high-fat foods and too much salt. Minimize sugar intake, avoid preservatives, processed foods, and chemical additives. Go easy on the caffeine and alcohol.

And exercise regularly. It should be a scheduled part of your daily routine, along with your devotional life. Make it a top priority. It's more likely to be that, if you do something you enjoy. There's no reason exercise has to be boring. Do something that's fun, and do it with friends. Just do it!

Appendix B

Three Rules for Telephone Callers[1]

1. Vocal Compensation

In a telephone conversation your voice is the only thing to which the other person can respond. The person at the other end of the line cannot see your face and body language. He or she does not know if you are smiling or frowning. To come across as friendly, you have to *sound* friendly. To come across as interested, you have to *sound* interested. To come across as caring, you have to *sound* as if you care. Your voice has to compensate for what your face and body cannot communicate. This is the rule of vocal compensation.

2. Auditory Accommodation

The absence of visual contact works both ways. Since you cannot see the other person, you have to listen all the more carefully. Because it is more difficult to hear when both people are speaking at once, you have to give the other person more opportunities to break in, and be more careful yourself not to interrupt. All the rules of interpersonal communication apply. The only difference is that since your eyes cannot help you, you have to rely on your sense of hearing. This is the rule of auditory accommodation.

3. Telephonic Inspiration

A telephone call is sometimes a convenient and often a necessary substitute for being there in person, especially when the distance is far. That is all the more reason for the pastor to want the telephone conversation to be as meaningful and helpful as possible. It is as easy to have a faith-sharing conversation on the telephone as it is in person. The telephone is a marvelous medium for prayer, and it is amazing how close two people can feel to each other and

1. From *Faithful Witnesses*, Participant's Book, by Richard Stoll Armstrong (Geneva Press, 1987), p. 92.

to God when they do pray together on the telephone. It is as if someone were whispering a prayer into your ear and direct to your heart, as the human voice and the Holy Spirit transcend the distance that separates you. The very absence of visual and tactile contact heightens the spiritual impact. That is what is meant by telephonic inspiration.

Index